THE SILENT WAR

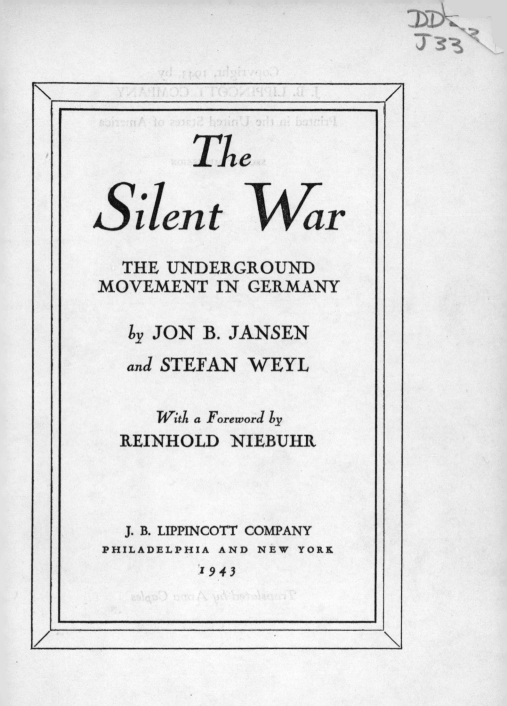

The
Silent War

THE UNDERGROUND
MOVEMENT IN GERMANY

by JON B. JANSEN
and STEFAN WEYL

With a Foreword by
REINHOLD NIEBUHR

J. B. LIPPINCOTT COMPANY
PHILADELPHIA AND NEW YORK
1943

This book is dedicated to the memory of those who have given their lives in the silent war inside Germany.

Feiger Gedanken
Baengliches Schwanken,
Weibisches Zagen,
Aengstliches Klagen
Wendet kein Elend,
Macht dich nicht frei.

Allen Gewalten
Zum Trutz sich erhalten,
Nimmer sich beugen,
Kraeftig sich zeigen,
Rufet die Arme
Der Goetter herbei.
                    —GOETHE

Cowardly weighing
Timidly swaying
Womanish quailing
Faint-hearted wailing
Will not thwart ruin
Nor set us free.

'Gainst every power
Defiantly tower
Never once bending
Brazenly standing—
Gods, thus called hither,
Hold arms out to thee.
            (*Translation by*
            J. B.-V.)

Introduction

The authors of *The Silent War* have in my opinion
rendered a real service to the democratic cause by this
vivid and revealing portrayal of the underground opposition to Hitlerism in Germany. Their story is valuable for
many reasons. It refutes the rising prejudice of those who
profess to believe that all Germans are Nazis. It proves
with what heroism and resourcefulness many Germans
have resisted Hitler's tyranny and still resist it. It gives
an intelligent account of the complex social forces at
work in Germany and reveals both the difficulties and
the possibilities of remaking Germany after Hitler's defeat. It must certainly convince all but the politically
stupid that the reconstruction of German life cannot be
achieved without a political program which will allow
the forces of residual health in Germany freedom to
achieve the rebirth of Germany from within.

Not the least value of this book is the light it throws
upon the tremendous handicaps which were placed in
the way of German opposition to Hitler because of the
tardiness of the so-called democratic world in opposing
him from without. It throws new light upon the tragedy
of Munich and upon all similar policies which preceded

INTRODUCTION

Munich; for it shows the effect of external appeasement upon the fate of the resolute band of anti-Nazis within Germany itself.

As a protection to their associates still working against Hitler within Germany, the authors of this book are using pseudonyms. I am personally acquainted with both of them and have the utmost confidence in their sincerity and integrity. They belong to a group of Germans who have won their right to be heard with respect, not only because the courage of their deeds supports their judgments, but also because their judgments in the past have been justified by the events. They knew that Hitler can and must be defeated. But they never shared the optimism of certain types of German liberals and radicals who always saw the fall of Hitler around the corner. They warned at an early date that Hitler's ascendancy would lead to a world war and that nothing short of his defeat in that war would destroy him. If present events have validated their past judgments we may hope with some reason that the future will justify their present analysis of the German situation.

Reinhold Niebuhr

Union Theological Seminary
November 12, 1942

Authors' Foreword

This book is an attempt to give the American public a picture of what the German underground movement is and what it is not, what it has accomplished and what it has not accomplished, what can be expected of it and what cannot be expected of it.

In describing this silent war inside Germany the authors labor under a number of handicaps.

The first handicap is the popular conception that the underground struggle against tyranny is a romantic affair and that opponents of the Nazis are able to rally and encourage their forces by printing and distributing great numbers of illegal newspapers and leaflets. From our contacts with friendly and understanding Americans we have found out how difficult it is for free citizens of a democratic country to comprehend even the most rudimentary facts about life under a Fascist dictatorship. Therefore, our first concern has been to give our readers an understanding of the grim everyday life of the anti-Nazi opposition in the Third Reich, and to put the apparently romantic aspects in the place they deserve.

Secondly, we have had to abstain from mentioning many important events, facts, names and places which have played and still play an important part in the underground fight. Concern for the safety of the fighters within the country must take precedence over all other considerations. In order to betray to the powerful and diabolically systematic enemy—the Gestapo—nothing which may be useful to him, we have had to change many details in our story. All names of persons have been disguised and frequently the names of places and dates. However, not a single detail in this book is fictitious.

Thirdly, in no sense can this book claim to be a history of the underground movement in Germany. That history can be written only after Hitler has been defeated, when the archives of the Gestapo have been opened and the records of the various groups in the German underground movement have been made available.

The story that we have written is based in all essentials on our own personal experiences and observations. However, if it had not been for our many years of association in a larger movement, if it had not been for the collective experiences of a group which shared our own conceptions—the New Beginning Group—we could not have had these experiences ourselves, nor would we have been able to assemble the more comprehensive information in this book. Some of our material has been published at various times and in various countries: in the *Inside Germany Reports* of the American Friends of German Freedom, in the *Deutschland Berichte* of the New Beginning

Authors' Foreword

Group, in London in the *Reports from Inside Germany*, in Paris in the *Rapports d'Allemagne* and in Scandinavia. Other parts have been taken from hitherto unpublished reports and letters from the Third Reich. Another important source was the *Green Reports* published by members of the German Social Democratic Party. We are indebted to the posthumous book of Otto Bauer, leader of the Austrian Social Democratic Party, entitled *The Underground Party*, for valuable insight into our problem.

Without the aid of the research staff of the American Friends of German Freedom, it would have been impossible to collect reports and other documents dealing with the whole period of the underground movement in Germany. We are indebted to Anna Caples not only for her intelligent translation, but for much valuable advice. We also wish to take this occasion to thank Karl O. Paetel for valuable information concerning the S.S. and the Gestapo.

The authors would like to say that their wives who participated actively in the underground work have also contributed in great measure to the preparation of this manuscript.

Jon B. Jansen
Stefan Weyl

CONTENTS

CONTENTS

i

THE SILENT WAR

THE SILENT WAR

1

Is There Still a German Underground?

Almost ten years have passed since Adolf Hitler took over the Reich Chancellorship. For almost ten years, the Third Reich, whose early demise was prophesied by so many of its enemies, while Hitler was promising it a thousand years, has continued in existence. For almost ten years a regime of violence such as the civilized world had not believed possible has spread its terror over Germany and the whole world.

After this decade of barbarism and brutality, is there still in Germany an opposition worthy of the name? After all of these years in which the Gestapo have ruled, aided in their cruel work of oppression by all the techniques of modern science, are there still enemies of Hitler who have escaped destruction? In 1942, is there still an underground movement in Germany?

This question has been asked frequently since the war started, especially since Hitler overran western Europe: Is there an opposition against the Nazis in Germany, as there is in the occupied countries? If such an opposition exists, why do we hear nothing from it? What is it doing?

It is not easy to answer these questions. The Nazi blackout is too effective. Goebbels, with the diabolical skill of his propaganda, twists facts until they are unrecognizable. Moreover, since the outbreak of the Second World War, inside information has been reduced to an absolute minimum. The organized system of supplying information about the situation within the Third Reich, which existed before the war, and continued to some extent until Norway, Holland and France fell, no longer exists. The reports that still trickle out come only by chance and do no more than throw light on some one problem.

We would be at a complete loss for information if it were not for certain events that have taken place in the Third Reich recently. And the official reports of these events have conveyed a special message. They have confirmed what we knew from all the inside reports sent before the summer of 1940, that the opposition still lives in Nazi Germany.

In an editorial on June 28, 1942, the *New York Times* said:

"Recent reports from Sweden telling of unrest and executions within Germany have a new note of significance for the opponents of the Nazi regime. They indicate that the measures of repression which have become routine in the occupied nations of Europe are now being applied, if as yet only in small measure, to citizens of the Reich itself. There is in these stories of executions in Berlin, Hamburg, Mannheim and other parts of Greater Germany a clue to what the future may hold for the Reich and its people in the further progress of the war. It is not a clue indicating when the war may end, but it does forecast how the war may end under Hitler's rule."

The great majority of the executions were in Berlin. According to a dispatch from the correspondent of the *New York Times* in Stockholm, 258 persons were executed on May 28th. Why? The correspondent states that they were charged with an attempt to dynamite an anti-Soviet exposition.

This explanation is certainly not true. The report goes on to say that those executed were Jews and Communists. But how in the world could Jews organize a bombing attempt at an exposition? Every Jew has to wear a yellow badge with the Star of David on it. Jews are not allowed to be outside of their homes after eight o'clock at night and, furthermore, Jews are not permitted to enter the Berlin Lustgarten, where the exposition was held. At best, only Nazi brains would be capable of believing that Communists would have made such a bombing attempt. Assuming that Communists decided to blow up something and, assuming that they were able to get hold of dynamite, they certainly would choose a more worthy object than a Nazi exposition. The Reich Chancellory and other government buildings are not far from the exposition grounds.

21

The most important key to understanding this "bombing attempt" is the date on which the executions took place. The 258 persons, undoubtedly completely innocent of any such attempt, were executed the very day after Heydrich was shot. The alleged bombing attempt in Berlin is only a reflex of the act in Prague. The executions in the capital city of the Reich were a warning to the German opposition.

After a careful examination of the reports of the Berlin incident any critical observer must be convinced that nothing about them is true, except that 258 people were murdered. This would not have been the first time that the Nazis had fabricated, even carried out, an act of violence in order to furnish cause for a terror campaign of their own. From the Reichstag fire to the explosion of the time bomb in the Munich beer cellar in November, 1939, there has been a series of incidents in which violence or attempted violence was alleged, some publicly known and some less well known. Every incident unloosed a wave of terror, thus serving the higher propaganda purposes of the Nazis.

At the end of February, 1933, the Reichstag went up in flames. The Nazis insisted that Communists had started the fire and then launched the first great Nazi wave of terror over Germany. It was accompanied by a carefully prepared propaganda campaign against the "danger of a Bolshevik revolution" in Germany and the rest of Europe.

In November, 1939, when Hitler and his leading

henchmen were so "miraculously saved," the story followed a similar course. For weeks afterwards there were arrests and shootings, and still more arrests and more shootings. So far, no one has been able to learn anything about the political background of the people who were the victims following this incident. And, of course, no one knows how many victims there were. This time the propaganda campaign was directed against England. The British Secret Service had organized the attempt on the Fuehrer's life. An official Nazi pamphlet published soon afterwards said: "We have succeeded in obtaining evidence that proves that never before in history has England planned a more brutal murder."

All acts of violence in Germany, big ones as well as little ones, were committed by the enemy, whoever he happened to be at the moment. In 1933, it was "the Bolshevik revolution." In 1939 it was England. In November, 1939, temporarily, Bolshevik Russia did not happen to be the enemy. The menace of Communism was carefully eliminated from Nazi propaganda. As long as the Nazi-Soviet Pact was in force, the honor of organizing bombing attempts and sabotage in Nazi Germany was bestowed on Churchill and his "Jewish clique," but not one day longer.

On June 25, 1941, the German press published a secret report from the Chief of the Security Police, Heydrich, to Heinrich Himmler, Reich Fuehrer of the S.S. and Chief of the German Police. The report was dated June 10, 1941 (twelve days before the attack on Russia), and read:

"The destructive activity carried on by the Communist International against the Axis Powers and particularly against National Socialist Germany, up until the conclusion of the German-Soviet Russian Non-Aggression Pact of August 23, 1939, is well known.

"Our hope that, following the conclusion of this Pact, Soviet Russia would behave in accordance with its provisions and put a stop to the insidious activity against the Reich proved to be an illusion. On the contrary, Communist sabotage and terror and a vast far-reaching development of their military, economic and political espionage services proved to be the determined, even the acknowledged, aims of the Russians.

"They have only changed their methods; they have employed a series of new techniques and clever disguises that have constantly posed new problems for us."

Heydrich had the following to say about the "new techniques" of Communist terror:

"The great number of terror and sabotage groups in the Reich, founded by order of the Comintern, which the police has uncovered, is indicative of the attitude of the Soviet Union toward the Reich. In addition to orders for acts of sabotage, their agents have received instructions to make attempts on the lives of leading personalities in the Reich.

"Although it might have been assumed that the series of acts of violence which the Comintern had carried out or which were in the process of being carried out would come to an end with the conclusion of the German-Russian Non-Aggression Pact of August 23, 1939, comprehensive reports, especially from territories occupied by the Reich, have given evidence that the Comintern does not intend to cease its criminal activities against the Reich.

"In addition to the ship sabotage groups created under instructions from the British Secret Service, whose aim it was, even in peace-time, to destroy German ships, there existed a much more extensive network of terror organizations set up by the Comintern, whose task was to destroy the shipping of countries which, at the time, were members of the Anti-Comintern Bloc. . . .

"Sabotage attempts against sixteen German ships, three Italian and two Japanese may be traced back to the activities of these Communist terror groups with branches throughout Europe. In two cases, extremely valuable ships were completely destroyed. At first the conspirators tried to destroy the ships by setting fire to them, but when these methods usually did not result in total loss of the ships, they turned to the use of dynamite in the case of ships traveling in the North Sea and the Baltic. Their principal headquarters are in the harbors of Hamburg, Bremen, Danzig, Rotterdam, Amsterdam, Copenhagen, Oslo, Reval and Riga."

As it was in 1941, so in 1942, only *the* enemy could be guilty of the bombing attempt.

And who is *the* enemy of the Nazis in the summer of 1942? *The* enemy is not only "Bolshevik" Russia, but also "plutocratic" England and "plutocratic" America.

That is why the bombing attempt in Berlin was laid at the door of Communists and Jews. The Communists, among the 258 beheaded, represent Russia, the Jews represent the Western Powers. Bombing attempts and sabotage, death sentences and executions—all serve only the political and propaganda ends of the Nazi regime.

It is important for us to understand what is behind this kind of Nazi terror propaganda. It is even more important that we analyze some of the official Nazi reports, which, although they may be cut and dried in their presentation, give a real insight into Nazi methods.

For example, the Nazis' own report about certain executions in Mannheim is an even better source of information than the dispatch from Stockholm quoted above. On May 22, 1942, the Berlin radio announced that the People's Court in Mannheim had sentenced fourteen former "Communists and Marxists" to death. "They were found guilty of listening to foreign broadcasts, mimeographing and distributing leaflets and organizing illegal cells to undermine the German home front."

Another report: On July 2, 1942, the D.N.B. stated: "For some time it had been noted that, in a Frankfort armament factory, suspicion and doubt were being sown among the workers through the spreading of mendacious and inciting rumors, mainly directed against the conduct of the war by the Reich and its allies. It was discovered that the thirty-one-year-old plant engineer, Heinrich Maas, a former Marxist, had been listening systematically to enemy radio stations and, with treasonable intent, passing on the inciting lies broadcast by the enemy to the workers in the plant. Maas was sentenced to death and four other workers who had helped him pass on the news were given prison sentences."

There have been many reports of this kind in the German press and radio in the last few months. Their primary purpose is to intimidate the opposition.

At the end of September, 1941, all German newspapers were instructed that they must publish a detailed report about the first death sentence handed down to a so-called "radio-criminal." His name was Johann Wild. The report from the official German News Agency ran: "Wild had been an active member of Marxist organizations both before and after the World War. After the [National Socialist] advent to power, he had listened to foreign broadcasts, thus placing himself systematically under the influence of the propaganda launched against Germany by the Marxist war mongers. When England and France declared war on the Reich, Wild hoped for the downfall of the new Germany, which he hated. Thus, in his opinions and in his beliefs, he sided with the enemies of the German nation, to whose mendacious and vehemently anti-German broadcasts he listened regularly. These enemy broadcasts supplied him with material for a pamphlet that contained libelous statements against the Fuehrer and other leading personalities of the state as well as against the army. He also incited his wife to listen to foreign broadcasts and to

27

spread their lying messages. The Special Court attached to the Provincial Court at Nuremberg Fuerth expressly stated that the prisoner was guilty of deliberate and wilful treason against his nation. Accordingly, he was sentenced to death. . . ."

As a matter of fact, Johann Wild was not sentenced in September, but in May, 1941. At the time of his sentence the Nazi papers contented themselves with a brief notice. For, at the end of May, 1941, the Nazis could report great victories, in Yugoslavia, Greece and Crete. At the end of September, Nazi Germany was faced with the third war winter. The wave of discontent and opposition was rising. With the attack on Russia, the worst fears of the war-weary citizens of the Third Reich had been realized. The most important source of information for all Hitler opponents was, and is, listening to the foreign radio, a practice which is becoming more widespread all the time, despite prohibitions and threats, even of the death penalty. Thus, Goebbels published a long story about Johann Wild's death sentence with the sole purpose of intimidating the mass of "radio-criminals," although four months had passed since the court had given its verdict.

Constant observation of Nazi propaganda, what it includes and what it leaves out, its phraseology and its contradictions, gives us a perspective on the witches' brew of Nazi propaganda and an insight into the hell of Gestapo terror. Official German press and radio reports contain much more material from which we may judge events in Germany than is generally supposed. Skilled propagandists though the Nazis are, from their own sources we can learn facts that are indispensable in judging the situation in the Third Reich.

The *Left News* of London, in its May, 1942, issue, publishes a careful summary of such reports under the title: "Two Years of Judicial Terror Against the German Opposition."

The author of this article is B. F. Heine, a member of the London Committee of the German Social Democratic Party. From his careful compilation, we have selected several items concerning executions and prison sentences which relate directly to underground activities. We have limited our selection to only one example for a specific underground activity. All are official German reports.

"Michael Schneeberger, aged 40, of Nuremberg, was a member of an anti-German organization. He attempted to smuggle seditious leaflets into Germany and was apprehended in the act. He used his firearm and was sentenced to death for high treason."

Schneeberger was executed on February 16, 1941.

"Johann Dombrowski, aged 38, of Gross Rakitt, who consistently over a period of years had been engaged in illegal activities tending toward setting up organizations of a banned party, was sentenced to death."

Dombrowski was executed on August 20, 1941.

29

"Paul Schurr, aged 33, of Frankfort on Main, was found guilty of circulating seditious 'chain-letters' and sentenced to death."

Schurr was executed on February 27, 1941.

"Ludwig Cyranek of Adscheid, president of the German branch of the *Internationale Vereinigung der Bibelforscher* [the German branch of Jehovah's Witnesses] was found guilty of actions threatening the public welfare, of disrupting the fighting power [of the Reich] and of membership in an anti-militarist association. He was sentenced to death by the Special Court, Dresden, on March 20, 1941."

"Karl Hoffmann, Erich Schulz and Willy Tosch, all three of Danzig, and Hermann Chill of Danzig-Ohre were found guilty by the People's Court of acts in preparation of high treason and of crimes committed in contravention of the law concerning explosives, and were sentenced to death. The four men were members of an illegal organization constituted outside the territory of the Reich, which by terror and sabotage aimed at undermining the striking power of the German army and at overthrowing the National Socialist Constitution of the Reich."

The four men were executed on October 12, 1940.

"Willi Gall, aged 33, of Pethau, and Otto Nelke, aged 42, of Berlin, were sentenced to death on a charge of disrupting the fighting power of the German nation and of preparation of high treason."

Gall and Nelke were executed on July 25, 1941.

Thus, using Nazi grounds for death sentences as an index, we find that underground activities include the following crimes:

Organized listening to foreign broadcasts.
Mimeographing and distributing of leaflets.
Organizing illegal cells to undermine the Home Front.
Smuggling seditious leaflets into Germany.
Setting up units of a banned party.
Circulating seditious "chain-letters."
Working toward overthrow of the National Socialist
    Constitution.
Undermining the striking power of the German
    army.
Disrupting of the fighting power of the Reich.
Terror and sabotage.

The catalogue is complete. No important activity is missing. Those underground fighters have paid with their lives. Many more than those we mention here have paid, many more than we even know about, than anyone can know about—with the possible exception of Heinrich Himmler. However, the examples cited give some impression of the broad range of underground activities.

So far we have dealt only with very definitely defined "crimes" against the Third Reich and against the National Socialist State that are punishable by death. However, in going through reports of executions in the German press we find less specific charges as the basis for death sentences, particularly, one known as "treason against the people." The number of the *Left News*, from which we have quoted, also contains a list of fifty "traitors against the people" who were executed. The list starts with Hermann Krueger, executed on October 9, 1939, and ends with Emanuel Schafferszik, of Sperlingsdorf, executed on September 15, 1941.

The author of the article makes the following comment about this list:

"In about forty cases the age of the victims is known. Ten were between the ages of 20 and 30; eleven between 31 and 40; thirteen between 41 and 50; and five over 50 years of age. Among them were three women, the youngest was 20."

All of these people were guilty of "treason against the people," but in analyzing more closely we find that this crime may include anything from "espionage for a foreign power" to "contacts with emigrants," from the shooting of an S.S. man to running away from work.

Even more indicative of the nature of Nazi justice than the death sentence imposed for "contacts with emigrants"—which might mean simply writing a letter to a relative living abroad—is the following case.

Is There Still a German Underground?

Early in August, 1940, the People's Court in Berlin condemned 36-year-old Eduard Grabbe of Vorarlberg to life imprisonment. The explanation of the sentence stated that Grabbe "by his inflammatory reports conjured up the danger of military entanglements for Germany," whatever that means. The President of the court, in delivering sentence, "expressed regret at the fact that the law did not yet make this type of offense punishable by death, although the death penalty would appear a perfectly adequate punishment."

A few days later, on August 14, 1940, it was officially reported that Eduard Grabbe "was shot for resisting officers of the law." Where the law of the Third Reich does not reach, the long arm of the Gestapo does.

Heine collected forty-seven official Nazi reports of anti-Nazis being shot "for resisting officers."

Of course, this list of examples of Nazi terror against the German enemies of Hitler can, by no means, be complete. But it does give us an idea of the vitality which we can expect from the underground movement in the Third Reich during the tenth year of Nazi rule. This grim account also tells us something of the tasks which this movement has set for itself and dramatically illustrates the willingness of the underground fighters to carry on their work, despite the odds against them.

The first mass movement against Nazi domination in an occupied country took place in September, 1942. The workers of Luxembourg answered the formal incorporation of their small Duchy in the Third Reich by a general strike. A few days later the B.B.C. announced that a certain Heinrich Adam had been executed as one of the leaders of the strike. Adam was accused of giving the signal to start the strike with the siren of the factory where he worked. Adam was not a Luxembourger; he was a German citizen.

These casualty lists for the German underground are like the casualty lists of the High Command. They certainly do not tell the whole truth, but they indicate the direction in which to look for the truth.

Anyone who wants to understand what is going on inside the frontiers of the Third Reich must already have realized that the war on the inner front is carried on without publicity. It is a silent war.

The Gestapo publish no communiqués and no casualty lists. They tell no one what losses the German people suffer in the underground struggle. The Gestapo kill without a sound.

Of course, the Gestapo do speak occasionally. They talk when talking will be to their advantage or when they cannot hide their secrets. The same thing is true in the occupied countries as in Germany.

In Poland, the Death's Head S.S. murders without publicity. It is only by chance that occasionally detailed reports about their deeds of horror come to light. An example is the shocking story of the Polish physician, W. B. Starski, which was published in the *Free World* (July, 1942) under the title, "I Was a German Hostage." On the other hand, in Czechoslovakia recently, the Death's Head S.S. committed their murders in the open, because they wanted to avenge the death of the hangman, Heydrich, to capture the alleged authors of the deed and, especially, because they wanted to intimidate and to frighten off the courageous opposition of the Czech people.

Intimidation is usually the motive when the Gestapo break their silence. The victims of the black terror do not even find peace in the grave. Their corpses are mobilized for the war of nerves which the Nazi regime is carrying on against all the oppressed peoples and against the entire world. The opponents of the Nazi regime who have been beheaded, hanged or shot have to intimidate the living Nazi opponents. This is an important phase of the war on the inner battlefront in occupied Europe as well as within the Third Reich.

It is a battlefront: We did not have to find this term ourselves to describe conditions in the unknown land of Germany. The term is not only apt; it originated with one whose authority cannot be challenged, Gestapo Chief Heinrich Himmler.

Even Himmler did not just happen upon this descriptive term; he did not apply it in retrospect. Long before the war he *created* the term in that sober spirit of brutality which characterizes Nazi terrorists. He outlined in advance what has since become a reality.

Preparations for action on the battlefront inside Germany were among the most important preparations for the war.

Even before Hitler purged the officers' corps of the *Wehrmacht* on February 4, 1938, he was in a position to force them to listen to a lecture by the S.S. Chief about the important role of the Gestapo terror in preparing for war and for the conduct of the war itself. In the spring of 1937, Himmler addressed the officers of the German *Reichswehr* as follows:

"In a future war we will have to deal not merely with the front of our Army on land, the front of our Navy at sea, and the front of our Air Force in the air, we shall have a fourth battlefront, Internal Germany!"

Himmler warned them:

"We must never forget that neglect of the internal battleground will lead to catastrophe."

In order to make a greater impression on the officers of the army, the Gestapo Chief conjured up the specter of 1918, the "stab in the back"—the malicious legend by which German officers and reactionaries had always explained their defeat in the First World War. Himmler said:

"Unless we can manage, by hook or by crook, to keep the fourth in check, the other three fronts, on land, on sea, and in the air, will again be victims of a stab in the back!"

In this speech, two years before Hitler unleashed the forces of war, Himmler omitted no argument that might serve to convince the officers. In conclusion he said:

"It is absolutely essential for you, gentlemen of the army, as well as for everyone in a responsible position, to understand the vital importance of that internal battlefront, which, in case of war, will mean life or death for us. To solve this problem, and to solve it ruthlessly, is the order the Fuehrer has given me, and he has given me unlimited powers to carry it out."

That was in 1937, two and a half years before Poland was attacked. Himmler informed the officers of the German army at that time that when war came he would immediately arrest large numbers of suspected persons and that more concentration camps would be needed. He demanded at least thirty 'Death's Head Battalions' (*Sturmbanne*) of the S.S. for the inner front alone. "Once the emergency arises, utter ruthlessness will be essential," the Gestapo Chief concluded.

Himmler kept his word. During the last days of August and the first days of September, 1939, there were mass arrests in every section of the Reich. In every large city, thousands of so-called "enemies of the state" were arrested and sent to concentration camps. Himmler had the additional concentration camps he had requested. In the camp at Buchenwald, which was built after 1937, more than 20,000 people are held in "protective custody." How many have been murdered by the S.S., no one knows. No one can control the activities of the S.S.; Himmler literally has unlimited powers.

Himmler got what he wanted and he got even more. Early in 1942, more than half a million men of the *Waffen-S.S.* were under his command, which meant one heavily armed S.S. man for every fifty German males over twenty years of age. Their chief has the right arbitrarily to arrest or to shoot anyone he wishes. The latest reports estimate the present strength of the armed S.S. formations at 900,000 men.

The Death's Head S.S. are feared like nothing else in the world throughout all of Hitler Europe. They are dreaded by all, civilians and soldiers alike, anti-Nazis and members of the Nazi Party, in the Third Reich and in the occupied countries. The *Schwarzen* (the black ones), as they are called, have become the symbol of terror. They are the symbol of the complete lack of rights of all people in the territories ruled by Hitler. Their very name means death.

The difference between German soldiers and S.S. men is illustrated by the warning that spread through all the occupied countries in 1941: "If the eagle is on the chest, it's all right. But if it is on the sleeve—run!"

The soldiers of the occupation army in Norway christened the S.S., "The Black Death." They are even more afraid of the S.S. than of the dreaded Russian Front. They say: "You may survive the Russian Front if you're lucky, but if the *Schwarzen* get you, there is no hope."

Today the S.S. is more powerful than ever before. Every conflict among the leaders of the Nazi regime has ended with a compromise and every compromise has meant more power for Gestapo Chief Himmler.

Beginning late in 1941, there has been a new series of significant changes in the top ranks of the Nazi regime. Changes were made in the High Command of the *Wehrmacht*, in the Manpower Commission, in the leadership of war economy and in the Reich Food Estate. In every case we find that the S.S. gained more authority. Even Himmler's oldest and deadliest enemy, the man who had always been the liaison with the *Reichswehr*, Hermann Goering, seems to have decided that it was better to fight on the strongest side. In July, 1942, he bestowed on Himmler the highest honor of the German Luftwaffe.

There is no doubt that in the last few months Himmler has had great successes, though it is not yet clear to what extent he has attained the demands which he made late in 1941. At that time he demanded that a large number of officers of the S.S. be put in leading positions in the High Command of the army, that the intelligence services of the army be incorporated in the *Sicherheitsdienst* of the S.S., that the S.S. have a right to increase their numbers from army ranks, and that a thousand fighting planes be given to the S.S. to form an *S.S. Verfuegungs Luftwaffe* under his own command.

This S.S. Luftwaffe is perhaps the most ominous news since the Reichstag fire. We don't know whether Himmler already has it. On the strength of past experience we can assume he will get it, at the latest, by the time the inner front meets its *first great* challenge from the people, either in the Third Reich or in the occupied countries. We cannot expect that National Socialism will go down otherwise than according to "the law through which it came to power," the law of violence.

The Nazi Fuehrers know that they can count on no

leniency. Neither the unhappy people of the oppressed countries of Europe nor the German anti-Nazis will have mercy. Himmler knows that, and the hundreds of thousands of S.S. men know it too. Every Gestapo official knows it.

When, at the time of the Munich crisis in 1938, war appeared to be inevitable, many Nazis believed that it was the beginning of the end. Even those in high places were extremely pessimistic. During those days a high Gestapo official in Berlin was talking to a friend about the consequences of a lost war. He said: "What shall *I* do then? What do you think *they* [the people] will do to us?" He opened a drawer and showed his companion a revolver. "That is always ready. Don't believe that I shall wait until they make mince meat of me."

This awareness that not only the existence of the Third Reich, but the personal life of every single Nazi, is at stake, has been constantly hammered into their followers' minds by the leaders of the Nazi Party since the war broke out. In the middle of March, 1940, a report came to us from northern Bavaria, from a source which has always proved to be well informed. Our informant said: "Recently, Gauleiter Wahl made a journey and visited all the higher functionaries of the party. He told them all in confidence that they should not be misled into thinking the report that Nazi Germany stood on the threshold of the decisive battle was only propaganda. It was meant in deadly earnest and had nothing to do with propaganda. The Fuehrer is determined to fight. It is a life and death struggle. We shall all be victorious with the Fuehrer, or we shall all go down with him. There is no other way out. Anyone who believes that he will be able to get out if things go wrong is fooling himself. There is only one way and that is to fight. It will be a terrible fight but the Germans will win because they are faster than the others, because they will be more ruthless than the others. We can have consideration for nothing; our very lives are involved!"

The Nazis will sell their skins at a high price. No one who has watched the development of National Socialism with his eyes open can mistake that fact.

The *New York Times* editorial, mentioned earlier, contains an excerpt from a conversation between one of their correspondents and a former S.A. man during the first winter of the war. The Storm Trooper was asked what he thought would happen if the Nazis were to start losing the war.

"There will be a reign of terror until they collapse. They will kill anyone who whispers against the regime. There will be wholesale executions with the Gestapo in control. Before they quit they will try to wipe out all traces of potential opposition. They are saving this reign of terror for the last; they are determined not to give up easily."

It is not our task to make prophecies. But after the experience of the past years, we cannot doubt that the silent war on the inner front will become an open war. In his speech to the army officers in 1937, Himmler declared that "the inner battlefront will be the decisive battlefront." The Nazi Fuehrers will not accept defeat

41

on the foreign front until a final decision has been reached on the inner front. They will defend their rule to the very end and with every means. The end of the National Socialist regime of horror will be horrible.

The Nazi leaders are prepared for such an end. Ever since they took power in Germany, they have been aware of the possibility of a *Goetterdaemmerung*. They have talked of the "thousand years of the Reich," and at the same time they were preparing for the fight on the home front. They have talked of a people who stood united behind Hitler and at the same time in the barracks and quarters of the S.S. they were erecting barricades for civil war. They have spoken of the enthusiasm of the German people for National Socialism and of the love of every German for Hitler and at the same time they were building an impregnable fortress for Hitler and his closest followers in the mountains above Berchtesgaden and all the time they were fanning the hatred of a considerable part of the German people into a flame that will not be extinguished. And, finally, since the war has been going on they have spoken constantly of the inevitable victory of the German war machine; and at the same time they were repeating over and over again the challenge: there cannot and will not be a repetition of 1918.

In the background of everything that the Nazis do and say is their fear of a "stab in the back" as in 1918. If it were not for this fear, the Nazis' preparations for the inner battlefront would be as hard to understand as the still scarcely visible force against which they are mobilizing, the inner German opposition and its vanguard, the underground movement. The Nazis learned a lesson from the collapse of Kaiser Wilhelm's autocratic rule, and from the collapse of Czarism and the Hapsburgs. That lesson was that every regime of force will find its limits when it is no longer strong enough to hold down a latent opposition. They know too that their regime will not survive a defeat abroad. They have done all that is in their power to decimate the opposition, to destroy its contacts and to wipe out its leadership. But they still know that that will not save them from the last showdown if their war machine cracks under the force of superior enemies.

The preparations of the Nazi leaders show that the decision on the battlefront inside Germany will be the last great decision of this war. In this decisive battle the German opposition and the German underground movement will emerge into the spotlight. Those forces will come out into the open, whose silent work and secret existence for almost ten years, whose defeats and sacrifices, whose determination and aims, we are going to describe in the chapters of this book to follow.

The Nazi leaders realize that the day of judgment is approaching. In his speech before the bier of the "hangman" Reinhold Heydrich, Himmler spoke plainly enough. The Chief of the S.S. and of the German Police said: "Heydrich will be with us if we, true to our oath, fight on to the end."

2

Mass Organizations Go Underground

The German underground movement lives on. Ten years of unparalleled Nazi terror have been unable to destroy it. Who are these men and women against whom the Nazis fight with such ferocity and whom they fear as the potential leaders of an internal revolt? What is their background? From what sections of society do they come? What traditions, what ideas and what goals have given them the strength to hold firm through all these years?

The active underground workers stem for the most part from the labor movement of Germany. Most of the death sentences against political criminals, pronounced by Nazi courts, have been directed against former "Marxists" and "Bolsheviks"—Nazi terminology for former members of working-class parties. And almost all the political prisoners in the prisons and concentration camps were officials and members of working-class political parties, trade unions and other free labor organizations.

44

This picture of today's resisters is quite in keeping with the picture of the pre-Hitler period. The German labor movement was the strongest bulwark against the rise of National Socialism, the most powerful social and political support of the Weimar Democracy. Nazi propaganda has succeeded in spreading the impression that Hitler was chosen by the majority of the German people in a free and democratic election. This does not accord with the facts. In time of great crisis Hitler was able to range under his banners unprecedented masses of desperate people. Nevertheless, he never succeeded in securing a majority, not even in the notorious terror election after the Reichstag fire. In this election (March 5, 1933) 17,000,000, or 44 percent of the 39,000,000 voters, cast their ballots for the National Socialist Party. The parties of the so-called National Government, the Nazis and Hugenberg's German Nationalist Party together, received 52.6 percent of the entire vote. In the elections for the National Assembly in 1919, the Social Democratic Party had received 45.4 percent of the vote. The party was at that time split into two wings, the Majority Social Democrats with 37.8 percent and the Independent Social Democrats with 7.6 percent of the votes. The parties of the "Weimar Coalition," Social Democrats, Democrats and Catholic Center, received jointly 77.8 percent of the total vote.

The majority for the National Government in 1933 was scant enough. And the conservative German Nationalist Party, with its 3,000,000 votes, tipped the scales

45

on the condition that Hitler adhere to the rules of the game of parliamentary democracy. Those who yielded to the illusion that Hitler would respect these rules could, therefore, be quite satisfied with the results of the March 5th election. Despite the further accretion to Hitler's own votes, many of his enemies were not disturbed. They said: "Didn't we tell you that Hitler would not get a majority?" "Didn't the vote of the working class hold up splendidly in spite of the terror?" "Wasn't it the bourgeois parties that lost out heavily?" "Won't the German Nationalists, for the sake of their own interests, have to prevent Hitler from using his position in the government exclusively on behalf of the National Socialists?" "Aren't the majority of the members of the government conservatives?" "Can't we work together with the Catholic Center and form a strong democratic opposition, so we'll be ready when the time comes and Hitler has been discredited?"

All these questions were predicated on the assumption that Hitler would adhere to the rules of parliamentary democracy. But this was not Hitler's idea. The terror had begun immediately after he had been named Chancellor. Storm Troopers and S.S. formations functioned as auxiliary police. Known opponents of the "national uprising" were arrested or disappeared in the cellars, in which the private armies of the incipient dictatorship had instituted their own private torture chambers. Goering—named as Prime Minister of Prussia—had begun to purge the government. Opposition newspapers were suppressed daily.

The day after the Reichstag fire, Hindenburg signed the Law for the Protection of the State and People, which put the Communist Party outside the law, confiscated its press and its property and forced those of its leaders, who had not been arrested during the preceding night, to flee or to hide. With the aid of this law Hitler broke the key position of the German Nationalists and obtained his majority.

The wording of this law and especially its interpretation showed clearly that it was by no means directed against the Communists alone. It could be used just as well against every political, trade-union, cultural or religious organization. The democratic Weimar Republic, born out of defeat in the First World War, torn by implacable party strife and clandestine civil war, driven to the verge of bankruptcy by years of depression, was already shaken to its very foundations.

The enemies of democracy had advanced step by step. As early as 1920, barely two years after the Hohenzollern rule had collapsed, the anti-democratic forces felt strong enough to attempt a putsch against the new state. The *Kapp Putsch,* the first counter-revolutionary attempt, was broken by the combined force of the workers in a general strike. Three years later, at the peak of inflation, Hitler tried his luck for the first time. His march from the beer cellar to the Feldherrnhalle was dispersed under police fire. Hitler failed because

47

the leading militarists no longer liked the putsch strategy nor believed it necessary. During the first years they had been amazed at, and frightened by, the might of the people which had destroyed the rule of the Hohenzollerns, but by 1923 they had got their self-confidence back. They had decided against putsches and for legality—that is, for their own kind of legality.

The forces of the past had begun to permeate the Weimar state and they would end by conquering it from within before it was delivered over to Hitler. More and more anti-democratic elements had gotten into positions of authority in the state administration and in the judiciary. They were finding their way into the governments and only the large cities and the state of Prussia remained as strongholds of Weimar Democracy. Field Marshal von Hindenburg was elected President in 1925 and his election was symbolic of the reactionaries' success in their plan for a legal re-conquest of Germany. In political tactics, Hitler was no more than an apt pupil of his early military sponsors. As the years passed, he too adopted their slogan: "We shall take power by strictly legal means."

The collapse of the prosperity of 1928-29 and the devastating consequences of world depression gave Hitler his great chance. Seven to eight million unemployed began to lose their faith in democracy as every prospect of work vanished. While the income of the workers shrank steadily, the peasants lost their markets and the shopkeepers their customers. Under Reich Chancellor

Bruening, the Reich's democratically elected government steadily relinquished its democratic forms. It came to rely on the "confidence of the Reich President" and governed under a succession of "emergency decrees." It was only in this way that the costs of the depression could be transferred to the mass of the population. At the same time, mass unemployment meant that the trade unions were being deprived, to an increasing extent, of the weapon of the strike as a means of defending the standard of living of the working people. Demagogic Nazi propaganda found fertile ground and, supported by the contributions of the great industrialists, sowed its vicious seeds.

In the elections of May, 1928, the National Socialists polled a total of only 809,000 votes in all Germany. By September, 1930, the brown flood had swollen to 6,500,-000 votes. One hundred and seven Nazi deputies entered the Reichstag and, rallying all their forces, began ruthlessly to put their "legal methods" into effect. At the end of July, 1932, with more than 13,500,000 votes and 230 deputies, the Nazis reached the peak of their legal power in the Weimar state.

The bourgeois centrist parties, with the exception of the Catholic Center, had been almost completely crushed. The labor parties had stood against the Nazi tide alone. In the July, 1932, election, the Social Democratic Party still had almost 8,000,000 voters behind it and was by far the strongest party after the Nazis. Communist voters cast more than 5,000,000 votes, so that the voting strength of the two labor parties together was not far behind that of the National Socialists.

However, the split between the two parties of the German working class cut very deep; the struggle of brother against brother went on with undiminished fervor. They hated each other more than they feared Hitler.

The leaders of the Social Democratic Party and of the democratic trade unions reflected the same achievements and the same weaknesses as the Weimar state; they had been caught up in formalistic democratic conceptions and they considered Hindenburg and Bruening as the "lesser evil." The Social Democratic leaders were convinced that, in order to avoid open battle in a situation unfavorable to the democratic labor movement, they must tolerate this lesser evil, at whatever cost.

The Communist leaders, on the other hand, considered anyone who so much as questioned their "party line," a "traitor to the working class" and a "social-Fascist." According to this party line, the "principal enemies" were the social-Fascist Social Democrats and the social-Fascist trade unions. It was these "chief bulwarks of German capitalism" which must first be beaten.

However, most of the members and sympathizers of both parties looked upon Hitler as their common enemy. The will to unite in the struggle against the Nazis developed spontaneously during the summer of 1932, but was not strong enough to overcome the official enmity of more than a decade.

Mass Organizations Go Underground

On July 20, 1932, Franz von Papen, Reich Chancellor by courtesy of Hindenburg and representative of the feudal *Herrenklub,* broke the last great stronghold of Weimar democracy by a coup d'état in Prussia. The Social Democratic and Communist workers of Berlin joined in a protest demonstration in the Lustgarten. Jointly, they demanded a general strike. But, the "strong men" of the Social Democratic movement, Otto Braun and Carl Severing, did not dare to demand that the trade unions call a general strike to protest the overthrow of the legal government of Prussia. They did not dare to do so, although they had the magnificently equipped state police force of 90,000 men to support the strikers. The Central Committee of the Communist Party declared that it had no interest in defending the Social Democratic government of Prussia, which had shown itself to be the "enemy of the working class." Thus the most important bastion in the fight against Hitler was surrendered without resistance. The Weimar Republic was mortally wounded.

Once more, in the fall of 1932, there seemed to be a chance to change the course of events. At the November 6th elections, the National Socialists lost 2,000,000 votes as compared with the elections in July of the same year, the first regression that they had suffered since the party's rise began in 1930. The two labor parties together polled 1,500,000 votes more than Hitler. The Catholic Center still carried more than 4,000,000 votes. Even supported by the conservative German Nationalist

51

Party of Hugenberg, the Nazis were in the minority.

Actually, it was this regression and the threat that National Socialism and the reactionaries would fail that hastened the end of Weimar. Goebbels himself, in his book *From Kaiserhof to Reich Chancellory*, tells how great the danger was and describes the grave difficulties of the Nazi Party at that time. The reactionary adventurer, Von Papen, had been followed as Chancellor by Von Schleicher, the "liberal general." General von Schleicher negotiated with the trade unions for coöperation against the Nazis. He threatened to expose the corruption of the Junker land-owners of East Elbia and to tell the true story of the scandalous subsidies granted to the great estates in East Prussia, a scandal in which President Hindenburg himself was involved. It was while Von Schleicher was in office that the encouraging November elections took place and showed the Nazis that "legal means" did not necessarily work to their advantage.

If strictly legal means were no longer effective, then trickery and intrigue would serve. Thus, it was Von Papen who helped to bring unity between the representatives of big industry, the large land-owners, the army and the higher bureaucracy on one side and the "plebeian" National Socialists on the other, and he too was responsible for winning Hindenburg's agreement. General Schleicher was out, and on January 30th Hindenburg appointed Hitler Reich Chancellor.

On the day before the German people were to elect

their "National Government" in such peculiar circumstances—on March 4, 1933, six days after the Reichstag fire—we took part in a mass meeting which we shall never forget. It was a symbol of the unresisting collapse of the powerful German labor movement. *"Berlin bleibt rot!"* The cry rose from the throats of a hundred thousand marching men and women. "Berlin . . ." a voice called out, ". . . will always be red!" the marchers answered. And from the windows of the houses in the inner city came the echo: "Heil Hitler!" "Germany Awake—Down with the Jews!"

It was Saturday, March 4, 1933, the eve of the elections Hitler had called in order to get a vote of confidence from the German people for his National Government. The Social Democratic Party and the trade unions had called a pre-election mass demonstration at the Lustgarten in the heart of Berlin, the great square between the old imperial palace, the Domkirche and the Altes Museum. Disciplined lines of demonstrators poured into this traditional meeting place from every corner of the city of four millions.

There had been many such mass demonstrations in the Lustgarten, many that had played a decisive role in recent German history. It was here that the old Emperor Wilhelm I had, in 1871, greeted the patriotic citizens of the new Reich. Here, his grandson, boastful Wilhelm II, had said on August 2, 1914: "I no longer recognize parties, I only recognize Germans!" It was here, after the Hohenzollerns had been overthrown, that the first assemblies of the young Republic took place. And, during the first tumultuous years of the post-war period, it was to this center that the German people came by the hundreds of thousands to demonstrate. They came to demonstrate for democracy, against the cowardly murders by the reactionaries, for political amnesty and against the "emergency decrees" with which the Weimar Republic was slowly being strangled.

On every May Day and on the eve of each of the numerous elections of 1930-33, the great square was filled with hundreds of thousands of citizens. And always at those times the red flags of the labor organizations and the black-red-gold of the Republic waved from the ramp of the palace and from the public steps of the museum. But, at the same time, there were the black-white-red banners of the conservative right and, in more recent years, in growing numbers, the black swastika in its white circle on the red field, the flag of the so-called National Revolution.

Demonstrations and mass assemblies meant something in Germany which they could not mean in England or in the United States, where the right of freedom of assembly has so long been taken for granted.

In Germany, the "freedom of the streets" was won late and it was only won from the Hohenzollern police state after a long, hard struggle. Before the First World War, every public demonstration in Germany was an organized protest against the autocratic authorities and a movement in favor of democratic rights. During the

Weimar Republic the "freedom of the streets" was defended just as jealously as before. In January, 1920, 113 people lost their lives because they wanted to demonstrate within the so-called *Bannmeile*, the legal precincts of the Reichstag. In 1929, the attempt of an overzealous police president to forbid the May Day demonstration cost the lives of thirty men and women. By March, 1933, Hitler was not yet strong enough to infringe upon this bitterly contested privilege.

On election eve, we were with our party division in Neukoeln, in the south of Berlin.

The street scene was no different than usual: red-black-gold flags at the windows, the red banners of the demonstrators, election posters on the walls, leaflets scattered on the streets, brass bands, posters: *"Berlin bleibt rot."* "Beat Hitler—Vote List No. 2—the Social Democratic Party." "Down with Fascism—Vote Social Democrat." "For the Democratic Trade Unions—Against Reaction—Vote List No. 2."

Policemen were stationed on every corner, mounted policemen at the intersections, police cars in the squares, the guards of policemen's helmets down, rubber truncheons in their hands, pistols ready to shoot. Before the railway underpass was an armored car, its machine-guns turned menacingly on the crowd. Police officers in twos and threes gave last-minute instructions to sturdy dispatch riders.

The workers' Marseillaise rang out:

The Silent War

"Wohlan, wer Recht und Freiheit achtet,
Zu unsrer Fahne steht zu Hauf! . . ."

Banners were raised: "Social Democratic Party of Germany—Berlin District—Unit III," "Association of Metal Workers of Germany," "Union of Wood Workers," "League of Construction Workers," "Union of Technical Employees."

The workers from the great factories of Berlin were in formation, eight or twelve to a line: Borsig, A.E.G., Knorrbremse, Schwarzkopff. There were old men who had taken part in the great election demonstration of 1913, war veterans of 1914, former munitions workers whose great strike in January, 1918, precipitated the collapse of the Kaiser's war machine. There were men who had been present when, on November 9, 1918, Philipp Scheidemann proclaimed the German Social Republic from the steps of the Reichstag; men who, during the Kapp Putsch in March, 1920, forced the mutinying generals to withdraw their troops from Berlin; men whose mass strike in 1923 had put an end to the adventure in the Ruhr. There were men who carried the first Social Democratic president to his grave in 1925, and who the next year, when the reactionary war veterans of the *Stahlhelm* tried to demonstrate in the streets of Berlin, repelled them by their mere presence. These were men who for decades had been building the mightiest labor movement in the world.

Long columns of unemployed marched by. Every

third worker of Berlin had been out of work, for a year, for two, for five years. There were young men who had not had tools in their hands since they finished their apprenticeship and others who had never even had a proper apprenticeship. There were many more who, for these very reasons, had left the democratic labor organizations. Some had joined the Storm Troops, some had joined the Communist League of Red Fighters. Those in the Storm Troops had it easier. The money of heavy industry bought them uniforms, paid for their barracks and for their food. After a nocturnal pistol battle, their members were always treated better by police and judges than were the defenders of the Republic. But their friends and acquaintances in the labor movement considered them traitors and treated them as such. The traditions of seventy years had survived the great depression; they had also survived the flood of Goebbels' propaganda. Even in March, 1933, a part of the unemployed were still trade unionists and Social Democrats.

A poster marked Union of Civil Service Employees passed by, followed by marching columns of letter carriers and streetcar conductors, railway employees and firemen, prison wardens and street cleaners, employees of state waterworks and state transportation systems—in gray, blue and green uniforms. In comparison with former years, their ranks had already thinned. The Nazis had announced severe reprisals for *"Parteibuchbeamte"* —state employees belonging to other parties. Many of these were afraid of losing their privileges and their pension claims. The Prussian police, formerly the strongest and most devoted fighting troops of the Republic, had gone on duty for several days with swastika armbands. Goering had already dismissed not only the important officers of the police but also dozens of governors and other local officials of the Prussian state government. The purge of the state administrative machinery had begun. Civil service employees were haunted by fear of losing their means of livelihood. But many of them had refused to be intimidated and were marching, loyal to their old organizations.

The delegations of the labor sports organizations marched by in rhythmic step: gymnastic clubs, football clubs, water sports clubs. The worker athletes had mustered thousands of boys and girls in colored shorts and white jerseys, strong, healthy and well-trained. The millions in Germany's labor-sports movement had great achievements to their credit, even if they had refused to participate in the formal competitions of conventional athletics.

Labor's cultural organizations were represented: book clubs, reading circles, Workers' Chess Associations, Labor's Union of Hikers, the Friends of Nature—whose youth hostels and camps were used every year by tens of thousands from the cities on Sunday excursions and vacation trips.

The Friends of the Children passed by and the Red Falcon youngsters in their blue blouses with loosely knotted red neckerchiefs. Then came the children from

Berlin's great barracklike tenements, children who would have spent their days in dark and airless courtyards if the labor movement had not provided them with playgrounds. The Socialist organizations of high-school and university students marched too and the hosts of Socialist labor youth in shorts and blue shirts.

From the cradle to the grave, the German worker was accompanied by his organization, party and union, sports club and cultural society, kindergarten and youth group, workers' benefit society and cremation fund. Generations had built up these organizations and in them they had achieved a real share in democratic liberty. These organizations had their own libraries, their own rest homes and pension funds, their own athletic fields, their own children's homes and summer camps. Most of them had been founded under the Hohenzollern Empire and they had been maintained and expanded through war, revolution and inflation. The Republic was their state, or at least it was supposed to be. Would Hitler succeed in destroying this work of decades without meeting resistance? That was the question that thoughtful observers asked themselves that day.

The "military" organizations of the German labor movement marched by, the *Reichsbanner* commandos and the *Hammerschaften* of the Iron Front. They were in uniform and marched with military precision. In 1933, the Reichsbanner could look back upon a history of tireless struggle in defense of democracy. After the World War, they had defended the Republic against monarchist reaction, against the *Freikorps,* against the Stahlhelm and the other armed battalions of the right. A few months before Hitler took over the Chancellorship, the Social Democratic Party, the trade unions and the Reichsbanner had joined together in the Iron Front, in order to present a united force against the Nazis. There were hundreds of thousands of determined men throughout Germany, in Berlin and Leipzig, in Cologne and Munich, ready to join their commandos at a moment's notice. They awaited orders from their top command to go into action and to fight for democracy and liberty with weapons in their hands. They waited in vain.

There was an incident in the parade which, trivial as it was, illustrated the situation that day in Berlin better than any long description. Near us in the line of march was an older man, Kurt Riemann. He was a Social Democrat to the inmost core of his being. Before 1914, he had been fired from job after job because of his convictions, but he had never given in. Riemann had held positions in the party and in the trade unions for thirty years; he was a veteran of the Berlin labor movement, a member of the City Council, a member of the executive committee of his union, treasurer of the cremation fund, honorary member of two workers' sports societies. His wife was active in the labor welfare organization; his daughter was married to an editor of the labor press. His son, a leading member of the workers' youth organization, was a good friend of ours.

At the last party meeting there had been a heated debate between Riemann and one of our younger friends. The latter had presented our point of view, namely, that we did not dare to wait until our movement was so weakened that it could no longer fight. It was high time that we took action. Many of the members present agreed with us, particularly the younger ones.

Riemann answered with a long speech in which he said essentially the following:

"Our strength lies in legal means, not in illegal ones. If we stick to the legal way our enemies will be destroyed because right will be on our side. We built up our movement through long years of devoted and painstaking work—and no Hitler can rob us of the fruits of our labor. Hitler is a demagogue; as long as he was in the opposition he was able to sway the discontented crowds. As Reich Chancellor he will have to show positive results; that he cannot do and so he will soon be out. What we must do is wait and remain calm. Unrest would only be grist for Hitler's mill. You people are still young, but we know from experience that one cannot rule over a long term with violence. Bismarck and Wilhelm II and Ludendorff all had to learn that. Certainly sacrifices must be made. The labor movement has become great through sacrifice. Our strength lies in our use of legal weapons. We must stick to them and justice will prevail."

61

That phrase, "legal means," was a fetish and the old and honorable fighters in our midst refused to believe that "legal means" had become one of Hitler's most important weapons. After the encouraging elections in November, any doubts these older members of the labor movement may have had vanished again. At the end of his speech, Riemann used the argument with which we were so familiar in those days: "Germany is not Italy!" —the German version of "It can't happen here."

In the inner city, not far from the Lustgarten, which was our goal, the line of march was halted. Something had happened ahead of us in the parade. A group of Storm Troopers standing on a balcony decorated with a mammoth swastika flag called out: "The Red Plague!" A young worker two lines in front of us answered: "Fascist Rabble! Murderers of the Workers!" Another Nazi shouted: "Germany, awake!" and the other Storm Troopers answered in chorus: "Down with the Jews!"

From every side, the demonstrators called out slogans which were no longer intelligible in the tumult. A police car speeded up to us. A young lieutenant stood beside the driver. "What's going on here? Quiet or I'll lock up every disturber of the peace!"

Riemann stepped out in front. "Quiet, comrades," he said, "don't let them provoke you!" "We won't stand for insults," the young worker in front of us retorted.

The police officer nodded. Three policemen sprang from the car and set upon the young man with their clubs. A few seconds later, before we had grasped what was happening, the bewildered boy was in the police car. As they drove off the officer turned and called to Riemann: "Be careful. You'll be next; we'll show you people we mean to keep order."

Two hours after this incident, Otto Wels, chairman of the Social Democratic Party, declared before hundreds of thousands of listeners at the Lustgarten: "Strict masters do not rule for long." This, in few words, was the appraisal of Hitler's rule by the forces supporting the dying Weimar Democracy.

And the Communists, who for fifteen years had been working to set up their own rule in the place of this democracy, had nothing better to say on April 1, 1933, than: "The momentary calm after the victory of Fascism is only a passing phenomenon. The rise of the revolutionary tide in Germany will inevitably continue. The resistance of the masses against Fascism will inevitably increase. The open dictatorship of Fascism destroys all democratic illusions, frees the masses from the influence of the Social Democratic Party and thus accelerates the speed of Germany's march toward the proletarian revolution."

The next weeks and months of the spring of 1933 were a nightmare of unrestrained violence on one side and complete impotence on the other. The tempest of National Revolution swept away the remnants of the Weimar Democracy faster than even the worst pessimists had dreamed could be possible.

By prohibiting the Communist Party and annulling

the Reichstag mandates of Communist deputies, Hitler attained what the election had not given him, an absolute majority in the German Reichstag. The leaders of the German Nationalist Party had anticipated that they would hold the balance of power with their 3,000,000 popular votes and their fifty-one Reichstag deputies and be able to control their new Reich Chancellor, Adolf Hitler. Hitler saw to it that these betrayers should in turn be betrayed. Their shrewd plan went up in flames with the burning of the Reichstag. Hitler abided by the rules set by the feudal reactionaries and the heavy industrialists no more than he abided by the rules of democracy.

He used his new power ruthlessly. His enemies had put great hope in the traditional resistance of Bavaria against every centralized authority in Berlin. But, on March 9th, only four days after the Reichstag elections, Held's Catholic state government in Bavaria was expelled by force. The governments of Baden, Wuerttemberg and Hamburg followed in rapid succession. The "Reich Law Concerning Governors," announced on April 7th, granted dictatorial powers to Nazi Party Gauleiters in each German state. Within a few weeks, Hitler had removed the obstacles that had paralyzed the framers of the Weimar Constitution. National Socialism had banished states' rights and the Reich government was completely centralized.

Franz von Papen was still the Prime Minister of the largest and most powerful state of Germany, Prussia.

As Hindenburg's lieutenant, he was also Vice-Chancellor. Hitler shoved him aside too—making himself Governor of Prussia on the basis of the "Reich Law Concerning Governors" and making Hermann Goering, the Minister of the Interior for Prussia, his deputy.

On June 1st, three months after the burning of the Reichstag, the Nazis' coalition partner, the German Nationalist Party, was deprived of its power. The Young Bismarck Bund, the conservative youth organization, was dissolved and the military organization of the German Nationalists, the Stahlhelm, was rendered impotent by the simple expedient of incorporating it as a Reserve in the S.A. The same fate awaited all the periphery organizations of the other conservative parties, whether they were a part of the National Government or in the "loyal opposition."

Late in June the political parties of the right and center disbanded "voluntarily," the conservative German Nationalists as well as the Catholic Center. Alfred Hugenberg, head of the German Nationalists and leader of the coalition which had brought Hitler to power, resigned from the cabinet on June 27th. On July 14th, the National Socialist Party was named the State Party. It was announced that attempts to continue party activities illegally or to found new party organizations would be severely punished. Germany had become a one-party state only five and a half months after Hitler's appointment to the Reich Chancellorship.

The real impact of the Nazi attack had been directed

against labor organizations. The Communist Party was the first to be outlawed and this act was applauded by the same conservative parties who a few weeks later were to be themselves disbanded.

Although they had talked about having to go underground and predicted the coming of the final conflict, the leaders of the Communist Party were dumbfounded. Before the night on which the Reichstag burned was over, the chairman of the Communist Reichstag group, Torgler, and many other leading members had been arrested. Soon afterwards, Thaelmann, chairman of the party, and even such an underground expert as Georgi Dimitroff, representative of the Comintern, were also arrested. That they had not even been able to bring their popular leader, Teddy Thaelmann, to safety was a great shock to the Communists.

The local party organizations were no better prepared. Almost all of the known leaders were arrested or had to go in hiding. From the very beginning it was evident that the Communist structure was riddled with Nazis. They had spies and agents provocateurs placed throughout the party even in the Central Committee. During those first weeks, the Communists lost the largest and the best part of their officers and functionaries.

A formal attack was not made on the Social Democratic organizations at first. However, publication of their newspapers became virtually impossible because of consistent prohibition and confiscation. All public assemblies were forbidden and the Storm Troopers broke up membership meetings, arresting or kidnapping the party officials present.

The despairing leaders clung to the fiction that the party was still legal. Otto Wels, Chairman of the Executive Committee, resigned from the council of the Labor and Socialist International, hoping that the formal breaking-off of international connections would save the party from being banned. Those younger members who insisted that the party should go underground, while there was still time to save something, were called "hare-brained radicals" and "Communists" and threatened with expulsion from the party. The demoralizing effect of this retreat, in the face of the increasing terror of the enemy, was intensified by the flight of the former Prussian Prime Minister, Otto Braun, who escaped to Switzerland immediately after the March elections. Other former dignitaries of the Social Democratic Party followed him. The Nazis skilfully furthered the process of inner disintegration by arresting the more radical party leaders, particularly those who were Jewish, and treating those Social Democrats who had held high office—high officials in the ministries, former Police Commissioners, etc.—with great courtesy, and retiring them with full pensions.

Actually, the decisive blow fell, not against the Social Democratic Party as such, but against the free trade unions. The trade unions were still the backbone of the labor movement. Their membership had declined almost by half since the peak of the post-war period, from

67

more than eight million to four. (This does not include the more than one million members of the "Christian unions.") Nevertheless, the unions still were, by far, the greatest mass organizations of Germany. Made up primarily of skilled workers they had been weakened but not seriously threatened by mass unemployment. The property of the trade unions still counted in the millions and various unions still possessed large office buildings, printing presses, schools and vacation homes. They still could be something of a political force.

Officially, the Social Democratic Party program was also the program of the free trade unions, but it would be inaccurate to say that the unions were controlled by the party. On the contrary, in a number of decisive questions, the unions had forced the party to bow to their will and during the depression years, the bonds between the party and the unions had become constantly looser. They and the Catholic unions had in 1932 joined in support of the government of the "liberal general," Kurt von Schleicher. There were rumors, during that critical time when the Nazi Party was skyrocketing to power, of negotiations between trade union leaders and Gregor Strasser, leader of the "Socialist" wing of the Nazi Party, which were not without foundation.

The union chiefs were convinced that no modern society could exist without labor unions and so assumed that even a Hitler dictatorship would be forced to some kind of coöperation with representatives of organized labor. After Hitler became Chancellor, they tried to avoid steps which would be considered hostile to the new government. Some unions, which had sent their funds abroad for safe keeping, were forced by anxious leaders to bring the money back to Germany, although they had more trouble getting it back in than in taking it out. When Hitler proclaimed on May 1st, the traditional holiday of workers of all countries, as the Day of National Labor, the union leadership decided to participate in the Nazi demonstration. Actually, a number of heads of democratic unions did march under the swastika banner on May 1st and applauded obediently as the Nazi Fuehrer demanded "Four years' time . . ."

The very next day Hitler abandoned the tolerant pose, and the illusions of the trade-union leaders vanished as he set about to destroy their organizations. The way these sturdy pillars of the Weimar Democracy were cut down should be a lesson to all. There can be no compromise with National Socialism.

It is the same story: The first of May was followed by the second of May; the annulment of the Communist Reichstag mandates was followed by the "voluntary dissolution" of the German Nationalists; the visit of Schuschnigg to Berchtesgaden was followed by the invasion of Austria and, finally, the Munich Conference was followed by the occupation of Prague.

Once the Nazis had rendered impotent the Socialist labor movement, the only enemy capable of serious resistance, there was nothing to stop them. The Nazis incorporated the far-flung network of societies and organizations into their own state. *Gleichschaltung*, meaning the summary conversion of all organizations and institutions into sections of the Nazi Party apparatus, was the slogan of the day. Youth leagues, sport clubs, cultural societies and savings associations were *gleichgeschaltet* by a simple process of appointing Nazi leaders and commissars. Threat of confiscation or suppression forced newspapers, magazines and publishing houses to fall into line, another form of Gleichschaltung. Editors and correspondents could conform or be fired. Schools, technical and academic institutes were cleansed of undesirable elements—gleichgeschaltet. On the evening of May 10th, the flames that rose from the pyre before the University of Berlin, consuming the intellectual heritage of centuries, lighted the Gleichschaltung of the German intellect. The National Revolution was triumphant.

The victory was complete. In a few weeks, the Nazis had not only destroyed the material base for organized resistance, they had also broken the spirit of resistance. But not in every individual. On the contrary. Uncounted executions and murders, the masses that have peopled the prisons and concentration camps, have proved that love of liberty and loyalty to the ideals of justice and democracy continued to live in the hearts of countless men and women, stronger than ever before.

But what could a single individual do against the overwhelming power of National Socialism? Once the great organizations of the German working class had been destroyed, organized mass resistance was unthinkable. Only a resistance of masses of the people could have halted the advance of National Socialism. The individual was impotent. That was the way it was later for the citizens of Czechoslovakia, who had to look on in powerless indignation as the German troops marched into Prague. It had been the same for German democrats—workers, intellectuals, peasants—who had to stand helplessly by, while their freedom was being taken away from them bit by bit, while their homes were searched and their friends taken to the cellars of Storm Troop barracks and to concentration camps. German and Czech historical and national backgrounds were different, it is true; the social and political problems were not identical; but both cases had one factor in common: the decisive bastions around which a successful defense could have been built had been given up without a struggle. In the case of Germany the democrats of Weimar had relinquished the bastion without raising a hand in its defense; in the case of Czechoslovakia, it was the democrats of the world.

Hitler, in speaking of the events of 1933, once said: "This great revolution was carried out without a windowpane being broken, without a hair of the head of a former enemy being touched." In the meanwhile the world has learned how much confidence to put in the words of the German Reich Chancellor.

Back in 1933 careful observers could have studied that "strategy of terror" which later had so much to do with the rapid conquest of western Europe. We shall probably never learn the total number of the victims in the first wave of terror. An official of the Berlin Bureau of Vital Statistics reported several years later that, during the first two years of the Nazi regime, 30,-000 people, in no way officially accounted for, had simply disappeared from Berlin alone. "Address unknown" was the only information that Germany's scrupulous census authorities could give about them.

During the first months of Hitler's rule, the terror and vengeance of the victor had unbridled sway. The life of an enemy of the regime depended on the whim of any neighbor who knew about his past. Former members of the labor parties, renegades, who had gone over to the Nazis earlier, and had been scorned and boycotted by their former friends, came back as S.A. "Storm Leaders" to take vengeance. Whole sections of German cities were painstakingly combed for "Marxists." The mere possession of old books, old newspapers, leaflets or pictures of long-dead labor leaders could have deadly consequences.

The enemy might be anywhere: your next-door neighbor, the janitor, the boss at the factory, a girl who worked in the office with you, a zealous Storm Trooper out on his rounds, the grocer whose bill had not been paid, the workman who had borrowed money from you and not returned it. The expanding Gestapo apparatus was swamped with denunciations. On a single day no less than 7,000 denunciations were handed in to the Gestapo central headquarters in Berlin.

Rumors about kidnappings, beatings, murders, reports about spies and traitors helped to create an atmosphere of insecurity and paralyzing fear. In later years, the Nazis learned to make use of the rumors that inevitably develop and fashion them into a kind of whisper propaganda, one of the means of intimidating dissatisfied persons who might go into active opposition. But during those summer months of 1933 no synthetic assistance was needed. With their own eyes they had seen the Republic crumble about them and witnessed the unspeakable terror of the Nazis—the German people were ready to believe anything.

Although they had been persecuted and defamed, though their leaders had been captured and had abandoned them to the will of a relentless enemy, the remnants of the labor movement did not give in. What has been built up over decades cannot be entirely destroyed even under the worst terror. The demoralizing effect of the democratic capitulation was more serious than the enemy's brutal attacks. But the fighting traditions of the past were not dead altogether. It would take many more years of oppression, of disappointment, and shattered illusions before the great masses of organized workers would give up their hopes of a return to the old order.

Within a few weeks, underground newspapers were springing up on all sides. Few of them were printed;

73

most were only a few mimeographed sheets, primitive in form and inadequate in content. The price that those who wrote and distributed them paid in personal sacrifice was out of all proportion to their possible effectiveness. Just the same, every one of these papers was a testimony: "We are still alive—we are still true to the old cause—Hitler could destroy our organization, but he cannot kill our spirit."

But these appearances of activity were just engagements fought in retreat by an army which had already been beaten. The workers of Germany had begun to get used to everyday life in a Fascist state, when they were roused from indifference by the thunder of the cannon in Vienna. It was February 12, 1934.

At the request of Mussolini, the Clerical-Fascist government of Austria had set their battalions to fight the decisive battle against democracy in their little country. Using the pretext that he was defending the independence of Austria against National Socialist Germany, Chancellor Dollfuss and his *Christlich-Soziale* government had removed one democratic right after the other, rendering parliament powerless and discarding the freedom of the press and freedom of assembly. These so-called defenders of Christian culture and European civilization believed that they could fight the Nazis more effectively by destroying the only bulwark that could have defended democracy in Austria, the Socialist labor movement.

In the last elections in Austria, labor had polled 40

percent of the total vote. The Communist Party was negligible. Since the World War, the Social Democratic Party had done its utmost to keep the tiny, economically impossible country of Austria alive. It had made poverty-stricken Vienna a model progressive municipality. The workers' military guard, the *Schutzbund*, had kept their weapons through all the years of political crises. But, when the leaders of the reactionary guard, the *Heimwehr*, declared that they would "settle things once and for all," Austrian labor rose up to defend its rights and to defend democracy.

It was an unequal battle. The economic depression had weakened the Austrian labor movement more than that of other countries. In Austria too the Social Democratic workers had waited too long; they had falsely put confidence in the good sense and the judgment of the rulers. Dollfuss's regime settled things with tanks and machine-guns, with grenades and howitzers. Martial law and the gallows finished off the job, and paved the way for the Nazi putsch five months later that cost Dollfuss his life.

Fascism and violence had triumphed once more. However, democratic Austria had not surrendered without a struggle. "Red Vienna" had defended itself. The Austrian Social Democrats fell, for liberty and democracy, with their guns in their hands. The names of the two labor leaders, Georg Weissl and Koloman Wallisch, whom Dollfuss hung, were on the lips of every worker. Groups of men and women gathered in the factories and in the working-class districts of Berlin, their faces flushed. The "extra" editions of the papers were torn from the hands of the newsboys. Crowds of silent readers stood before the billboards of the newspaper buildings. The workers would not leave their radios. A change was noticeable even in the Storm Troopers during those days while the fight was raging in Vienna; they seemed quieter, unmistakably impressed that the democrats in Austria were defending themselves in armed combat.

The end was frightful. The proud new homes of Vienna's workers lay in ruins; the courageous fighters were in prisons or their bodies stacked in mass graves, their wives and children at the mercy of the victors, and those victors knew no mercy. The Social Democratic Party and the Schutzbund were banned and their leaders in exile.

Was it worth so much sacrifice? Hundreds of thousands of German workers asked that question during the days of February, 1934. Every friend that one met asked the question. But what about Germany's unresisting defeat? For weeks and months all the underground groups weighed these problems. They discussed and tried to analyze "the lessons of the Austrian revolt."

Kurt Riemann, the old Councilman, asked his son, Walter, the same question:

"Was it worth it? Didn't our comrades in Vienna die in vain? Don't you think that perhaps we were right to avoid battle against the overwhelming superiority of our enemy?"

Walter answered: "Did fewer of our comrades die because we avoided battle? Our victims were unarmed; many of them didn't even know what they were dying for. The Austrians knew why they were sacrificing their lives. And haven't you always told me that the labor movement became great through sacrifice? You're right, the Austrians didn't save democracy but they showed us that you can fight against Fascism. They saved the honor of international Socialism, our honor too. Although they were defeated, they have given us new faith in the strength of our ideals."

In November, 1937, Walter Riemann was killed in Spain. He died for the cause of freedom.

3

Ten Thousand Heroes Lost

In 1934 the *Manchester Guardian* published a report on the underground movement in the Third Reich, telling of its "ten thousand unknown heroes." The author of this article was Frederic A. Voigt, who had for many years been the correspondent of that newspaper in Germany. Voigt was a wise observer and an excellent journalist and had a thorough knowledge of modern German history. At that time, he was, as far as we know, the only British or American newspaperman who enjoyed the confidence of any of the significant underground groups, and he had won great respect in our circles.

It was not till several weeks after its appearance that we saw a copy of Voigt's report; his paper had already been banned in the Third Reich, but one of our friends brought us the clipping from Switzerland.

Ten thousand heroes? We had mixed feelings about Voigt's story. We could not decide whether we should be pleased or annoyed. Of course we were happy to have recognition from such an outstanding observer of German conditions. We realized that a report of this kind was worth more than anything we or anti-Nazi emigrés abroad put together might write. But we took exception to such a one-sided presentation of the underground struggle and the stress on heroism.

In fact, it was this very attitude that we were trying to combat in our everyday work, the tendency to regard our underground activity in a glamorous light, which so often led to a false evaluation of the hard realities of the underground struggle and to a romantic conception of our fight against the Nazis' superior police forces. These were the conceptions with which adventure-hungry young people plunged themselves into the fight and then were not able to hold out. Our primary concern was to prepare ourselves for a long, hard struggle, demanding self-denial and sacrifice.

Otto Bauer, the great leader of the Austrian Social Democratic Party during the post-war period and the helpful and understanding friend of the new underground movement, wrote in his posthumous book, *The Underground Party:*

"At the beginning, great numbers stream into the underground parties, attracted by the romance of clandestine activity and the adventurous appeal of the fight with the police. They do not hold out. Only those with the deepest convictions, only those whose belief in the invincibility of Socialism is deeper than a passing fancy, and in whose hearts determination to hold out in the unequal struggle is rooted more firmly than love for adventure and liking for conspiracy, persevere in the un-

79

derground struggle. If they hope to win out against the police, they must cautiously consider every step they take; they must think through all their deeds carefully; their every action must be disciplined. It is only thus that they will develop a cadre in the underground fight, which will combine the highest ethical idealism with the most sober appraisal of their own strength and the strength of the enemy, a courageous philosophy based on reason."

Looking back on that early period today, it seems that our own attitude was rather one-sided and Frederic Voigt's report came closer to realism than we thought. Of course, we were then in the midst of our struggle against the illusions and the romanticism which had contributed so much to the collapse of the old labor movement and which later contributed so much to the tragedies of the first years under Nazi rule. Even we realized that there were hundreds of thousands of former members of the old labor movement who carried on courageous resistance, individually or in small groups, that there were tens of thousands who preferred prison and concentration camp to submission to the Nazis, that thousands were being murdered by Hitler's henchmen.

For us, the problem was not whether we should be heroic or not. The question we asked was: are the sacrifices demanded by this heroism in logical proportion to the ends achieved? Is the risk involved in a given deed proportionate to the possible good to be attained? Can the activities of the underground groups seriously threaten Nazi domination or hasten the collapse of this barbaric system, or are these courageous martyrs making their sacrifices in vain?

One might say, and rightly, that no soldier who falls in the fight against Fascism has really died in vain. The spirit of the dead, the magnitude of their sacrifice, lives on among those who survive. But that exactly was the problem: the underground organization *itself* must survive, even at the cost of uncounted victims. The task of the underground movement in the first line was not to disturb the Fascist rulers, not to make difficulties for them, not to annoy them. Its task was to organize the resistance of the people against the rule of violence, to bring together the isolated centers of resistance and to utilize any serious blow to the system in order to help toward its downfall. This task could not be fulfilled if the most determined fighters were sitting in prisons and concentration camps or had already been killed by the Nazis.

In fighting against a terrorist apparatus like that of the Gestapo, the most difficult problem is always to determine the limits of the activity of an underground organization. Underground fighters can make mistakes in the direction of too much activity as well as in the direction of passivity. During the first years of Hitler domination, most of the mistakes were in trying to do too much.

One night in the spring of 1934, the inhabitants of Gartenfeld, a small working-class quarter near the Siemans Works, were roused from their sleep by the sound of firing. Trucks filled with police and Storm Troops raced through the town toward the cottage development on the outskirts. Shooting continued for more than an hour, then stopped as suddenly as it began.

Two ambulances returned toward the city. In the meanwhile the district was surrounded by Gestapo, police and Storm Troops. Every house was searched, more than two dozen people, almost all of them former members of the Reichsbanner, were arrested. The Storm Troops were particularly brutal in the treatment of their prisoners. One, in whose home leaflets were found, was beaten so badly that he was permanently crippled.

Gartenfeld was in a kind of state of siege the next day. No one could leave his house without special permission, and hearings were conducted all day long. In the end more than fifty people were arrested and it was late in the night before the police and the Storm Troops withdrew.

Probably all the details of the Gartenfeld tragedy will never be known. From what we were able to learn, the action was directed against a group of young Reichsbanner people who had buried about a dozen rifles and some munitions under the beans and potatoes in a vegetable garden. Gartenfeld was an outlying district and they believed that their little arsenal was safe. Thorough as they were, the Nazis could not dig up all of Germany in order to look for a few rifles and hand grenades.

But, if you possessed weapons, you also had to take

care of them. That was why two brothers, who were members of the group, Karl and Erich Lorenz, were assigned the task of exhuming the little treasure every few months to oil and clean the rifles and bury them again. No army took better care of its weapons. Things went all right for several months. National Socialism celebrated its first triumphs. One democratic form after the other was destroyed, one labor organization after the other was broken. Karl and Erich, unemployed, under suspicion as former members of the Reichsbanner and as Social Democrats, cared for their little arsenal, preparing for the great conflict, the overthrow of Hitler.

We were not able to find out whether the Lorenz brothers had been under observation for a long time, whether they were denounced, or whether it was simply by chance that they were discovered in the midst of cleaning their guns. In any event, the Nazis arrived to find Karl and Erich with all their arms laid out in the garden shack. Surprised with weapons in their hands, they both opened fire. Evidently they were able to barricade themselves in the little house and to beat off the first police attack. It was said that at least eight Nazis were wounded, but of course there was never any doubt how the unequal fight would end. Erich was the luckier of the two, he was killed on the spot by a Nazi bullet. Karl was badly wounded and fell into the hands of the victors, still breathing. They literally trampled him to death.

The Reichsbanner men arrested in Gartenfeld were

tried for high treason and armed resistance. All of those who it could be proved had even a slight acquaintance with the Lorenz brothers were sentenced to long prison terms.

Such events were the order of the day in 1933 and 1934. The victorious Nazis were particularly energetic in dealing with the military organizations of the opposition, the organizations which had been their most active opponents in the preceding years of struggle.

Pretty much the same tactics were used against the Reichsbanner, the guard of the democratic left, as were used against all of the great democratic mass organizations. The central core of the organization was destroyed by the arrest of the most active leaders. The others were intimidated, their offices confiscated. Attempts were made to corrupt any wavering elements in the leadership—in short, the Nazis used all the techniques that had operated so effectively against the trade unions. Uncounted victims from the ranks of the militant democrats fell during the first year of Nazi rule.

The fate of the members of the Communist "Red Front Fighters Bund" was even worse. In the eyes of the Nazis, they were the "Murder Communes." In addition to the vengeance, which the local Storm Troops wreaked upon them, were the anger and bitterness of the special courts. Mere suspicion that an individual had participated in one of the countless street fights of the previous years was sufficient ground for the death penalty.

84

Ten Thousand Heroes Lost

Despite the degree of danger and the hopelessness of their situation after their organizations had collapsed, despite the shocking discrepancy between their few revolvers and pistols and the machine-guns and tanks of the police, the little underground groups did not give up their resistance. They did not give up their hopes or their preparations for "der Tag." Their story is a tale of unknown heroes fighting against that same National Socialism which, only six years later, was to challenge the entire world.

The Nazi press was silent. Only a very few people in the near vicinity learned about happenings such as that at Gartenfeld. Most of these were silent too. And in the democratic countries abroad, after 1933, interest in the atrocities of the Nazis waned. A pall of silence was laid over the silent war going on beneath the surface of everyday life in the Third Reich. This silence was broken only occasionally by courageous publications of democratic newspapers, especially the organs of the European labor parties.

We only mention this as a fact, not in a spirit of bitterness. Apparently human nature can comprehend only a certain amount of atrocity, before its sensitivity is deadened. After a certain point, it cannot take in any more bloodshed and misery. The concerns of everyday life make their demands on one's attention.

The same thing that happened with the atrocities of the Nazis in the Third Reich in 1933-34 is happening today with Nazi atrocities in the occupied countries.

When Hendrik Willem van Loon heard, at the end of June, 1942, that his 27-year-old nephew had probably been killed by the Nazis, he said:

"I don't understand people any more. We tell them these tales of Nazi ruthlessness and brutality time and again, and they only half listen to you, as if to tell you: 'Oh, you must be exaggerating. No human beings could be as cruel as that.' Sometimes I fear we will never learn, until the bombs start falling here."

These moving words furnish perhaps the best answer to the question: Why does the world know so little about the silent war within the Third Reich? It is not only because the organization of terror is so complete and because the Nazis have shut Germany off from the rest of the world. It is also because human capacity to comprehend the sufferings of others is limited.

This human quality was an advantage for the Nazis. The world unconsciously became more lenient in its judgment of their brutalities. The Nazi press said nothing; it had every reason to be silent. It was silent about murders and executions, about death sentences and barbarous penitentiary treatment, about the misery and the sadism in the prisons and concentration camps. It was also silent about the unnamed and unknown enemies of National Socialism, about the opposition and the sacrifices it made.

The risk taken by militant Reichsbanner members who "were trying to keep their powder dry," was hardly different from the risk of the no less militant writers of illegal leaflets and illegal newspapers, of the couriers and contact men, of the leaders and the simple soldiers of that first year of underground struggle.

In 1933 and 1934 there were dozens of underground papers in every large city, supplying a certain group of readers, more or less regularly. There was every kind of anti-Nazi activity, from simply getting information to distributing leaflets, from compiling confidential reports for distribution among a narrow circle of friends to posting placards and painting slogans on walls.

But even the most highly qualified activists "survived" the years of 1934 and 1935 only in rare cases. By "survive" the literal meaning is not always intended; in most cases the activists withdrew into private life or landed in prisons and concentration camps.

This is the story of an especially qualified group and its end:

One evening in September, 1933, at a time when there were great crowds of people on the Hermannplatz in Berlin, thousands of leaflets fluttered down from the top story of one of Berlin's tallest buildings, the Karstadt Building. The wind carried them over all of the Hermannplatz and into the adjoining streets. These leaflets told a story of corruption among leading Nazis. The passersby read them eagerly. Actually, before the police could intervene effectively, so many people knew the very concrete story contained in the leaflet that it spread through the city like wildfire.

This "action" was unusually successful. All of Berlin

was talking about the leaflet for days. Then, as now, corruption among Nazi leaders was one of the favorite topics of conversation among restive citizens of the Third Reich.

The action was also successful from a second point of view. The Gestapo sent a special detachment to the scene at once. The Karstadt department store was locked and all customers and employees were carefully searched and cross-examined. No one could leave the building before he had been examined down to the skin. The officers worked half the night but they could find no suspicious characters.

This is the inside story:

It happened that there was going to be a special exhibition in one wing of the building. Among the artisans employed to build the exhibition booths were a number of members of an underground group. They learned that there were a number of empty rooms in the building which were always kept locked.

This gave them their idea. They got other members of the group to make leaflets and brought them to the store hidden under their tools and working material. They were able to get into one of the empty rooms with a skeleton key. Just before leaving work the fateful day, they took the leaflets into the locked room and laid the package on one end of a wooden plank, which they balanced over a windowsill. On the other end of the plank they put a tin can, filled with water, so that the plank balanced. Tiny holes had been punched in the can, so that the water flowed out gradually till the end of the plank with the leaflets on it became heavier and they fell down on the Hermannplatz. In the meanwhile the authors of the deed were already far away.

That was how they did it. The members of the group did not let success go to their heads and try a repetition. Nevertheless, scarcely six months later, fate caught up with them.

The Gestapo got hold of a harmless letter. The only reason why it was of "interest" to them was because it was written to a man whom they had under observation. Just because the letter seemed so completely harmless the Gestapo were all the more suspicious and examined it very carefully. They discovered that it had been written on the same typewriter as the famous Karstadt leaflets of a half year before.

These details were revealed in the subsequent trial of members of this underground group. Only two of them were able to escape arrest. One member "hanged himself in his cell." Sentences for the others ranged from a year and a half to fifteen years in the penitentiary.

In spite of their unusually good qualifications and in spite of their painstaking precautions this group was wiped out, betrayed by a typewriter. For all underground groups, a typewriter was a costly and precious possession. Without one, they could not write their reports, their leaflets or their underground newspapers. Their poverty compelled them to use the same typewriter over and over again. All too often lack of funds prevented the taking of necessary precautions and typewriters were frequently brought into court as evidence against their owners.

However, underground groups were destroyed much more often by failure to take human weaknesses into account than by such scarcely avoidable technical risks. It was a rule in all really serious groups that no member could be accepted who drank or who for any other reason might not be fully responsible for his actions. But even living in the catacombs, a human being is a human being, and human qualities such as need for companionship, love and hate have caused countless tragedies.

One of our friends, while in the Luckau prison, became acquainted with a certain Fritz Kraus. Kraus was a metal worker of about 35, had been a member of the Communist Party since his early youth, and had traveled all over Europe. He was politically trained, a good comrade and even in prison he was looked upon as a leader. At the same time he was a quiet person who kept his own counsel. Our friend had shared the same cell with him for many months before Kraus told him his story.

At the end of 1932, just before the Nazis took power, Kraus had gotten a job at the A.E.G. Turbine Works and had moved to Schoeneweide, an industrial suburb of Berlin where there were a number of large electrical and chemical plants, as well as railroad shops and many small factories. In the course of 1933, the old party organization was completely destroyed, but even the

Gestapo were not able to arrest all the former functionaries in this stronghold of the labor movement.

Kraus was not known in the factory nor in his neighborhood and, knowing how careless the Communist organizations were, he was cautious enough to avoid making any contact with the party during the stormy period
of Hitler's National Revolution.

Kraus was certainly a person with a thorough knowledge of people and unusual ability in dealing with them.
He had those qualities that are indispensable for an underground organizer, a healthy distrust of people whom
he did not know well and complete confidence in those
with whom he worked.

Kraus had another advantage: he knew his own limitations. For example, he was not able alone to write a
leaflet, much less an underground newspaper. It was also
difficult for him to make a speech, although he could
express his thoughts well in individual discussion. He
had grown up in the tradition of the German labor
movement, where, for decades, it had been axiomatic
that no political action should be undertaken unless
based on political theory.

Therefore, Kraus recognized that his first job in
preparing for future underground work was to find
the right assistants. He remembered an old acquaintance,
a girl who had been a student at the University and
long a member of the Communist Party. She had recently returned to Berlin and was working as a secre-

tary at the Oberspree Cable Works not far from Schoeneweide.

Erika Liebmann was exactly the person Kraus was looking for, with unquestioned loyalty to the cause, critical of the mistakes of the old party and with good theoretical training. She was also experienced in writing and had her own typewriter. The two of them began to organize the district. The first "member" of their group was a young unemployed man who lived with two friends in a garden cottage on the outskirts of Schoeneweide, about fifteen minutes' walk from the nearest houses. Their place soon became the headquarters for Kraus's group.

The old tool-shed served as an excellent hiding place for papers and equipment. A path from the cottage, through the woods to the nearest tram stop, provided a quick getaway if things should get "hot."

The three young men had been born and raised in Schoeneweide. They knew almost everyone in town; one by one they brought old acquaintances from the labor movement to Erika and Kraus. They were very careful that their identities should not become known and only the inmost circle knew the correct names of the members.

New members were never permitted to come to meetings until Erika and Kraus, after long conversations with them in the woods or in crowded coffee houses, had carefully examined their backgrounds and decided that they were qualified to participate in the group's activities. Not one of them knew where Kraus lived.

After several months of careful selection and training of his people, Kraus succeeded in organizing a good group. Its membership included representatives in the most important factories in the vicinity of Schoeneweide, in the A.E.G., in the Accumulator Works, in the Kahlbaum Chemical Works, in the N.S.U. Auto Factory and in the Lorenz Radio firm. Many of them had been members of the Communist Party or the Social Democratic Party; others had been trade unionists. The greatest caution was required of each of them, no individual actions, no careless propaganda. Their duties were: first, careful observation of conditions in their factories and among the people with whom they came in contact and reports on these to the central committee; and, second, careful exploration and recruiting of trustworthy new members.

The next step was to make contacts with the outside world. Here, too, Kraus went to work with unusual care. Because of his broad circle of acquaintances in the old days, it would have been easy for him to make contacts with the official Communist Party. But Kraus avoided that. He knew that the Gestapo were arresting one central committee after the other. If he met one of his old friends by chance, he acted as if he had given up all thought of further political activity.

Instead of getting in touch with groups in Germany, he used his summer vacation to make a hiking trip through the Riesengebirge. From there, it was an easy matter to stroll over the frontier into Czechoslovakia. A week before, one of his "adjutants" had crossed over into Czechoslovakia by a nearby, but different, path and had asked an old friend of Kraus, the editor of a German-Czech trade-union paper in Reichenberg, to meet Kraus in a hotel off the beaten track in the mountains. With this man Kraus discussed the technical possibilities for transmitting reports about conditions inside Germany abroad and getting money and information, particularly about what was happening in the international labor movement, into Germany.

Kraus had thought of everything. There was just one thing he overlooked: his own wife's jealousy of Erika Liebmann. Kraus tried in vain to prove to her that his relations with his closest colleague were exclusively concerned with their political work. She didn't believe him, and, while Kraus was in the Riesengebirge, his wife went to the police and reported that he was being unfaithful to her under the pretext of political activity. She told them that the garden cottage was their lovers' rendezvous.

The Gestapo investigated. The wife was told that the matter was of no consequence, so that she would not become alarmed. Kraus was arrested the moment he returned home and so were the three young men. The garden cottage was placed under observation day and night. One of the young men broke under the Gestapo's torture and "told all." Then practically all of the members of the group were arrested.

94

TEN THOUSAND HEROES LOST

In the trial against "Kraus and Comrades" before the People's Court, Kraus received eight years' penal servitude for high treason. The others got from three to six years.

Mrs. Kraus collapsed and soon after the trial she had to be sent to an insane asylum.

It was inevitable that many victims should be claimed in the struggle against the Nazi regime. But the majority were sacrificed unnecessarily, because the opposition judged Nazism falsely. The common failing was to anticipate a rapid collapse of the Hitler rule and to try to continue a part of their legal mass movement underground. Tens of thousands had to die, hundreds of thousands had to go to concentration camps before the movement was freed of the old ideas of underground work which had been carried over from the time of the Anti-Socialist Laws of Bismarck, from the First World War, or at best from the experience of the Russian Bolsheviks.

An example of the consequences of such false ideas is described in a little book written by one of our closest friends, Evelyn Lend, and published in the United States in 1938 under the title, *The Underground Struggle in Germany*. The author writes:

"I remember particularly vividly one incident in the first days of July, 1933: I happened to meet in the streets of Berlin a friend of mine who was a member of the C.P. We talked for a while and I asked him what he was doing these days, whereupon I received the surprising answer: 'I am just going to sell literature [meaning party literature].' 'What do you mean, selling literature? You don't mean to tell me that you go around to strange people offering them Communist pamphlets for sale?' 'That is exactly what I do mean to tell you.' And he showed me his briefcase, which contained about a dozen copies of a pamphlet entitled *Thaelmann's Thirteen Questions to the Social Democratic Workers,* which had been published long before Hitler and which, even from a Communist point of view, was somewhat obsolete and without any meaning in the fifth month of Fascist rule. I tried—without success—to convince him of the dangers of his undertaking, which to my mind were completely out of proportion to the possible effects he might hope to achieve. A fortnight later I heard he had been arrested by the secret police. Of his further fate I know nothing."

That is a typical example of the heroism and the courage with which many Communists attempted to continue their mass activity under Hitler. Such methods led directly to prison, to concentration camp or to the grave.

This Quixotic stubbornness had its own inner logic. It was a natural result of the "short perspectives" endorsed officially by Communist leaders, who considered Hitler's accession to power as a "revolutionary crisis," which must inevitably lead to a victory of the Communists.

Starting out from such a premise, the Communists felt that mass propaganda was called for, such as distribution of leaflets and preparation for armed revolt. Never were the *Military-Political Lessons* of Lenin studied by greater numbers than in 1933. Nor were the Communists the only ones who turned to Lenin at this time. The decisive differences between the situation in Russia in 1917 and in Germany in 1933 were largely ignored. People overlooked the fact that in 1917 in Russia, after three years of war and grave military defeats, the population was armed, whereas in 1933 in Germany, there was an alliance between the state executive and the armed sections of the Nazi movement, that seven million unemployed were crying out to be saved from their misery, and finally, that there was an anti-Nazi movement which had been disarmed and decapitated without resisting.

It was the bravest part of the anti-Nazi movement, the part which was most willing to make sacrifices, which forgot that a successful battle must begin with a correct evaluation of the situation and not with skirmishes between advanced guards. The Russian Revolution of 1917 had not begun with fighting in Petersburg, nor did the Czechs start their revolution in 1918 by firing on the Austrian soldiers. In both cases the actual revolutions were preceded by careful and thoughtful preliminary work and by correct estimation of the situation, in one instance by Lenin, in the other by Masaryk.

Though they differed in many respects from the Communists, the section of the Social Democratic Party which resisted the Nazis also falsely evaluated the situation. To them, Hitlerism seemed only an interruption in the Weimar Democracy that could not last long. They refused to recognize that such a system of medieval barbarism could exist in the modern world. They tried to maintain their organizations, to collect dues, to hold meetings as well as they could under the new conditions.

One of these mass organizations, with which we came in contact during our first year of underground work, was made up of thousands of Social Democrats in Hamburg. It was an organization which had first-rate contacts, excellent information, and, in spite of being underground, still exerted considerable influence in the old Hanseatic city. The members considered that their group was a kind of counter-government of the city state, which was only biding its time. They were partly right, that is, until the organization was snuffed out in a single night.

We made contact with the "Hamburg organization," only after careful consideration.

We felt that for the long term Berlin was the most important center of the underground movement, but we also realized that one of our most important tasks must be to get in touch with illegal groups in the provinces. It was just because we did not believe that the Hitler dictatorship was only an episode and because we considered the chief task of an organization to prepare for the time when there would be a serious crisis of the regime, that we felt it of decisive importance to build up a network of contacts throughout the entire Reich.

The Nazis had begun by directing their main vengeance against the leaders of the labor organizations, on the correct assumption that a democratic mass organization, robbed of its leaders, was no longer an effective force, even if subordinate sections were left comparatively undisturbed for a time. In the eyes of the Nazis, an army without officers was not much more than a helpless herd. It did not seem to them that isolated groups could be dangerous. It was, therefore, the more opportune for us to restore broken contacts, once more to give individual groups in the provinces the feeling of solidarity, to exchange experiences and to establish relations with the best people among them.

Hamburg was especially fertile ground for our purposes.

An American acquaintance told us that, visiting Hamburg in 1934, he happened to get into a conversation in a restaurant with a young man who spoke excellent English. As always, in those days, the conversation turned quickly to politics. The young man expressed his scorn for the Nazis so unmistakably and so loudly that the American asked him whether he was sure that there were no police or customs officials in the restaurant. They would certainly be able to understand English. His companion looked at him in surprise: "But I am a customs official myself, and these are all my colleagues from the harbor customs authority."

Conditions for opposition to the Nazis in this old Hanseatic harbor city were more favorable than in other cities. Hamburg had always felt itself to be a "bit of England." It was only unwillingly and with reservations that the free port had joined Bismarck's Reich. For decades, Hamburg had been sending Social Democratic deputies to the Reichstag. At the last elections for the City Council in April, 1932, the labor parties had polled 46 percent of the votes and the National Socialist Party only 30 percent.

The citizens of the second largest port of Europe had always looked more to the rest of the world than had other parts of Germany. The city's prosperity depended on commerce and shipping. In Hamburg they had no tolerance for autarchy and the other fine arts of Nazi economic policy. Likewise, they considered summary *Gleichschaltung* an unjustified intervention on the part of Berlin in Hamburg's private affairs. In addition to the governor appointed by the Reich, there was a locally elected mayor and President of the Senate who, as customary, was a representative of the old Hamburg ruling house. Even the Gestapo for a long time did not hasten to carry out to the letter their orders from headquarters. The notorious anti-Semitic window displays of the *Stuermer*, which sullied the streets of all the cities of Germany, did not last long in Hamburg.

For quite a period the labor movement of this second largest city of the Reich was able to profit from these conditions. However, the fight within the labor movement was particularly bitter in Hamburg. The Social Democrats and the trade unions had always worked closely with the middle-class parties; their leaders belonged to the extreme right wing of the Socialist movement and that drove the Communists automatically to extreme radicalism. In no other section of Germany were there more determined fights between the labor organizations, nor had there been anywhere else more bloody conflicts between the military organizations of labor and the Storm Troops before Hitler took power.

After Hitler became Chancellor, the Nazis set up the "Hanseatic Special Court" to take their revenge. In a single trial concerning a shooting at the end of 1932, in which six Communists and two S.S. men had been killed, nine death sentences were handed down and several other defendants were sentenced to life imprisonment. Those who received only fifteen years were lucky.

But for many months the real severity of Nazi terror was directed almost exclusively against the remnants of the Communist Party. As late as the fall of 1934, former trade-union functionaries were able to use the "German Labor Front" for meetings of their own old guard. The number of members of the Social Democratic Party who came more or less regularly to meetings and paid their dues numbered thousands. The Socialist youth held meetings in the camps and youth hostels in the country round about.

On the night of May 1, 1934, a May Day celebration

took place in the woods with more than two hundred people present. Seamen smuggled whole cases of leaflets from Copenhagen and Rotterdam into the harbor and these found their way into the factories. During this period Hamburg scarcely belonged to Germany.

One of our friends, Leo Koch, was assigned the task of making contacts with Hamburg. He knew the city and had a relative there, an old and respectable aunt. That meant that he would have a safe place to stay and a plausible excuse for visiting Hamburg, should there be an "accident." Even the Gestapo could not object to people visiting their relatives.

The first contacts were made with extreme care. One of the girls in our organization had, shortly before Hitler took power, been to Hamburg to attend a large youth congress. She had made the acquaintance of a number of local officials of the youth organizations and had corresponded since with two or three of them. Albert Roloff, from Hamburg, had been in Berlin for a few days during the summer of 1933 and had spoken with us. At the time of his visit we had simply discussed the possibility of coöperation and had left it at that, though we had agreed in principle that it would be a good idea to make permanent contacts. Roloff spoke particularly about a rather large group of younger functionaries which he had organized.

This was a beginning. Roloff would be excellent as our chief contact and we would also get in touch with others, not only among the youth but also in the Social

Democratic Party and in the trade unions. Leo went to Hamburg and after a few days he had interested twenty to thirty people in our work. Of course he brought them news. After all, one learned more in Berlin than anywhere else, and the mere fact that he had news from the capital and from abroad made him a welcome guest. Everyone was eager to have him meet his friends—that was particularly the case in Hamburg's carefree atmosphere. The fact that no one in Hamburg knew Leo's real name gave him a certain protection.

In the weeks that followed, Leo spent many weekends in Hamburg. Our contacts became more firm. Little groups met regularly, and finally Leo had a meeting with the leading people of Hamburg's underground party organization.

In reporting to us later, he said: "You'll have to grant the Hamburg Committee one thing, they don't let anything disturb their calm. National Socialism or no National Socialism, they continue their organizational work as if nothing could happen to them. Coming to Hamburg from Berlin, you almost feel as if you were in a different country, and the people there look upon us as emissaries from another world. We speak different languages.

"They have excellent contacts in all circles of Hamburg's economic life, and that is why they know so much. Returning seamen tell them amazing stories about the growing feeling against the Nazis in other countries, which means in the international seamen's homes, because where else do foreign seamen meet people? The leaflets that come to Hamburg from abroad are written by people who have no knowledge of German conditions; how could they?

"I spent two hours trying to explain to them what the terror was. They listened politely, but they didn't believe a word I said. Speaking as diplomatically as I could, I tried to show them that an organization, built like theirs on the basis of residential membership, would be delivered helplessly over to the Gestapo at the first blow. They smiled at me indulgently and that was all.

"Finally, I spoke frankly and prophesied that it wouldn't be two months before they would all be sitting behind bars, that of their really fine organization not a fragment would remain. After that they explained to me, polite as ever, that the meeting was over.

"I had no choice but to instruct our contact people in Hamburg that they must withdraw from the large organization as carefully and unnoticeably as possible. It was a hard decision for them and it was not easy for me to demand from our new people that they part with their old friends. I discussed the problem with them all night before I convinced them. But there was nothing else to do. We had to try to save at least the kernel of a later organization from the coming disaster."

We all agreed that Leo had done the right thing; and then the collapse came as he had feared, only a few weeks after his last visit in Hamburg.

Subsequently Leo found out from our friends that

the Gestapo action had started when they surrounded and searched the large housing development on the so-called Duellberg. Very early in the morning all of the streets approaching this area were blocked off. The great police cars bore down simultaneously from all directions. Double and triple guards were placed at all street intersections. Machine-guns were mounted at strategic points.

With two sentries before the entrance of every house, the police began the systematic search of the first block, from attic to cellar, every apartment, every room, every desk, every bookcase. All of the residents were fetched out of bed and assembled in one place.

Hundreds of members of the Hamburg organization were arrested. Many of them were sentenced to long terms in prison or disappeared into concentration camps. Some of them "died in prison" or were "shot while trying to escape."

Despite our efforts we were never able to find out exactly what led to this action of the Gestapo. But one detail of this tragedy is illustrative of the spirit which was so widespread in 1934. During occasional house searchings, the Gestapo had discovered some rather peculiar snapshots, pictures of window displays of a large stationery shop. The various pictures showed the window from various angles. In some pictures the focal point was a card stating "Composition Books—10 pfennigs." Others featured "Large Correspondence Pads—25 pfennigs"; still others, "Fine Writing Paper—50 pfennigs." Usually when the Gestapo found these snapshots, they also found another picture, this one of the memorial in the Hamburg Cemetery to those who were killed in the 1918 revolution.

For a long time, the Gestapo were apparently unable to make head or tail of these baffling snapshot collections. Then one day a certain Erwin Schultz was arrested. He was denounced by a neighbor who reported that suspicious groups of people often came to his house. When they searched Schultz's apartment, the Gestapo again found the photographs: the memorial to the revolutionary dead and a whole group of photographs of the show window, neatly and carefully fastened together with a rubber band and, with them, Schultz's old Social Democratic Party membership book, with stamps recording dues payments up to March, 1933.

Schultz broke down during cross-examination. The story was told that the Gestapo threatened to take his only child away from home and send her to a state orphanage. In any case, the Gestapo learned from Schultz what the snapshots meant. The photograph of the revolutionary memorial was the membership card of the underground organization. The pictures of the shop window were receipts for payment of dues, hence the different prices.

German thoroughness and the traditional exactness of the Socialist labor movement in money matters once more celebrated a tragic triumph.

The destruction of the Hamburg organization was

not an isolated event. During the first period of underground work under Hitler, those same mistakes, which had such dire consequences in Hamburg, were made everywhere. Basically, it was one problem: the difficulty that most people experience in freeing themselves of the habits and the assumptions to which they have been accustomed under democracy. Even when people realized in theory that under Fascist rule there could be no large meetings, no "organizational life" or "political activity" such as was usual in democratic conditions, in practice almost all of them proved unable to adapt themselves to the new circumstances.

For underground work requires, above all else, renunciation—renouncing meetings with many of your friends, especially regular meetings, renouncing places of entertainment that you used to frequent, renouncing the use of the telephone, even of the mails for any purpose that is not completely "innocent," renouncing so many little comforts of daily life. It may be easy to make up one's mind to these petty renunciations, but it is very hard to remember the decision, day in and day out. Carelessness, desire for comfort, forgetfulness—the Gestapo understood all too well how to put such human weaknesses to work for their own purposes.

Our Berlin organization told what had happened to underground organization in one of its regular reports in 1934:

"One year after the collapse, the remnants of the old organizations are very largely annihilated. That does not mean that they have given up their faith or that no more connections exist. But it does mean that the movement and its activities have been reduced to microscopic size. . . .

"There are instances of great devotion. A funeral of a comrade was attended by many workers. Within hearing of the police the widow said at the grave, 'I know you were not shot in an attempt to escape.' And a worker said, 'You fell for the workers' cause; you shall be revenged.' The police did not intervene; they merely photographed a number of those present. . . .

"Of the former Social Democratic movement it is the youth above all who maintain the contacts. Numerically, extremely few are left. . . . But the young ones learn quickest of all. A year ago they merely kept in contact, met for outings or social evenings and went together hiking through the country. In the meanwhile, many of them have learned more than they could have during many years under normal conditions. Slowly they are acquiring political maturity and organizational skill. They are small in number compared to the millions of German youth. But these few are the core of a new generation which can defeat Fascism."

4

Organization for the Future

What did the men and women of the underground anti-Nazi movement in Germany actually do? What were they trying to achieve? "The overthrow of the Hitler government?" What did that mean? What means would lead toward that end? Sabotage? Inciting of strikes? Armed revolt? Assassination of leading Nazis?

In the middle of 1935, a member of the leading committee of our organization went abroad to attend a conference. In private conversation one of the members of the Executive Council of the Labor and Socialist International, a former Cabinet Minister and a man deeply interested in underground work in Germany, said to him:

"We have just devoted a great deal of time to a consideration of the problems of your work. But I must admit that I have been unable to get a concrete picture. What do you really do? How, for instance, do you spend a day?"

The question was understandable, even for a man who had grown up in the labor movement, who knew not only the problems of his own country but also those of many other European countries, and who had been in touch with German groups ever since 1933. With this background he still found Nazi Germany terra incognita and the day-to-day problems of underground work a closed book.

Our man said, "I believe that I can best give you an impression of our life and activities by describing my own special tasks and those of two of our friends.

"My first and most important function is teaching. You are probably amazed that I lead off with such a subject but, in a certain sense, we are an educational organization.

"In the course of a week I have to give two or three lectures. Some of them deal with the current problems the various groups are facing. Then we have courses of lectures dealing in a general way with our aims and our philosophy. Such courses serve a double purpose: first, to inform our people, and second, to give them a broader comprehension of our work. An individual member must often feel that the tasks he is asked to perform are quite incidental, sometimes completely absurd. His job may be to maintain contact with a certain person or it may be to deliver reports. He has to take a paper from one place to another or he has to convince an elderly lady that she should permit a meeting to be held in her home. In doing these things, he is risking many years of imprisonment. Is he going to overthrow Hitler through such petty acts? We have to show the rank and file members that their individual work has a meaning, show them how it fits into the larger whole. We must explain our organization, make the direction in which we are going clear to them, tell them why we believe that our struggle is worthwhile. We must point out that there are certain inherent factors in Nazism that can lead to its downfall. Using our knowledge of history, we must show the role that underground organizations can play and have played in the past.

"Everyone who goes into the opposition under Nazism runs the risk of isolation. Each of us is living under a glass bell. Life in the Third Reich is hard enough for those who are older and experienced. How much worse it must be for the younger ones. For them the underground organization has to serve as a substitute for all those things that used to be furnished by the great democratic organizations: special schools, libraries, companionship. We have to provide the books for them that are no longer in libraries. Our information service has to supply the news that does not appear in the newspapers and magazines. We have developed a variety of courses on historical, political and economic subjects. We have to try, as well as we can under illegal conditions, to take the place of the labor colleges. This involves finding suitable teachers and places in which the courses can be held. It is no easy problem to find a place where a group can come together without arousing suspicion.

"I doubt whether in your entire political life you ever had to rack your brains to find a place where you could talk to another man or where you could hold a committee meeting. That is a great problem for us, one of our greatest.

"Two or three people can meet in a coffee house for a brief discussion. However, that costs money and we haven't always got it. In the summertime everything can be arranged out of doors, but then we are dependent on the weather and it takes time to travel to a park or a picnic ground. In short, organizational work is impossible unless you have many homes available in which people can safely meet.

"There are differences of opinion as to what qualifies as a safe meeting place. As a rule, an apartment that is used for meetings more than once a week is not safe. The home of people known from the past as anti-Nazis is also not safe. An apartment in a building whose superintendent is an enthusiastic Nazi *Blockwart* must be excluded as well as an apartment house with a tenant belonging to the Storm Troops. If you have reason to believe that any resident in the house is connected with another underground group and may therefore be under observation, you should, if possible, avoid it. I could enumerate a dozen other grounds that make a house unsafe, but I shall only add that on no account should meetings be held in the homes of leading members of the organization or in apartments used for technical purposes, such as photograph darkrooms or stations for couriers. Furthermore, an apartment which serves as a "cover address" for mail from abroad should not be used for meetings.

"It has twice happened to me that I had to stay away from home for several nights. Once it was because the Gestapo manifested a great interest in another man in the same apartment house and I didn't want to be taken along at the same time. The second occasion was when a good friend of mine was arrested and we could not find out why. In both cases there were no untoward results. But where was I to live meanwhile? Go to a hotel? You know that you can't walk in the door of a respectable hotel in Germany without having to fill out the regular police registration. A hotel with a doubtful reputation would be the surest way to be caught in a police raid.

"Finding quarters for underground purposes is one of our most perplexing tasks. Of course, in Nazi Germany anyone who makes his home available for illegal meetings is subject to punishment. But there are people who are willing to do it as their contribution to the fight against Hitler. It is best to use the homes of substantial middle-class citizens. Small working-class homes are not safe. So we have endeavored to make contacts with physicians, attorneys and other well-to-do professional people who are anti-Nazis. Many of these people have been useful and important, and we have brought them into the regular organizational work. Others give their homes for meetings and "cover addresses." In return for the help they give us, they expect us to inform them about political questions and hold discussions with them.

"So you can see that in underground work educational problems are immediately bound up with organizational problems and consequently with questions of personnel.

"I can illustrate the personnel relations within our group best by describing the work of one of my closest friends, let us call him Max.

"Max came from the Socialist labor youth. He is in charge of the youth section of our Berlin organization. It includes about one hundred young men and women who average about twenty-five years of age. No one knows whether it may not still be many years before Hitler is overthrown. These young people belong to the generation which will one day play the decisive role. Therefore a large part of Max's work must be concerned with training and education. He knows a good many of the people from the past and that makes it easier for him because he has a good idea of the potentialities and the individual environment of each member. Max is really in a unique position. We have people who are more intelligent or more experienced than he. But, they could not do Max's job simply because they would not know the background.

"A man who can supervise one hundred people is a very great asset for underground work. Max has a special talent in his unusual ability to get along with his boys and girls. Of course, a man in such a responsible position cannot risk having a hundred people know about his specific activity. He maintains direct contact with only ten or twelve, who in turn are leaders of smaller groups.

"What kind of people are they? The majority are young factory workers. Most of them belong to organizations of some sort, hiking clubs, football clubs, etc. The Nazis have taken over all these societies, but they used to be part of the labor movement and their membership has not changed much. The parents, the brothers, sisters and friends of the members were almost all in the old labor movement. They are working in factories themselves and meet their old friends constantly. It is no exaggeration if I tell you that there is scarcely a large factory, scarcely a working-class residence district and scarcely a large organization with working-class membership, with which we could not establish contact. Unfortunately we cannot take advantage of all these possibilities because we have not enough qualified people to maintain regular and permanent relations with them. You cannot take an unlimited number of new people and new groups into an organization unless you have others to serve as leaders. Otherwise such groups are apt to be more of a danger than an asset. Also I should explain that all of the hundred people in Max's group are not members of our organization per se. Many of them come together in small groups made up of members of the old labor youth organizations. They know that their leader has contact with one of the underground organizations, and that he regularly receives advice and information for his group. They know something of the policies and the aims of that organization, but they know nothing of the identity of the leading people in it or of the organizational structure.

"You receive the *Reports from Inside Germany* published by our *Auslandsburo* [office abroad]. I know that these reports have won recognition and are generally considered reliable. How do you think that our friends abroad get this material? Most of it comes from these organizational units. It is these people who are our most important reporters. From them we are able to get a picture of what goes on in the factories and in various organizations. We learn what the German workers are thinking, and what lower Nazi functionaries have to say. Not long ago Max sent abroad some interesting information about the secret rearmament in Germany which he had compiled from our regular factory reports. To assemble reports from about one hundred people, rework them and pass them on is no small labor, but it is only a part of Max's job.

"The young people have personal problems and often need advice. One of the boys is planning to get married. Is his wife trustworthy enough to be taken into the organization? Another has a sister who is engaged to a Storm Trooper. What should he do? Should he find some pretext for moving out of his father's house so that he won't have to be under the constant surveillance of his future brother-in-law? Another has a chance to get a job with more pay, but he is now working in an important factory where he maintains contact with a number of anti-Nazi workers. What should he do?

"What should a man do when a wage decrease has been announced in his factory and the other workers "want to do something" about it and they don't know what. Of course our man cannot stand passively on the sidelines; on the other hand he should not put himself in a position where he will probably be arrested without accomplishing any good, because he has a responsibility, not just to himself, but to the organization. In another factory, the Labor Front leader may be one of the "radicals" who honestly believe in the Socialist side of Hitler's National Socialism. He wants to help the workers and, of course, will come into conflict with the boss, who is also a Nazi. Two of our young men handled such a situation so skilfully that there was an open fight between the two Nazis, and the Labor Front man was fired on the spot. The incident impressed the workers in the factory who hadn't made up their minds completely about Hitler. The old trade unionists, who had always told them that the Nazis' "friendliness to the workers" was pure hypocrisy, gained a great deal of prestige. When, shortly afterwards, another worker in this factory was arrested for political reasons, our two friends were able to take up a collection among their colleagues for his wife and children.

"The ten or twelve closest colleagues of Max all have their special tasks. A number of them are highly skilled workers. One of them is charged with finding people

needed for our technical work: for example, a book-
binder who can bind messages into the cover of an innocent book to be taken abroad by a courier, or a car-
penter who can build a first-class secret drawer or hiding place in the home of one of our leading members.
Recently a new problem has been added to Max's responsibilities. In a few weeks the first class for compulsory military service will be called up, including some
of our own boys. This brings up the question of how
we can stay in contact with our people when they are in
the army. We are not completely unprepared because
some of our men have been in labor service, but at the
present time no one knows what the new German army
will be like and we have to draw up our first general
instructions now.

"So much for Max and his work. Now let us speak
about Grete.

"Grete belongs to our technical staff. Our technical
office is ostensibly a patent law firm. The 'chief' really is
a patent lawyer and has some 'clients' among our sympathizers, with whom he carries on regular 'business
correspondence.' Of course, the firm keeps records for
taxes and complies with all the necessary formalities. It
is not unusual that a patent lawyer should have a rather
mixed clientele. Of course, it is rather embarrassing when
genuine clients wander into the office, but it is usually
possible to discourage them by naming high fees.

"Grete was employed in this office in a completely
normal manner. She answered an advertisement in the

paper, she has her social security card and is a member of the Labor Front. She keeps regular office hours, though she has to put in a great deal of overtime. Her boss is very strict. Private phone calls and personal visits in the office are forbidden.

"In this office the reports are assembled, both those from Berlin and from other parts of the Reich. Also reports from abroad come first to this office and are prepared for distribution. Part of the correspondence with groups in the provinces is taken care of here and all the technical arrangements for organization trips are handled through this office. The material is put in proper form for couriers traveling to the provinces and abroad. I do not know much of the technical details of this work as it is not necessary for me to know them.

"Grete also has other work to do, since we believe that, except in unusual cases, an organization member should not be limited to purely technical work and lose contact with the political side of our activities. Grete is the leader of a group of young people who work in a large factory. Not one of them knows her real name or where she works. In this particular factory, former trade unionists still maintain strong ties of friendship among themselves. From time to time we send special information to the most trustworthy people there. We should like to win the former chairman of the trade union council over to our organization. Grete has twice been invited by him to Sunday afternoon coffee. But a man of this type will not be satisfied to be influenced by a girl. Fairly soon she will have to find some pretext to bring him together with one of the older trade unionists in our organization.

"This spring Grete was in Prague for two weeks and worked in our Auslandsburo there. Such trips have to be arranged with the greatest care, but we believe firmly that people working inside should be familiar with the work of the groups abroad and vice versa.

"You understand that the work that each of the three of us does complements that of the others. My work could be described as primarily political. It is my task to see that our evaluation of National Socialism, our own philosophy and the general methods of our work are understood by our members and that through them as large a group of anti-Nazis as possible is influenced. Max's function is chiefly organizational, keeping a hundred people together. And Grete's chief responsibility is in the technical apparatus, without which the rest of our work would be impossible.

"But you also see that we try to avoid too strict a division of labor. I also have organizational work to do, providing meeting places. In keeping one hundred people together Max is necessarily doing a vital political job and is constantly faced with political and theoretical problems. And Grete also has political tasks.

"We do not want to fall into the same errors as the Communists. In 1933 they thought they could become an underground organization by devising a complicated scheme of organization. They provided for a very strict division of labor; they appointed 'political commissars,' 'organizational leaders,' treasurers, chiefs in charge of literature, reporters and a dozen other kinds of officials. They worked out a complicated system of 'groups of five,' cells, district committees, state committees. It looked very pretty on paper, but it had no relation to reality. This very schematization was one of the chief reasons why their organization was destroyed in spite of the devotion of most of their members.

"As a matter of fact, I have still another job. I have to maintain a series of contacts with people in the provinces. I happen to come from the Rhineland and lived and was active politically there until a few years ago. Many of my good friends are still there, many have been arrested and others have become passive. But I have been able to develop some organizational nuclei. Every two or three months I make a trip to my old home, to keep contacts alive and try to find new ones. It may be that I shall try to find a job in Cologne or Dusseldorf and stay there for a year. Strengthening our organization work in this industrial area would be very important. I don't know, though, whether I shall be able to get away from Berlin. There aren't so many of us and we have so much to do."

The work in the provinces was especially important. Early in 1935 one of our leading members had made a trip to central Germany and, in the soft-coal-mining district there, got in touch with a man who, because of his personality and his broad experience, could be of great value to our work.

Werner Michaelis had been the head of the union local in one of the mines. He was fired in 1933 as "politically unreliable," but otherwise nothing had happened to him. For months he took absolutely no part in political work of any kind. Then, early in 1934, he used his last savings to buy a bicycle and began systematically to look up all his old friends in the entire district. He would just "drop in" on them. If he noticed that a former acquaintance seemed nervous and didn't like his visit, he would explain that he was looking for work in the neighborhood, drink a cup of coffee and go on. But, if he got the feeling that his host had remained loyal to the old cause, he would stay, ask questions about the situation in his friend's town and plant, tell of his own experiences and get his friend to introduce him to other friends who were politically interested. After a few months, Michaelis had established a loose contact with about forty former trade union leaders in one of the most important industrial areas of Germany. His contacts were not limited to miners. He soon got into touch with workers from the Leuna Works of the I. G. Farben Industrie, the great chemical trust, which employed over 20,000 men and had once been one of the bulwarks of the labor movement. He also had contacts in the Mansfeld Copper Works and in the Junker Works at Dessau.

Michaelis' case was not an exceptional one. On another trip in northern Germany, one of our people met a railway employee, also a former trade union official. This man was still in his job and not under suspicion. As a railway worker he got around the country and had made contacts with old colleagues in many cities.

We found out that such loose organizations had been built up all over the country. Most of them were composed of older people, trade union officials with decades of experience in the labor movement.

Therein lay their strength, but also their weakness. In rare cases were such men able to adapt themselves to the completely new problems which Nazism presented. They wanted to go on doing what they had been doing all their lives, defend the rights of the workers. They attempted, often taking great risks and making great personal sacrifice, to achieve immediate goals, perhaps to prevent a wage reduction in a certain factory or to prevent the closing down of a workers' coöperative. Some of them believed that it was possible to utilize positions in the Nazi Labor Front in the interests of the workers, while others tried to get the workers in their factories to boycott the Nazis' compulsory labor organization. Some of them hoped to build a large underground trade union movement; others soon became convinced that there was nothing to be done except to keep in touch with old friends, so that they would be ready when the time came. They represented various shades and degrees of opinion on political and organizational problems.

The same thing was happening among the remnants of labor's political parties as among the unionists. In March, 1933, the organized opponents of Hitler numbered millions. By the spring of 1934 there were still many hundreds of thousands who considered themselves part of the old movement. Of these, during 1933, tens of thousands did some actual underground work. But even the first year showed how quickly their numbers diminished. The best and the most active, those who enjoyed the most confidence among their colleagues and were consequently the best known, were arrested. When the Gestapo struck it meant not only that the men arrested were lost to the movement, but with the disappearance of a leader many members always withdrew from the underground work. Often, a few months later, the second group of leaders, which had taken the place of those arrested, was also caught and the underground group reduced still further. For instance, in a middle-sized industrial city, there might have been 30,000 organized workers before Hitler came to power. In the first summer, perhaps one to two thousand were trying to continue the work of their old organizations. However, after the first wave of arrests, and by the winter of 1933-34, only two or three hundred would have been left. Finally, by the summer of 1934, only a few dozen determined people would remain. If they continued to manufacture and distribute leaflets; if this handful, by working more ardently than ever, attempted to continue the kind of mass propaganda that a few months before had been carried on by hundreds, their fate was sealed. It was only a question of a brief time till the last active remnants of a movement of millions were destroyed.

But simultaneously and quite independently of these activist groups, a new kind of association of former members of the labor organizations was developing. A former Social Democratic municipal official invited a few old friends to see him regularly and they sat around and talked. Younger people who were members of a workers' sports club continued to go on hikes together. Members of another youth group met on week-ends at nearby youth hostels. Older party members met regularly to play Skat.

Scattered over the entire Reich there were thousands and thousands of such little groups, groups that were completely isolated from each other, each meeting together for some innocent and non-political pursuit. Many of them had no intention of doing anything illegal or underground. They wanted only to be among friends, to have as little as possible to do with the Nazis. At that time, 1934-35, membership in the Hitler Youth and other Nazi organizations had not yet been made compulsory. For many of these groups the outdoor sports or card-playing, which had originally been only a pretext, became their real reason for existence.

However, others developed into political discussion circles. They talked about current events and had spirited arguments about the cause of the democratic defeat and the possibilities of fighting Hitler. Very often a member of such a group got in touch with an active underground organization and brought political information back to his friends. Members sometimes took advantage of their vacations to make trips abroad and get information from anti-Nazis outside the country.

These little circles and clubs were not underground organizations. The people who belonged to them were "anti-Nazis," representing a broad and wavering section of the German people. The very looseness of their organization was a protection from Gestapo interference. The extent and the influence of such groups varied greatly. Their actions and their very existence depended on the state of public opinion. Every time the Nazis had a new triumph, either at home or abroad, their influence diminished. But every crisis the regime went through gave them new impetus, increased their influence, made them the center of oppositional sympathies in their area. When the regime collapses, the local leaders of the democratic mass movement against the Nazis may very well come out of such circles. Their significance lies more in their possible future role than in what they do today. But even now such loose groups afford a bridge or an approach to the masses of the people, the only one there can be under a totalitarian dictatorship.

The Nazis succeeded in destroying the democratic organizations, but they were far from succeeding in winning over all the people from these organizations or even in changing them. Many retained their former beliefs, but they were now isolated.

It did not take us long to learn that we could not unite all these varying groups. In one district an attempt was made to create a single organization out of such semi-social circles as had sprung variously from youth groups, from Social Democratic Party units and from trade unions. The organization included more than a hundred people. A few months later a small circle in one of the towns of the district was discovered by chance by the police and the members were arrested. As a result practically the entire organization throughout the district was lost. Groups from diverse backgrounds, with different political ideas, different aims, different methods of work and no conspiratorial experience could not be brought together in a successful organization.

However, people like our friend the unionist Michaelis wanted to be in touch with our organization. He wanted us to work with him and his people. Why? Because there were questions which he and his friends could not answer alone; they were faced with problems that they needed help in solving. They wanted to get information from outside; they wanted to send their own reports on for the use of others. They wanted a chance for discussion and advice on theoretical issues, more knowledge of the real nature of National Socialism, how it had come to power, what hope there was of overthrowing it. They wanted clarification about the meaning behind the acts of the Nazis. They wanted to learn from the mistakes of the past, in the hope that some time, somewhere, they could help in building a new movement. They wanted literature. They wanted to know what was going on in other parts of the Reich and abroad. They needed assistance in conspiratorial methods, in technical devices for their work. It was important that they should know of arrests of other people with whom they had some contact; they wanted to be warned of spies. And, most important, they had to have the feeling that they were not alone, that the little or much that they did was only a part of a movement. They wanted constant and living proof that there was an underground movement.

To answer all these needs was the task of the organized movement. Under the Nazi dictatorship an underground organization had to bring together the most progressive and the best qualified parts of the loose, wavering, unorganized forces that were the expression of popular anti-Nazism. It had to try to furnish leadership for this movement. Under the given conditions, it could never do this fully, but the extent to which it succeeded was the only measure of its effectiveness, the only justification for its existence. In the constant ebb and flow, the appearance and disappearance of these loose anti-Nazi circles and groups, the task of the underground "cadre" organization was to furnish continuity.

A cadre organization could only include a relatively

small circle, because its demands on its members were very great. It had to be highly centralized, it had to encompass a group not too large to be personally controlled. But, at the same time, it had to extend its contacts over the entire Reich; it had constantly to be in touch with the representatives abroad. Its technical and conspiratorial methods had to be highly developed.

The members of this organization had not only to be completely devoted, loyal and ready to do anything their work demanded, but these "professional revolutionaries" also had to be many-sided individuals. In addition to a mastery of conspiratorial technique there was the need for ability and talent in handling people. In addition to a broad knowledge of political problems was the need to be able to deal with many special problems. The underground organization had, during many years of struggle, to train the leaders of the coming democratic revolution. Within itself the underground organization must develop all the prerequisites for the creation of a new Germany.

That was the task, and certainly none of the organizations under the dictatorship have succeeded in fulfilling this task. Only when the Hitler regime collapses will we see how far they were actually able to go.

We always knew that it would be a long time before that day came, that the chances for our success were not great, but we determined to do what we could.

At the end of 1933 a brochure was published in Prague with the title: *New Beginning—A Secret Ger-*

man Manifesto. Later it was translated into French and English, and in 1935 an edition appeared in the United States. In the foreword to the British edition, H. N. Brailsford, the famous labor journalist, wrote:

"This pamphlet, the work of sincere minds, struggling to think out their task in new conditions of appalling difficulty, should serve two uses in its English dress. It should enable us to follow with sympathy and understanding the struggles of our German comrades in the years to come. With their fortunes are bound up those of the whole European working class. For the Old World there can be neither peace, nor liberty, nor cultural progress, while the Nazi reaction holds the German nation in its grip. No debt is more imperative, no duty more intimately linked with our own destiny, than that which we owe to the German working class. Until it stands on its feet again, there is no secure future for us."

This little book was written in Germany in the summer of 1933. It was a first and imperfect attempt to formulate the most important questions facing the German underground movement and to answer them on the basis of the experience up till then. There is no question that the author, who used the pen-name, Miles, was expressing the opinion of only a part of the underground movement of Germany. And, a part of his theories later proved to be wrong. The value of *New Beginning* was that it rejected a whole series of illusions about the nature of National Socialism and that it analyzed the special tasks confronting an underground organization in a Fascist state.

The brochure states:

"It would be an absurd illusion to believe that the Nazi seizure of power in Germany was merely an episode, interrupting for a longer or shorter period the postwar history of German democracy. Such ideas reveal a complete misconception of the state of affairs and the tendencies governing the political life of the Fascist state.

"Once in full possession of power, it will, to avoid the formation of an opposition in the future, abolish, step by step, the miserable remnants of the old democratic parties and bloodily suppress the germs of new parties. This is necessary owing to the fact that, after all, any non-Fascist party would be bound to become the reservoir for all opposition tendencies which, even under Fascism, are called forth as a result of crises. . . ."

During the very first months of Hitler rule, the author of this brochure realized that even a widespread opposition would be helpless against a state apparatus like that of the Nazis with its tremendous concentration of power in the hands of a ruling party.

"Even in periods of severe crises the growing dissatisfaction of the masses is diffused over the surface of the whole population, while the power of the Fascist state is at once concentrated and ubiquitous. It can contend with the insubordination of single groups separately, as regards both time and locality. It can placate

131

some with small concessions, others it can strike down, while it can play one group off against another. It can deflect anger or grievances from itself against certain elements in society. In short, it can 'divide and rule.' "

An underground organization under the Hitler dictatorship "can only be successful when the Fascist regime, weakened by internal and external difficulties, presents a sufficiently vulnerable surface for attack, when the masses have been stirred to anti-Fascist action by a crisis of the system."

In 1933 it was too early to speculate in concrete terms about such a crisis of the Nazi system. But, only two years later, the German anti-Nazis predicted that the Hitler regime would lead to war and suggested that a military defeat could bring the overthrow of Hitler.

But one question had to be answered in 1933, namely, which part of the German people could be expected to be in the forefront of mass resistance to Hitler? In what sectors of the society of Germany should the underground movement concentrate its efforts?

"In a country such as Germany, where the proletariat constitutes a large majority, the economic factors are of especial significance. It was clear in the first few weeks of the Fascist reign of terror which way things were going. . . . Under Fascism every fresh sharpening of the crisis must vastly intensify the suffering of the proletariat.

"This aggravation of the misery of the workers, nevertheless, will not lead to a spontaneous uprising on their part. The destruction of their mass organizations has made it impossible for the workers to come together for united action. Their forces are completely scattered. The structure of the Fascist dictatorship will only be shaken when a determined united Socialist organization transforms the suppressed murmurings of the masses into the clear expression of their will to fight, and thus into a political factor. . . ."

In the spring of 1934 we called our closest associates together for a conference. The participants came in small groups to a little-frequented lake not far from Berlin. A few days before, advance agents had picked it out as the safest spot. As it turned out, some of the participants had at the last moment to make a detour of several miles. A few thousand Storm Troopers had happened to choose the woods through which they were to pass for military exercises. Otherwise the conference passed without incident.

Almost all of the participants at the conference were former officials in various sections of the labor movement, trade unionists, Social Democrats, a few former Communists, leaders of the old labor youth organizations. Most of them were workers, some were students and there were a few professional people. A number had been employed in the party or in the trade union movement. All were young, only a handful over thirty. But practically all of them had been in the labor movement for at least ten years.

The subject to be discussed at this conference was a

proposal for the setting up of an organization in the factories. It was, of course, closely related to the factory council elections which the Nazis had called for in all plants.

The coming factory elections posed a concrete political question for the underground organizations for the first time.

The Nazi leaders were well aware that, in spite of all their political triumphs within the country during 1933, they still had a long way to go before they "united the German people in the spirit of National Socialism." And they knew that they were further from success among the working class than in any other group. After the sham Reichstag elections in the fall of 1933 they had been able to tell the world that in Germany there was only a "hopeless minority of uneducables." But even in those farcical elections, despite Gestapo terror, in the working-class districts of Berlin, Hamburg and other large cities, as many as 30 percent had dared to vote "Nein." Nevertheless, in the spring of 1934, only a few weeks before the bloody day of June 30th, the Nazis had decided to call for a vote of confidence among the workers of Germany.

In each factory, candidates were to be chosen by the employer in consultation with the official Nazi "trustee of labor" in the plant. The workers had nothing to do with the choice. They could cross out the names of single candidates or, for that matter, they could cross out all the names. In case the majority of candidates were voted down, it was provided that the Labor Front should appoint the factory council members itself.

Though undemocratic, the "elections" would give the workers a chance, meager though it was, to vote on National Socialism. The underground organizations had to decide what their policy would be, what they should advise the workers to do.

There were great divergences of opinion among the conferees. At one extreme was the thesis, "We can have nothing to do with this Nazi swindle"; and at the other, the not less ill-advised proposal that we should try to elect those candidates who would, as far as possible, represent the interests of the workers.

Those supporting the first point of view made things easy for themselves. They could point out very correctly that this was not a genuine election, that it could not alter Nazi policies in the least and that Hitler was interested only in fooling the people in Germany and probably abroad. "Therefore," as one man said, "it is not our task to try to influence these so-called elections. Our only duty today is to prepare for the future. Today we can do nothing other than win as many trustworthy people as possible in the factories for our organization."

Another answered him: "Of course, you and I and many of the more experienced workers know that these elections are only a Nazi maneuver. But there are others, especially among the younger workers who have been taken in by Hitler's promises, who take the elections seriously. If the majority of the people had always known in advance what Hitler was after, then we wouldn't be sitting here hiding out in these woods to-day. You would be in your offices getting out your newspaper and I would be handling the affairs of my union. I agree with you that our most important work is the work of preparation, but that does not mean that we do not have to take a stand on current problems as they arise and use every opportunity to influence as many people as possible for our side. Although the results of these elections will not cause the Nazis to alter their policies, nevertheless they do give the workers this one opportunity to say yes or no. You all know that they are talking about the elections in every plant, you know that the other workers will ask former trade union officials, those in whom they have confidence, for their opinion. If, in this situation, members of the underground movement lay down the line, 'We are not interested in this question, it makes no difference how the elections come out,' they will be isolating themselves from the rest of the workers, and shutting themselves off from their confidence. We cannot, on the one hand, set out to build a factory organization and, on the other, fix our eyes firmly on distant goals with no consideration for the problems which at the moment trouble the people whom we expect to influence and win. If we take that line we shall be nothing more than a small sect, people who sit at home and are right; we shall never become a political organization."

Another member made the point that, in spite of the

hostility of the regime to the workers, many of the lower officials of the Labor Front, particularly "old fighters" from the pre-1933 Nazi cells in the factories, honestly believed Hitler's promises. If they were elected to the factory councils they would try to represent the interests of the workers. He said he had found in many factories that the workers were planning to vote for the "radical" Nazis on the list of candidates.

"We know that their own good intentions will lead to their downfall," another conference member added, "but, if we use our influence to get such candidates elected, and subsequently they come into conflict with higher Nazi authorities and achieve nothing, then the workers will have an excellent opportunity to see just what the Nazis' Socialist promises mean."

The overwhelming majority of the conference members were opposed to this proposal. One of our leading members said:

"It is certainly true that there are radicals among the Nazis. It is also true that we can, on some occasions, take advantage of the contradictions between the conceptions of certain unimportant Nazis and the real policies of the party. But our policy concerning the factory elections is not simply a matter of tactics in a single situation. If, at this first election, the entire underground movement takes the position that the workers should vote for radical Nazis, but for Nazis just the same, it will mark the first step toward our capitulation as an independent political force. If we tell the other workers that there are 'good' Nazis and 'bad' Nazis and that they should support the good ones, they will have a right to demand from old trade unionists that they permit themselves to be listed as candidates in order to serve the interests of the workers. The next step would be that workers who are against Hitler would have to try to achieve positions of prominence in the Nazi Labor Front. Finally, our entire activity would be limited to attempts to maneuver within the Nazi system. The bourgeois parties tried to do just that and we know how far they got. The army and the industrialists are still trying to 'restrain' the Nazis and we shall see how much success they have. You can't maneuver with the Nazis. Certainly not when you are as weak as we are today. Those who are recommending 'Trojan Horse tactics' seem to have forgotten that the entire Greek army stood, weapons in hand, ready to hasten to the aid of the little band that got into Troy in the horse. Where is our army today?

"When we talk about building an independent organization within the factories, it isn't because we believe that we shall be able to 'conquer' the factories under Nazism, but because we know that it is the workers in the factories that Hitler is having the most difficulty in conquering for himself, and because we know that the workers will be the first to fall away from him. It is also because we hope that the members of the tiny cells that we can build up and maintain in the plants and factories will become the leaders of a great revolt, not just a revolt of the workers but of the majority of the German people.

"These are the considerations which must determine our attitude toward the elections of factory councils. Our line must be: Cross out the Nazis' names; cross out as many candidates as you can; vote against the entire list; make your ballot invalid. Force the Nazis to put in their own commissars. Then the workers will have an excellent opportunity to see whether they are genuinely represented."

The conference agreed to follow this line and the results of the elections showed how correct it was.

Although the Nazis used their entire propaganda resources, although in most factories there was no pretense of a secret ballot and the workers risked being fired or arrested, the elections turned out a complete defeat for the Nazis. Despite all efforts to keep the election results secret, the actual vote was known in very many cases. In the majority of plants in all parts of the Reich, the workers rejected the Nazi candidates. A year later, no less a person than Robert Ley, leader of the Labor Front, admitted it.

The German underground movement would not claim that it alone was responsible for the outcome of the elections. The Socialist traditions of the old labor movement played a great role and so did the undisguisable hostility of the Hitler regime to the working people. But the underground movement made its contribution to this Nazi defeat.

139

Hitler had gotten his original majority in the Reichstag with the help of intrigues and a coup d'état. Time and again through his farcical "plebiscites" Hitler advertised a 99 percent united German people before the world. But, *Hitler never got a vote of confidence from the workers of Germany*. He got it neither in 1934 nor in the spring of 1935, when he repeated the experiment of factory council elections a second and last time. After two years of Nazi rule the results were the same. In some cases the returns were even less in the Nazis' favor than in the previous year.

One of our members, a former trade union official, who worked in a factory in a northern German industrial city, gave us a report about the local celebration of National Labor Day on May 1, 1935. On that occasion the members of the newly elected factory councils were to be sworn in.

"It was a rainy day and unusually cold for the time of year. Grumbling, the workers from all the plants in the city were forced to march to the celebration. Labor Front officials had received strict orders that the men from each plant must come in a body. The meeting place was surrounded by a cordon of Storm Troopers who were to see that no one left the spot before the conclusion of the solemn ceremony. First we had to listen to the Fuehrer's speech broadcast from Berlin. Then a big shot sent from Labor Front Headquarters made a speech. Evidently he had not been properly informed in advance. He got up to read off a list of the plants and the names of their newly elected factory councils, but time and again there was a painful pause. In the majority of the factories, the Nazi lists had been voted down and the local Labor Front representatives had not yet been able to appoint commissars.

"It suddenly began to hail, they couldn't hold the workers any longer, they broke through the Storm Troopers and the solemn ceremony of the state came to a sudden and not very solemn end."

The Nazis learned the lesson of the two unsuccessful elections quickly and thoroughly. In the beginning of May, 1935, a great wave of terror descended on the German workers. In all parts of the Reich, former trade union officials were arrested, among them many who had only the most remote connection with the underground movement or no connection at all. The Nazis, though, had the right instinct: these people were the backbone of resistance in the factories. The concentration camps filled up again. In the courts the judges handed down heavy sentences indiscriminately. As a result the loose network of contacts that had grown up among old trade union leaders was in large part destroyed. The informal anti-Nazi circles were weakened and their influence diminished. Hopes that they would be reactivized were in vain.

During this period of isolation, when activity was reduced to a minimum, the contacts of underground organizations with the anti-Fascist movement abroad were of special importance, both for political and organizational reasons. A feeling that they were allied with progressive international forces was an essential counterbalance to their oppressive isolation. Moreover, technical help from outside was indispensable in fighting against the increasingly powerful Gestapo.

Those who had survived the first period of underground struggle could see clearly and unmistakably the limitations imposed on an underground system within the Third Reich. All underground groups recognized, sooner or later, that they could continue their work only with coöperation abroad. Only in the democratic countries could their files and documents be assembled, only there could reports be studied and evaluated. Friends outside of Germany would have to prepare the theoretical material they needed and help to combat the mental isolation inevitable under Nazism, and they would also have to maintain the regular contacts with the international labor movement. Finally, the necessary financial support would have to come from friends in other countries.

Experience had already shown us that centralization of the individual groups in the country multiplied the danger for the entire organization. On more than one occasion when there were arrests in Berlin, we found that these could be traced back to too loosely organized provincial groups. So the Auslandsburo took on a new importance as a technical and organizational center. For instance, we found that it was usually wiser to route contacts between Munich and Berlin through Prague, that it was better to send important communications and reports from western Germany to Belgium or France, those from Hamburg to Denmark and those from the Ruhr district to nearby Holland. Often, when the leading committee in Berlin wanted to send a communication to all the provincial groups, it was more efficient and less dangerous to have a courier take it first to Prague, have the necessary copies made there and then send them to the groups in Germany by way of Switzerland, western Europe and the Scandinavian countries. As these working methods were developed, it became necessary to place "frontier secretaries" in all of the democratic countries bordering on Nazi Germany. The frontier secretaries and their assistants carried out an invaluable function for the underground organizations until Hitler's invading armies put a stop to their activities.

The removal of a part of our technical apparatus abroad was thought a safety measure, but at the same time it increased the danger for the work in another way. In their functions, the Auslandsburos were a part of the underground organizations. However, they were in democratic countries, in environments where the importance of the strict conspiratorial rules of underground work were far from being understood. That was especially true when the Auslandsburos were staffed by people who had been important figures in the old democratic mass movements but had no experience in the kind of work being done in Germany under Nazism.

The situation was complicated by the fact that the organizations abroad had much work to do that had no apparent connection with underground work—for example, refugee relief. A clerk in an office whose function it was to give advice and material help to refugees was working in what was, to all intents and purposes, an unpolitical job. But he was in a position to receive valuable information about work inside Germany. Unless the staff of such an office was chosen with the greatest care the organization in Germany might be placed in real danger. For example, in 1936, it happened that an employee of a refugee relief committee in Prague had been bribed by the Gestapo. Through him the Gestapo were able to obtain information of great value in their campaign of extermination of the underground movement in Germany.

The difficulties that arose and the contradictions that existed, as a result of the discrepancies in function and in experience between the organizations inside and abroad, could be removed only when the organizations abroad were considered as a part of the underground movement, adapting their work first to the needs of the groups inside and subordinate to them.

There were many differences of opinion between the groups inside and outside, and the most ardent disputes centered around the question of who was entitled to leadership in the new movement.

From the very beginning, many of the underground organizations were opposed to certain conceptions that had prevailed in the old democratic parties. The age problem—the majority of the underground groups were made up of younger people—took on a political color. The leaders of the old parties and trade unions had to bear the stigma that their policies had led the German labor movement to defeat in 1933. As bitter experience showed, it was a long time before those who had been leaders in the past realized the full consequences of what had happened. In March, 1933, with Hitler already two months in the Reich Chancellory, the leading officers of the Social Democratic youth organization in Berlin were threatened with expulsion from the party. Because they had firmly demanded that their groups be reorganized on an underground basis, they had—according to the Party Executive Committee—"endangered the safety of the party."

The authority of the leaders of the old parties, of the men who had been political chiefs and officials under the Republic, and were now in exile, was seriously shaken. This lack of confidence was enhanced when, as the years passed, it became more and more evident that the German emigration, with few exceptions, had accomplished little either politically or in theoretical work.

From the history of revolutions we know of political emigrations from which great leaders have arisen, men who were to guide the destiny of their countries. Russia's Lenin and Trotsky, Czechoslovakia's Masaryk, Latin America's Simon Bolívar, China's Sun Yat Sen,

Italy's Garibaldi, all spent many years in exile. But they were all representatives of young, rising movements, not of political groups that had been in power and failed. From the history of revolutions we also know about the exiles of the past, the French Royalists of 1800, the White Russians after 1917, the same Trotsky, after 1927. It is only in the rarest cases that the leaders for the reawakening come from the ranks of those who were once beaten.

The Hungarian emigrant, Siegmund Kunfi, painted a disconsolate but realistic picture of a gathering of exiles.

"If you know these people their assembly seems rather ghostly. When you close your eyes you feel that there are spirits in the gloomy hall. They are human beings sitting there like others but their future is behind them. Their eyes look fixedly backward. To them the flush of dawn is comprehensible only in the colors of the sunset. The beautiful gift of adaptability keeps most of them from knowing that something terrible has happened to them, that they have been uprooted, scattered by the storm, that they have become the flotsam and jetsam of history. . . ."

Executive Committee Abroad, or Representative Abroad? That was the question. It was answered in a different way by the different sections of the German underground movement. In our organization there was never any doubt—the Auslandsburo could not serve except as representing the organization working in Germany. Every important decision was made in the special interest of the work inside. Almost all conferences were held in Germany itself, with the leaders of the Auslandsburo participating; and they came to Berlin in spite of the personal danger that such an illegal journey involved. The last of these trips took place in 1938 shortly after the Munich Conference. Important political and theoretical discussions necessarily developed out of the problems of the work inside and they were carried on inside.

In organizations of the Socialist and trade union movements, the relations between groups inside and abroad were long disputed. In the course of the years, the matter was usually settled by events, especially after the war came. No question existed for the Communists; for them Moscow and the committee abroad appointed by Moscow remained the unquestioned authority. Countless Communist groups split off from the party for just this reason. Today, the problem no longer exists. Since Hitler's armies have overrun most of the European continent, there can be no question of any real contact between the organization inside and outside.

In the great wave of arrests of 1935-36, parts of the new cadre organizations which had been built up so painfully were destroyed. In our organization, too, a number of members were arrested. Others had to flee abroad. But worse than the direct blows of the Gestapo was the feeling of resignation, of the hopelessness of continuing the work, which attacked every section of the underground movement in 1935 and led to disputes and demoralization even in the most progressive groups. This defeatism was an inevitable result of the terrible and unresisting defeat of 1933, and at the same time it was a logical consequence of the shattering of those illusions with which a great part of the underground movement had started its fight against the Hitler regime. In our own ranks we had to fight against conscious and unconscious defeatism as energetically as we had fought against illusory hopes a year or two before.

For both tendencies held an equal threat for underground organizations. We had long and earnest discussions. Since theoretical discussions, concerning the strength of our enemy, the possibility of continued work, the proper working methods, must under the circumstances have immediate practical consequences, it was inevitable that differences of opinion had far-reaching effects. They led to expulsions, splits, sometimes to the formation of new groups.

In the difficult conditions of illegal existence in Germany we tried long and hard to formulate our political philosophy. The great defeat had shaken faith in democracy. The experience of Germany, Italy, Austria and growing Fascist trends in other European countries seemed to imply the end of the democratic era. Developments in Russia reinforced honest doubts as to whether democracy and Socialism could be reconciled. In all countries and in every sphere of life the influence of the machinery of the state was expanding. Did not

148

that mean that we were on the threshold of a totalitarian epoch? Did not that mean that any fight against Nazi dictatorship, any hope of bringing democracy back and achieving a Socialist society, was futile?

These were not just abstract questions. In answering them we were also answering the question: Shall we continue to fight or shall we liquidate? For all practical purposes it did not matter whether it was proved by scholarly arguments that "we are living in a totalitarian era," or if it was concluded on less theoretical grounds that "there is no point in trying to hold out."

These questions were not only an expression of a defeatist tendency within our movement. German democracy *had* failed. The democracy of western Europe was retreating step by step before the Fascist aggressors. The old liberal Europe had crumbled, and with it the labor movement which had grown up inside it. There seemed to be no path that led to the future.

Democracy, freedom, Socialism would have to find a new and militant content. Without social revolution, democracy was no longer feasible in Europe. Unless there could be democratic freedom there was no use in fighting for Socialism. The struggle in the new underground organizations was at the same time a struggle for new ideas and for new goals. It was a part of the great controversy, around which, in the final analysis, this war is being fought.

5

A Formula for Survival

"Underground work is a contest between the police and the revolutionaries; the smartest side wins."

That is the way a veteran of the Russian underground movement put it and he was accurate. The first essential of political activity under a dictatorship is not to be caught, not to be arrested. That may sound easy, but more than average intelligence, superior tenacity and a high standard of self-discipline are required, only to fulfill the first prerequisite of not being caught.

We had a man in our organization in Berlin, a student at the university and still very young, who was the son of a well-to-do and respectable business man. There were groups of young people at his house two or three times a week. They danced and chattered; often there was a bottle of wine. When he was at home the telephone rang constantly, mostly girls and young men of his own age calling up to make appointments or ask about mutual friends, all perfectly natural and innocent. In short, this student was one of our most valuable contact men.

In 1935, the film, *The Scarlet Pimpernel*, was playing

150

in Berlin, the famous story of an aristocrat and dandy, whose chief concern in life seemed to be his personal appearance, but who, on the side, was the leader of a secret organization to save French aristocrats who had been condemned to death.

It happened that it was the birthday of one of the servants who had been with our friend's family for twenty years. To celebrate the occasion he took her to see *The Scarlet Pimpernel*. After the picture she said: "These movies are so fantastic and incredible. I'd as soon believe that you are involved in some dark conspiracy."

The fact was that he was involved in a "conspiracy" but he was a good conspirator. A person who had known him for years, who lived in the same house, had no idea what was behind the activities in which he was openly engaged under her very nose.

In fact, the term "underground" is completely misleading. It belongs to a long past time, if it is not completely a figment of the imagination of fiction writers. Hidden vaults, the faint glimmer of candle light, trap doors, sinister plotters with false beards are all very well in the movies. In the sober reality of the Third Reich one would not get very far with such trappings. A prosaic office in a large office building is much to be preferred and much safer than a romantic dungeon.

You can't hide from the scientific surveillance of a modern police state, but you can mislead the police. And the best way to mislead them is to live as conventionally and as openly as possible. The more you resemble a normal everyday citizen in every respect, the less apt you are to be suspected. And as long as you do not arouse suspicion and scrupulously observe a long series of rules of caution, you may be able to carry on underground work for years on end. Once you are suspected, even catacombs will not help.

Thus, the first law of underground work is: lead a normal life. Maintain in all circumstances the appearance that you are the same as other people, that you have an ordinary job, the usual family ties, friends, interests, habits. Be one among many.

But an underground worker is not "the same as other people" and he doesn't lead a "normal life." That is only on the surface. Every move that he makes must be thought out in advance. The innumerable little acts of everyday life that for others are a matter of course he must consider and plan carefully. It is only on rare occasions that conspiratorial activity involves unusual daring or exciting deeds—but it always requires iron self-control, keeping little things constantly in mind, a continual war against the natural inclination to do the usual and the most convenient thing.

For example, you get up early in the morning to go to the subway station during the rush hour in order to make a short telephone call without attracting attention, although it would have been infinitely easier to make that phone call from home. Or you spend two hours traveling from one end of Berlin to the other, in order to give a friend a short message in person, although it would have taken only a minute to tell him over the telephone. Or you always keep the illegal material on which you are working in a safer house than yours and never give in to the temptation to keep it at home over night, to save a long street car ride in the cold. To do these things day-in and day-out, year after year, never allowing yourself to think "nothing will happen this one time"—that is the reality of conspiratorial work.

Make a habit of punctuality. If the man you are to meet has to wait on the street corner for five minutes, he may arouse suspicion. If you miss him because you are late, it may be days before you can reach him by way of intermediaries—the homes of important underground functionaries must be kept strictly secret. Such a delay can have dire results.

Whenever you are engaged in work connected with the underground—an errand, a meeting with a friend —you must have a plausible explanation ready in case you are questioned. We had a strict agenda for every meeting of two or more people. The first five minutes were spent deciding what the persons present would say if questioned about their reasons for being together and the nature of their contacts with each other. Birthdays and similar occasions were used when, contrary to usual practice, we wanted to bring a rather large group of people together. Once one of our members postponed his wedding for four weeks so that it could be held on a day when two of our important contact people from another city could come to Berlin. No journey could be made without providing a convincing "legal" excuse. Our most important members had to devote all of their energies to underground work, and did not have time for regular jobs on the side. However, you can't appear a normal citizen without a regular occupation. One of our leading men was an agent for an insurance company. That gave him an excuse to travel around the city, and if he was caught in a tight place he could always explain that he was selling a policy. Another member was a taxi driver and for a long time he was one of our best couriers. Another hung out his shingle as a genealogist. Genealogy is a respectable profession much in demand in the Third Reich where everyone has to prove his Aryan ancestry. A genealogist or his assistant might easily have to make journeys into the provinces.

One of our underground "offices" was the home of a girl who happened to live near a large public swimming-pool. Her chief associate went swimming every day all summer long so that after her swim she could have a cup of coffee with her friend. She carried the illegal papers needed for their business in the hem of her bathing-robe. They were on "silk" paper and so she was relatively safe in case she was searched on the streets or in the subway.

The hobbies of our members also served organizational purposes. Underground workers joined philatelist societies and amateur photography clubs so that they could meet with other members without arousing suspicion.

Even if he is ill, a member of an underground group cannot allow himself to be a "normal person." One evening a message came from one of our friends, who had been sick for some time, that he must see one of our leading members immediately. The trouble was that his illness had been diagnosed as acute appendicitis and he had to be operated on the same night. As an important official of the underground movement, he knew many names and addresses by heart; he had just remembered that once before under an anesthetic he had told wild stories for hours on end. He was terrified that this time he would give away important secrets and didn't dare to go to one of the big hospitals for the operation as his physician had arranged. It was not simple, on a couple of hours' notice, to find a reliable physician who would agree to perform the operation safely in his private clinic.

But the most painstaking observance of the rules of conspiracy and the greatest conceivable foresight do not in themselves make an underground worker. He must at the same time be willing to let any rule go by the board, to attempt anything if the circumstances demand and the end to be achieved seems worth the risk. He must be able to make the decision himself whether to undertake the action in question. In making a decision, he cannot forget for an instant that, not only his life, but even the very existence of the organization may be the price if he makes a mistake. An underground functionary has often to make crucial decisions without any opportunity to consult his friends. For example, he may have to decide at a moment's notice whether he should enter a house, about which he isn't sure, to warn an important man that the Gestapo are looking for him, knowing the while that the Gestapo may be waiting behind the door. He may have been sent from Berlin to Cologne on a special mission for the underground organization. Arrived in Cologne, he may learn that a potentially important contact can be made for the organization if he travels to Essen before returning to Berlin. His orders were to go to Cologne only; he alone can decide. If he goes to Essen, he is acting on his own and not in accordance with his orders; he may be running into some unforeseeable complication that will have grave consequences; on the other hand, if he does not go, he may be passing up an opportunity which he will not have again. All too frequently, a responsible underground representative has to decide on the spot whether or not a given person is to be trusted. Often one has no choice but to be guided by a hunch and to hope for luck.

Many of us really did have good luck. There is the story of the time the Gestapo knocked on the wrong door in an apartment house. For hours they searched the home of a completely innocent man while our friend, whom they were really after, heard the disturbance next door, realized what was up and was able to flee. One of the girls in our organization was searched twice on the streets by Storm Troopers looking for illegal documents. The first time she had the documents hidden under half a dozen eggs in a paper sack of groceries. The Storm Trooper was so afraid of breaking the eggs that he didn't find the papers. The second time the Storm Troopers were satisfied with a careful search of her briefcase, with nothing in it but books from the Public Library. In her coat pocket they would have found quite different things. Then, there was the time when the leader of our organization abroad was returning from one of his many trips into Germany and was arrested on the frontier under suspicion of smuggling foreign exchange out of the country. Luckily, he was able to prove that he was not guilty and it did not occur to the officials to examine him for other offenses. A few months later the same man ran into a blizzard while crossing a "green frontier" in the Riesengebirge from Czechoslovakia into Germany. (The frontier that one crosses without passport is a "green frontier" and it is easiest if it is mountainous territory.) He lost his way and had to spend the night in the woods. The next morning, his hands and feet frozen, he was found, not by the German frontier guards, but, as luck would have it, by the Czechs. To be sure, fortune is fickle. Another of our friends, a twenty-year-old boy, caught in a storm in the high mountains while crossing the frontier into Switzerland, was frozen to death; apparently he had not dared to ask the frontier guards for help after he lost his way.

It would be a bad conspirator, indeed, who did not rely on his luck. But, in principle, the rule must be to exclude chance as much as possible, not to depend on your guardian angel, but to develop methods of work which will enable you to prove smartest in the contest with the police. That is largely a technical problem. The same rules apply in the underground fight against the police of a totalitarian regime as apply in war. Just as it is absurd to try to fight tanks and dive bombers with shotguns, it is absurd to try to combat the power machine of a modern state, equipped with the best scientific techniques, with the obsolete arsenal of the conspirator of fiction.

Such methods of communication as invisible ink belong in a museum—not because all chemical combinations are known. At the beginning of our activity one of our members, a chemist, worked out an especially good formula which is still not known to the Gestapo. But what good are such things? When examined before a quartz lamp—a matter of course in every modern police laboratory—any paper will yield its secrets. Every secret ink falls down when tested with iodine vapor in a vacuum. The careful use of secret inks was some protection during the early days of the Nazis, but as the Gestapo perfected their technical facilities and enlarged their experience we had to abandon these methods.

Our solution of the problem of communications was micro-photography. Several of our members became enthusiastic amateur photographers, and it was possible to rig up a private studio and darkroom in one of their homes. Eventually we were able to reproduce on a piece of film, measuring one half inch by one inch, four, six, even eight typewritten pages. In this way long letters and reports of all kinds found their way over the frontiers, rolled up, sewed up or soldered, in an amazing variety of objects. Because of the information we were able to get out of Germany this way, our office abroad was able to supply the material published in *Inside Germany Reports* in the United States and in similar publications in various democratic countries of Europe. Organizational problems between the groups inside and outside the country could be dealt with adequately, and, at the same time, precious information was being transmitted in the same way to the isolated groups inside Germany.

One has to be ingenious and constantly discover new places to hide the material. Once the films were packed in a teddy bear which was sent as a Christmas present to a little girl in Prague, but she, thrilled with the new toy, cried bitterly when the grown-ups eager for the news inside tore her teddy bear's head off. One time we had to hold up the trip our secretary abroad was making to Berlin for twenty-four hours because, at the last moment while she was packing, it was discovered that in bathing she had inadvertently used the sponge in which the report she was to take with her had been buried. Nothing was left of the film but a sticky mess. The photographer swore because he had to do his work over again, but "the packer" was justly proud. If even his fellow conspirators couldn't recognize the suspicious object, he was doing all right.

To avoid any device that could arouse suspicion was the fundamental principle that guided us in the use of codes. There are innumerable books about code systems and there are codes without number that would have been adequate for our purposes, that is, codes that to all intents and purposes were proof against solution by the uninitiated. But our problem was to find a code which could not be recognized as such. The Gestapo would leave no means untried to find the key to a coded list of names and addresses. We know how many means are at their disposal—nothing could be worse than to have them find the key to such a crucial document.

After months of experiment we developed a system by which we could reduce our information to the form of tables of scientific data, such as a natural scientist might use. One of the girls in the organization was assigned to no other task than to keep these tables up to date. Day after day she made complicated numerical computations, and in decimals and fractions we had an undecipherable record of names and addresses in Germany and outside, times and places of appointments and other indispensable information.

A few weeks before the war started, friends in the underground in Germany succeeded in sending a pamphlet nearly a hundred pages long to their friends abroad. They had taken endless pains to assemble the material for this pamphlet, because they hoped it would give a real insight into the nature of National Socialism. Once the pamphlet was written, it had to be copied carefully on the kind of paper required for a good reproduction, with attention to margins, the absence of erasures, etc. Then it had to be photographed in miniature with a homemade apparatus and the precious film concealed and sent abroad by a reliable courier. That was during the time of the Polish crisis. In order to warn the world of the enemy which they knew so intimately from their own experience, these men and women of the underground worked for weeks in constant danger of their lives.

One day the police came to the apartment where one of our secret photograph studios was located, because they suspected that counterfeit currency was being manufactured there. The man whose apartment it was—in private life a division chief in a large firm—had sent his secretary to the bank to deposit money and some of the bills were found to be counterfeit.

Of course, that was pure chance. But our lives and our work depended on chance. We endeavored to plan exactly and to take advantage of the best scientific techniques. But almost all of our efforts to achieve the maximum in technical perfection failed for one reason, lack of money.

We knew just how we should go about setting up photograph studios and offices. We knew the kind of storage places that would be safest for illegal papers. But we didn't have the money to do what we wanted to do. How we used to envy the spies in novels. They always had the finest technical equipment; money miraculously seemed no object when the transmission of even the smallest military secret or the most insignificant court intrigue was involved. On the other hand, we who were fighting against a real enemy, whom we already knew to be the enemy of all, couldn't even approximate the technical facilities available to an ordinary money smuggler. Professional smugglers, most of whom were working purely for financial gain, were in a better position than we. For example, every time a smuggler had a job to do he could employ skilled workmen to insert secret pockets in new suitcases. He could purchase any kind of special aid for his work he wanted. Of course, even the most skilfully contrived secret pocket is not 100-percent safe, but such methods would be protection enough if one were not already under suspicion. And, during the first years after 1933, it was just those foreign exchange smugglers who drove the Gestapo to greater watchfulness and thoroughness and thus forced us to find more and more complicated tricks for our own conspiratorial work. But we didn't have the great sums of money that many of these people had. Month after month, we had to use the same toilet-accessories bag till it began to look suspicious because of the many times it had been opened and sewed up again. A new one would have cost five dollars and that was a lot of money for us.

Most of the members of the underground organizations were workers. It is well known that the wages paid in the Third Reich are small. Moreover, during the first years of the Nazi regime there was still much unemployment. Our people contributed what they could, but it wasn't much. Intellectuals and professional men with larger incomes who were in sympathy with our work, and especially those who were Jewish, left the country in the first months and years of the Hitler regime. Moreover, it should not be forgotten that anyone found guilty of contributing money to underground work was seriously punished. In the early years of general uncertainty and anxiety it required real courage to have anything at all to do with a person whom one suspected of membership in the underground movement. To give him money seemed much too dangerous for most people. Who was willing to go to a well-to-do friend and say: "I am a member of an underground organization. Will you give me some money for our work?" Ordinary methods of raising money were eliminated, first, on grounds of secrecy, and second, because people able to give considerable amounts would have nothing to do with the underground movement. Only for support of the families of arrested men did we find it relatively easy to collect money. It was impossible ever to make a proper budget or to count on having specific funds in hand. For this reason alone, time and again, carefully prepared plans had to be discarded.

No underground organization can maintain itself on its own strength alone, nor ever could. It must depend

on financial help from outside. The underground movement in Germany was supported from abroad. But there
were substantial differences in this respect between the
various groups.

From the very beginning, the remnants of the Communist Party were in a different situation from all the
other organizations. It is not true that the Communists
lived exclusively on the bounty of Moscow—ordinary
members in particular made real financial sacrifices for
the party. But it is a well-known fact that the Communist Parties of all countries, especially the underground
parties, were financially dependent on the Communist International and, as a result, on every fluctuation in Moscow's policies. Every change in German-Russian relations, every change in the responsible leadership, was
reflected in the budget of the German Communist Party.
The great Russian purges, which incidentally claimed
many victims among German Communists, and the Non-
Aggression Pact naturally reduced the funds of the underground Communist organization to a new low. However, during the period when Moscow was interested in
the Communist movement in Germany, the underground leaders had considerable sums of money at their
disposal, most of which naturally went to the members
of the G.P.U. machine and to the higher officials. Nevertheless, during the "good" years, the money problem
was one of the lesser problems of the Communist organization. Active Communists even complained about the
danger of corruption, for in underground work it is

obviously impossible to render exact accounts for the expenditure of organizational funds.

It was quite a different story in the underground organizations that grew out of the Social Democratic movement and the trade unions. They were accustomed to raise all of their own money and they had a tradition of the most scrupulous exactness in money matters. For decades no Social Democratic treasury had permitted five cents to be spent without a voucher. The Social Democrats had a difficult time learning to adapt their financial methods to underground conditions. All of the property of the trade unions, including their money, had been confiscated. The Social Democratic Party Executive Committee had succeeded in rescuing a part of its funds. But who had a claim to this money? There was no longer a unified party. Some of the local underground organizations refused to accept the authority of the old party Executive Committee for political reasons. Others had been unable to make connections with the committee abroad. Most of the members of the exiled bureau had no understanding of the changes that had taken place in the remnants of the party that remained underground in Germany, so they were not always able to distribute what money they had effectively among the various groups.

A somewhat similar situation existed in the international headquarters of the various trade unions, and the Socialist and labor parties in the democratic countries were faced with the same problem. How could people who did not know the conditions in Germany know to whom they should give money, how much was needed, or how they should get it to them?

In 1935, one of the largest and most generous international trade union federations sent a leading German unionist on a trip through Germany to find contacts and representatives in various cities. He posed as the representative of a foreign business house. One of our friends accompanied this man on a part of his rather dangerous journey and the unionist told him the following story:

"The international federation called a meeting of its finance committee before my trip. It was insane to discuss the details of such a trip with a half a dozen people, but the federation could not spend a penny without the explicit approval of the finance committee. They began to calculate: cost of railroad ticket from X to Berlin, from Berlin to Hamburg, from Hamburg to Magdeburg, etc. The total costs came to so much—approved. For decades this union, like all the others, has had a fixed rate of ten marks a day to cover the expenses of representatives who attend conferences or make journeys for the union. My trip was supposed to take twenty days, two hundred marks—approved. After concluding this business, the finance committee members were ready to let me travel. I tried to explain to them that, in taking a journey of this kind, unexpected difficulties could arise, and they finally appropriated an additional fifty marks for me. It was only after I got angry and threatened not to go under such conditions that they agreed to give me a little more. But they didn't understand what I was talking about—it was in contradiction to all their traditions, to the habits of years."

It happened that, when the unionist came to Magdeburg, he found all the local representatives of his organization had been arrested the week before. In order to make new contacts in the city he had to make a special trip to Hanover to find an intermediary. Of course, if his expenses had been pared down as originally proposed he could not have made the journey.

On his next trip into Germany, this trade union official was arrested and sentenced to fifteen years in the penitentiary.

This federation was one that had for many years been particularly interested in underground work and had been especially helpful and generous. But even such an organization could not comprehend conditions so basically different from those in democratic countries.

However, without the financial help of the labor organizations in democratic countries, the underground work in Germany could hardly have gone on, and the German anti-Nazis recognize the debt they owe for this assistance.

As, in the years following 1934, public opinion in the world lost interest in what was going on in Hitler Germany, the flow of money decreased in direct proportion. The more world Fascism expanded, the greater became the number of those who needed help, while the number of organizations in a position to help grew smaller. After a year, the Austrian labor movement followed the German into the underground. What had been a generous friend became a companion in misery. Then, for several years, every cent which the labor movement and liberals throughout the world could get together had to go to help the Spaniards who were fighting so heroically for their freedom. Even in National Socialist Germany, anti-Nazis took up collections for Republican Spain.

After the outbreak of war, not only did it become technically almost impossible to send money to the underground movement in Germany, but the great organizations of the democratic labor movement of Europe became, with their countries, the victims of the same enemy whom we were fighting when they had supported us. The United States became practically the only hope for the German underground. It was not always easy to find sympathy and understanding for the fight of German anti-Nazis among Americans. There had been more interest at first, but when years passed and there was no revolution in Germany people forgot the underground movement. It was only natural that help should go first to the victims in the countries conquered by Hitler. However, some American trade unions and some progressive Americans have done much for the underground movement. The American Friends of German Freedom, from the time it was founded in 1936, kept alive an interest in the inner German opposition and an understanding of its problems. It also rendered direct technical and material help to the underground movement. Not only did it contribute money, but its members when traveling in Europe served as couriers to underground centers.

The importance of adequate funds in our work could not be better illustrated than by an incident which occurred in our own organization in the summer of 1935.

The Gestapo had struck a heavy blow against the underground trade union movement; among others a certain R. was arrested. R. had been a member of the executive committee of a large trade union and he was our representative in an underground organization made up of unionists from factories throughout the Reich. A few hours after his arrest R.'s wife came to one of our leading members with his passport and his address list in code. It was essential that these valuable and incriminating documents be placed in a safe place at once. Our friend had an acquaintance named Mautner, who was a member of the staff of the embassy of a large European country. Mautner did not belong to our organization, but he was an ardent anti-Nazi. He had promised us that if a particularly urgent case arose he would be willing to take important documents to the embassy where they would be out of the Gestapo's reach. This case was sufficiently urgent since the lives of many people were endangered by R.'s arrest and by the list, so our friend decided to ask Mautner to help. Later he told us his story.

"I called Mautner in the morning in his office and he promised to meet me late in the evening in a coffee house, but he said that he was not sure whether he could be there on time. I had to be away from home all day; in addition to my regular organizational work, I had to get in touch with a number of people because of R.'s arrest. I hid the documents temporarily in my house and went about my business. You will remember that that was a time when all of us were particularly hard up, that the money which we were expecting from abroad had not yet come. During the course of the day I spent the little money I had in my pocket for carfare and telephone calls and then I had to pay for a taxi to get to an unexpected appointment. So far so good. But in the evening when I went home to get the all-important package I found that I only had just enough money for carfare to the coffee house. What would happen if by some chance Mautner couldn't keep the appointment? Not being a member of the organization he would not have the same attitude toward the importance of keeping appointments as we would. I had only talked to him by telephone and couldn't explain how urgent the matter was. I did not dare to go in the coffee house, order a cup of coffee and wait for Mautner. If he didn't come I might be arrested with my incriminating documents just for not being able to pay my bill. Nor did I dare use my money to call up one of our people and ask him to meet me somewhere, because if the person I called wasn't at home I couldn't get to the coffee house.

A FORMULA FOR SURVIVAL

"Finally, with a heavy heart, I decided to forget all our rules and regulations and wait on the street. For nearly half an hour, I walked up and down before the coffee house, the sidewalk burning my feet, R.'s passport and the precious address list in my pocket. To my great relief, Mautner came at last."

A few days after this happened the Gestapo came to the home of another trade union official. He happened not to be at home and got the warning in time. Meanwhile we received information indicating that the Gestapo had a spy in a certain center abroad, who might have been the cause of the whole series of arrests, including R.'s.

We had to work fast. On the evening of the day the Gestapo went to the home of our second unionist friend, he left with a member of our group on a "walking trip" in the Riesengebirge, and from there got to Prague. The same night one of the girls in our organization left for Paris, allegedly on business for a large art gallery, but really to inform the international trade union headquarters about our suspicions of a spy. (As a result of our warning, the Gestapo got no more information from this source.) The next day, another of the girls in the organization took Mrs. R. and her small child to Brussels, a passport having been procured for her in the meantime. These emergency measures had cost us one thousand marks. Luckily the money expected from abroad had arrived in the meanwhile.

The Gestapo were not able to send nearly as many ✓

professional spies or agents into the underground groups as is generally assumed. Espionage did play a sinister role in the destruction of the central machinery of the Communists. Later it was discovered that the Nazis had been able to win over high officials in the Communist Party even before 1933. So the greatest danger came from their own members who were renegades to the Nazis. The most notorious case is the story of Alfred Kattner.

Alfred Kattner was one of the assistants to Ernst Thaelmann, chairman of the Communist Party. He was assigned the task of arranging for the conversion of the central party machine for underground purposes, and among other things he had to find secret dwelling places for party leaders. This man had, for a long time, been an agent of the Nazis. As a result of information given by him several party leaders were arrested the night of the Reichstag fire. He delivered Thaelmann himself over to the Gestapo. There must have been few secrets in the Communist Party that Alfred Kattner did not know. The Nazis had planned to use him as star witness in a trial of the Central Committee members of the Communist Party; however, after the bad reception of the Reichstag fire affair, they lost their taste for public trials.

Early one morning in the summer of 1933 a number of cyclists drew up in front of the cottage in a suburb of Potsdam where Kattner lived. By the time the neighbors, awakened by revolver shots, had notified the police it was too late. Kattner was dead. The men who had shot him had gone and it was never learned who they were.

But the secret police would not let the death of so useful an agent go unavenged. Goering, at that time still chief of the Gestapo of Prussia, ordered that four high Communist officials who were serving long prison terms be taken from the Brandenburg-Goerden Prison where they were being held to Berlin for "questioning." The car carrying the prisoners was in the middle of the Grunewald on the outskirts of Berlin when the S.S. driver halted. The four men were shot "while trying to escape."

Kattner was not the only one who turned informer. Over and over again the Communists painfully built up a new Central Committee only to have it destroyed after the Gestapo had learned the identity of its members. The atmosphere of plot and intrigue in which sections of the Communist Party apparatus were involved, especially the G.P.U., and the long-term isolation of members in this sort of work from normal life and from the real labor movement, create a special type of person, the professional agent. Little as Jan Valtin's book *Out of the Night* tells about the German labor movement, it does aptly describe Communists of this kind.

A pure plotter or secret agent is necessarily isolated from society; he is isolated even from oppositional trends and organizations in society. A secret agent lives and works in a vacuum. He has no friends and no contacts outside the very narrow circle of his associates.

When a member of an underground anti-Fascist organization works in a factory he will naturally try to make friends with other men working there who think the same way he does. Without telling them that he is a member of an underground organization, he will try to win their confidence, he will try to strengthen their oppositional feelings, he will try to get them to look to him for leadership. A secret agent who is sent into the same factory, perhaps by the G.P.U., will anxiously avoid any contact with oppositionals. He will cry Heil Hitler louder than anybody else and only associate with the most die-hard Nazis. The first man feels solidarity with the other workers. Alone as he is, isolated as he is in his real function, he still feels that he is a part of the labor movement.

The second man feels, at best, some abstract attachment to the "cause." In pursuing his task the people around him are of no consequence. He has one definite and limited job to do. He is more a technician than a man with a political aim. His task may be a part of the anti-Fascist struggle, but the fact that he dare have no contact of any kind with persons of the same point of view means that he is not only isolated because of the demands of conspiratorial work, but that he is psychologically isolated. He lives in an artificial atmosphere, obeys a different set of laws. He is forced to accept the thesis that the end justifies any means which "the cause" to which he is committed, or the secret laws which he has sworn to obey, may demand. He abandons all accepted standards, estranges himself from normal human intercourse. He is driven to an amoral attitude. In the service of "the cause" he may feel justified in betraying his closest associate, even in committing murder. In *The Demons,* Dostoievsky describes the pure conspiratorial organization in all its frightfulness; it is a story taken from actual experiences among Russian revolutionaries.

In such surroundings, agents of the Gestapo and renegades who have gone over to the Nazis from the left, can feel comparatively at home, because they belong to a psychological type, not unlike that of the professional secret agent. In an environment which lacks any genuine comradeship and confidence, the best conspiratorial methods are no defense against spies.

What protected the underground groups of the non-Communist labor movement from penetration by Nazi spies to an amazing extent was the fact that these groups had developed out of a large democratic movement. Their tendency had always been to work closely with the great masses of the population, not to cut themselves off from them. Grown up in this tradition, the transition to underground work was terrifically hard for the members, but the same tradition protected their underground groups from degenerating into mere conspiratorial societies.

There was much similarity in the pasts of members of the underground German labor movement. They had read the same books, they had pretty much the same ideas, they spoke the same language and knew the same people. What a person in the labor movement took as a matter of course the Nazi spies could learn only with great exertion. Leading members of the German Socialist movement were informed about Marxist theories and Marxist ways of thinking. Anyone who claimed to have been in the labor movement for a long time and did not know the Communist Manifesto, or did not know that the Social Democratic Party had split at the party congress at Halle in 1920 would immediately be suspect. Anyone who did not know the role that the great labor leader, August Bebel, had played in the Germany of the Kaisers could hardly have been a real member of the old party. Active members of the German labor movement belonged to a well-defined type. To act this part convincingly was well-nigh impossible.

In the first years after their seizure of power, the Nazis set up courses in Marxism to train agents to go into the underground movement; but they failed. The only real agents the Gestapo had in the underground were, like Kattner, renegades from left-wing ranks who joined the Nazis.

But there were very few renegades. The persistence of the old traditions protected the underground organizations from that too. In the German Socialist movement, the standards of integrity were very high. Moral and ethical considerations played an important part both in political and private life. Idealistic motives are found more frequently in a movement which considers itself the vanguard of a new and ideal world than in other political groups. Men and women who grew up in this movement seldom became conscious traitors.

The real danger was not from people who turned Nazi, but from those who broke down after arrest and turned state's evidence. Sometimes the police forced such people to do jobs for them, perhaps take a trip, visit certain people or write a letter. Such people are not spies. They are usually decent average people, who simply are not strong enough to resist the threats and torture of the Gestapo. Anyone who has ever fallen into Gestapo hands knows that it is impossible to say in advance with certainty how you will hold up under torture. No one can vouch for himself beforehand, and it is even less possible to vouch for your friends. The real and the only test will come in the Gestapo's chamber. If a member of an underground organization does not stand this test, it is usually already too late for his colleagues to defend themselves. This was the greatest danger to the underground movement and only too frequently it was through their merciless torture that the secret police were able to reach and destroy whole groups.

It was a case like this that came within a hair's breadth of wiping out all the most important people in our Munich group. A courier had gone from Munich to Cologne. As customary, it was agreed that word of his arrival would be sent back immediately. Several days passed with no news, and the Munich group had to assume that Neumann—that was the name of the courier

—had been arrested. The usual precautions for such an emergency were taken by the group: all the people whose names were known to him retired from active work, were "isolated." No one could be sure how Neumann would stand up under questioning and certainly no one could know what the Gestapo would do. Several of our Munich members had to go into hiding. One man had to give up his job.

About a week after his disappearance Neumann turned up in Munich again at the home of one of his friends, a man who had only a distant connection with the organization, but knew a number of the active members personally.

Neumann told this story. Just before the train arrived at Cologne, he had been arrested with others in a Gestapo raid. However, in the crowd at the Cologne railroad station he had been able to get away from his captors. He had gone into hiding for several days and now had to flee from Germany. He asked the man to put him in touch with one of our local functionaries—we shall call him Wiener—who would give him money and tell him how to get over the border.

The message was sent on to Wiener and he discussed the matter with the other members of the Munich committee. They were suspicious of Neumann's story. It was decided that Wiener should not see Neumann, but that money and the necessary information should be given him in a roundabout and safer way. An appointment was made, but Neumann did not show up.

The next day one of our people happened to see him on the street. He was with two men, unmistakably agents of the Gestapo. The committee members had been quite right in their caution. It was apparent that Neumann had "broken down."

The situation was very disagreeable and, to make it worse, that same evening Neumann came again to his friend and told a fantastic story about why he had not been able to keep the appointment to get his money. Again he asked to be put in touch with Wiener.

The leading committee of the group had a difficult decision to make. Apparently Neumann had not yet given in entirely to the Gestapo; he appeared to be trying to gain time. If the group refused to have anything to do with Neumann, and did not help him to escape, then he would have to continue down the path on which he had already started. In that case the fate of the entire Munich group was sealed; little as Neumann knew about the leading personalities in the group and their present addresses, he knew too much. But, if someone went to meet Neumann, he was risking immediate arrest.

The final decision was to take the risk. The plan, after careful preparations, was to get Neumann to come to a certain place, ostensibly to meet important people of the group, and when he got there to take him across the border, whether he liked or not.

This kidnapping scheme worked. We cannot tell the details, but one of the reasons why it was successful was the professional jealousy that existed between the

Cologne Gestapo and the Munich Gestapo. They had entirely different sets of plans for Neumann. One group wanted to make a series of immediate arrests with his help and the other wanted first to observe the organization over a period of time so that they could find out about as many members as possible. Our friends profited by this conflict. A stroke of luck like that was unusual. As a rule, a "Neumann case" led to the destruction of an entire group.

To repeat: our real danger was not from spies and not from renegades. The chief enemy of underground work is the inadequacy of the human being, the very banal fact that one is dealing with people and not with perfect material. That is why it is so tremendously important that underground leaders have a knowledge and understanding of people. The rules of conspiracy have to be maintained, but at the same time the confidence of the members must be won and kept by a reciprocal show of trust in them. Iron discipline is required, but the initiative of the individual must not be destroyed. Sometimes it is necessary to tell a new member more than might seem proper according to pure conspiratorial principles just to demonstrate that you trust him. If you know that a friend or colleague has come under Gestapo suspicion, you cannot simply drop him, although the safety of the group may seem to demand that contacts be discontinued. You must use tact and consideration, not just suddenly isolate him completely from the organization which probably was the most important thing in his life, or he will become bitter and depressed and will be lost to you forever.

What about safety first? Of course. But the surest way of avoiding trouble and arrest is to do nothing. The maximum observance of the rules of conspiracy is often identical with complete passivity. Everything that you do in underground work, sooner or later, leads to danger. You cannot escape from this circle.

You can conceive of a perfect underground organization, but you cannot achieve one. Time and again, reality will destroy your best plans and stubborn dogmatic adherence to a perfect organizational scheme will lead to ruin just as certainly as will negligence in observing rules.

The underground organizations had to learn how to survive the blows of a much stronger enemy, to carry on after the heaviest losses. No one was spared the terrible fate of seeing his friends go to prison or to their deaths because of his own mistakes. There is not one underground group that can boast that it never had an "accident" in the course of its work. Many groups were completely destroyed by the Gestapo. Others, in spite of arrests in their ranks, succeeded in reorganizing and maintaining the continuity of their work.

In underground work, accidents are numerous and unpredictable. A courier is hurt in an automobile accident; illegal material is found on him. A man feels so safe that he doesn't learn an address by heart but writes it on a piece of paper and is arrested with it. Another breaks down when he is questioned. In a dangerous situation a man loses his head and puts a suitcase full of incriminating material in a lake without weighting it down sufficiently; later the papers are washed up on the shore and given to the Gestapo. Or, a man is burning illegal documents in his fireplace and a half-burned page goes up the chimney and falls on the street.

Through bitter experience, the underground workers had to learn that there was no absolute safety for them. As a German revolutionary once said before a military tribunal, they are often "dead men on leave." Anyone who works underground in Germany, not one who simply reads an occasional leaflet and passes it on, but anyone who pits his entire strength in the fight against the Nazi regime, knows that his span of life is limited. Two years, three years; perhaps, in an exceptional case, five years. The underground workers in Nazi Germany know that most of them will not be able to escape their fate. Nevertheless, there have always been men and women who were ready to take up the unequal fight and carry on.

6

The Enemy at Work—
Surveillance, Arrest, Prison

"A fly can't cough here in Germany without our finding out about it," a Gestapo agent boasted during the first winter of the war, a time when discontent was beginning to reach considerable proportions.

Naïve bragging of this sort is actually an expression of the real conviction of the Gestapo that they are able to keep a great country and 80,000,000 people completely under control. The Chief of the *Sicherheitsdienst* (Security Service), Reinhard Heydrich, said the same thing in "scientific" terms.

In 1941, Heydrich, the man with the "cobra eyes," writing in *Boehmen und Mahren*, a magazine published in Prague, described Gestapo methods in dealing with the internal enemy. He set down the following as the aim of the Gestapo: "Completely to comprehend the enemy in the foundation of his existence—exhaustive knowledge and criminalistic treatment of his organizations as well as of his personnel, and finally, systematic combating, crippling, destruction and elimination of the enemy by our executive force."

The construction of the apparatus of terror and surveillance necessary to carry out this task had begun long before Hitler entered the Reich Chancellory. In the same article Heydrich wrote: "The Sicherheitsdienst of the S.S. was founded long before 1933. When National Socialism took state power, it set up, in addition to the regular police, the *Sicherheitspolizei* [Security Police], with its subordinate divisions, including the Secret State Police [Gestapo], the criminal police and the Sicherheitsdienst [Security Service]."

Existing police organs were centralized according to carefully worked-out plans; new special divisions were created and finally the entire centralized machinery of control and punishment was merged in organization and personnel with the most dependable part of the National Socialist movement, the *Schutzstaffel*, known as the S.S.

The methods the Gestapo developed in fighting the inner German opposition are now being used successfully in the occupied countries. The "New Order" of violence in Europe is being built up on the experience the Nazis had in their silent war against the underground movement in the Third Reich.

Of course there are many differences, but they are differences in tempo, in the extent to which certain brutal means of oppression are employed and not differences in the methods themselves. For one thing, the rule of the Nazis in the occupied countries is newer, and also, because of national resistance in those countries, the Gestapo can count on less support from the general public.

In Germany itself, the Gestapo's systematic work is supplemented by two especially important auxiliaries:

First, in their organized surveillance and espionage at home, they have the help of the Nazi Party and its peripheral organizations. Hundreds of thousands of petty Nazi officials hand in regular reports about the people who live in their neighborhoods or are members of their organizations. They include the *Blockwart*, who is the lowest Nazi party official, charged with responsibility for the people living in his block; the air-raid wardens, the Labor Front representatives and the various officials of every conceivable kind of Nazi organization. Through these reports the Gestapo get a grasp of the current "situation."

Second, the Gestapo may always count on voluntary denunciation to deliver many potential enemies of the state into their hands. During certain periods the wave of denunciations has reached fantastic proportions; for instance, during the first year of Nazi rule. It was very easy to settle "old accounts" of a personal or political nature by denouncing your enemy to the police. Every foreign political success of the Nazis is accompanied by a new wave of denunciations. This volunteer police activity often furnishes the Gestapo with valuable tips.

These two aids to Gestapo work do not have the same

significance in the occupied territories. In principle the various Nazi organizations serve the same function. The organizations of the Quislings, Munters, Degrelles and Doriots are "extensions of the Gestapo," as are the Nazi organizations within the country. The same is, of course, true for most of the organizations of Germans living abroad. But all of these agencies do not take the place of the fine network of Nazi organizations within Germany itself. One should not forget that every German is forced to belong to one or several organizations, the Labor Front, Civilian Defense, the Farm Estate, etc. If he should not be so reported by his Blockwart, then his Labor Front official, his air-raid warden or the Nazi representative in his unit at the factory may find something "suspicious" about him. Thereupon the Gestapo machinery is set in motion. Regular surveillance begins and woe to him if . . .

There are almost no loopholes in the supervision of the German people. The same cannot be true in the occupied countries. The less successful the "silent" methods of domination, the more the naked fist of the oppressor is revealed, the more brutal is the terror, the less inhibited the firing squad.

The "silent" methods were perfected over a long period in the Third Reich and they have been extremely successful. The following incident is typical:

One morning in June, 1933, a block of houses in the northern part of Berlin was roped off by Storm Troopers and the police. Soon after six, three Storm Troopers and two policemen, all in civilian clothes, came to the home of one of our friends. They searched for three and a half hours, but found neither weapons nor "material hostile to the state" in the apartment. Before they left, one of the Storm Troopers said to our friend: "Just don't think, young fellow, that you can put anything over on us! We know exactly what you're up to. You're always having meetings in this house with all kinds of suspicious people." He named a number of days on which such "meetings" had been observed. He was quite right. The dates he mentioned were days on which a few people had met in the apartment.

Something that was even more significant we only found out by chance a few months later. Our friend had been under constant surveillance by his Blockwart for more than a year and a half, for one full year before Hitler had moved into the Reich Chancellory. Yet our friend was only a petty official in a labor youth organization, by no means an important person. In their methodical preparatory work the Nazis had not overlooked the smallest detail. That is what has given them such striking power on all their battlefronts, on the battlefronts outside of Germany as well as inside.

Sometimes, however, the Nazis did not reap the fruits of their methodical preparations. Sometimes, at the last minute, something went wrong. The most agreeable incident of this sort of which we know, agreeable, that is, for an anti-Nazi, happened in Norway in 1940.

About two weeks before the Nazis moved in to "liberate their northern brothers," a group of leading members of the German Gestapo was sent to Oslo.

As the gentlemen were supplied with all possible legal pretexts, some even traveling with diplomatic immunity, the Norwegian Government, anxiously guarding its neutrality, was able to take no measures against the unwelcome guests. The Gestapo officials used their time well; they must have put the finishing touches on the preparations for invasion. But luck was not with them in every respect.

Among the ships that tried to enter the Oslo Fjord in the gray morning hours of April 9, 1940, was the cruiser *Bluecher* with more than 4,000 men on board, among them those who were to be charged with the "internal administration of Norway." They included the Gestapo personnel with all the records and files listing German and Norwegian enemies of the Nazis in the new "province." A delegation of Quislingites awaited the Gestapo at the harbor, but they waited in vain. For, acting contrary to the forged orders of Quisling and his German helpers, the batteries in the Oslo Fjord opened fire. The *Bluecher*, with its 4,000 passengers, went down and with it the Gestapo and their carefully compiled records.

In Germany, the Gestapo did not find the system of voluntary denunciation an unmixed blessing.

One evening, in the spring of 1934, six of us, four men and two women, were at the home of a friend. The men were playing cards and the women were knitting. Suddenly the doorbell rang. Our hostess went to the door. We heard a rough voice and three men marched into the room—the Gestapo.

They began to search the apartment. After several fruitless hours, the chief of the group turned to the man of the house: "Where is your printing press? You'd better speak up now if you know what's good for you." The man explained that he had no printing press. "Well, where's your mimeograph machine?" Our friend insisted that he had none. The Gestapo had no choice but to believe him for they had already turned everything in the apartment inside out.

Then one of the Gestapo men said: "What, in the name of Heaven, were you doing between eight and nine o'clock that sounded as if you were printing an illegal newspaper?" We were dumbfounded. Then Emil solved the problem by bursting out laughing: "That's what comes of Hans always slamming his cards down on the table as if he wanted to break it." We all laughed, even the Gestapo.

As they started to the door, one of them turned around and said: "Goodnight, and to hell with the damned busybody who sent us up here."

Emil's explanation happened to be the true one, but it was a narrow escape nonetheless. Only the week before some confidential records had been transferred from this house to another hiding place. Things like that happened all of the time. Once the Gestapo searched the home of a friend of ours because her coffee grinder made so much noise a neighbor was convinced she was printing leaflets.

In both cases, there were no untoward results. But no one can know in how many cases such "suspicious noises" have meant catastrophe for underground groups.

Vital as was the role that voluntary denunciation played for a time in the Third Reich, necessary as it was to the Nazis during the first years, it still cannot be compared in importance with the systematic work of Secret State Police Chief Heinrich Himmler. The job done by self-appointed denouncers, by the Storm Troopers and by the Nazi Party in hunting out "enemies of the state" in the first year of Nazi power was tremendous. But as the Nazi Party consolidated its power, the Third Reich became a matter of course to Germans; with the rise of organized terror, the influence of the spontaneous terror of the National Socialist movement became less important. Only during the period of the National Revolution, 1933 and 1934, was terrorism the expression of a spontaneous popular movement.

Since June 30, 1934, organization has been dominant—organization that extends into all sectors of national life. It is not merely cynicism to speak of "organized spontaniety." It is a part of the Fascist rule, both in Italy and in Germany. For example, in the Third Reich, although there undoubtedly was anti-Semitism, there was never a spontaneous pogrom against the Jews. Every pogrom had to be carefully organized.

A report in our possession, published in Prague in

July, 1935, and based primarily on an underground report sent from Berlin the previous month, illustrates the improvement in the Gestapo methods of work during the first two years of Hitler rule:

"There is a difference between the first great wave of terror in 1933 which introduced the Nazi rule and the present. At that time, the regime was trying ruthlessly to root out every trace of the old labor movement. Fascism's own primitive desire for revenge was a considerable factor in this. . . . The real difference between the earlier period and today is that the present wave of terror is a proof that the Nazis are trying to combat new centers of resistance among the workers of Germany. . . . The Nazis did not succeed sufficiently in demoralizing the working class so their terror machine has had to become more brutal. It is not, as in 1933, engineered by the Storm Troopers; it is the Gestapo pure and simple.

"The Third Reich has become an *Ordnungsstaat* [a state of order]. It is the task of today's well-developed Secret Police to uncover centers of resistance and to see to it that they are destroyed in an organized manner, eschewing the unscientific methods employed in the early days. The Gestapo methods have really become 'more highly scientific.' We know that the Gestapo often observe underground groups and leave them alone. There have been many instances in which active enemies of the regime have been taken by the police, questioned for a few hours and then released, in spite of evidence against them, so that they get the idea that the police are 'dumb.'

"It is obvious why the Gestapo do this. They are no longer satisfied with the arrest of one or two underground workers. They want to get the whole group every time and they want to be sure that they are getting the key persons in the new organizations. The Gestapo are much more interested in underground contacts and in leaders than in individual enemies of the state, whose arrests often serve only as a warning to their colleagues. . . . In examining a prisoner the Gestapo are often less concerned about getting a personal confession out of him through their own kind of third degree —ten to sixteen hours of uninterrupted cross-examination, beating, wheedling—than they are in getting him to tell something of his contacts."

That is what Heydrich meant by "systematic elimination." It is not a question of single underground workers. The Gestapo cannot concentrate on individual "criminals against the state." Their job is "completely to comprehend the enemy." They have done astonishingly well, though we should never forget that they have all the facilities of a modern police system at their disposal. For individual Gestapo officials are no supermen; on the contrary, most of them are only mediocre. That will be confirmed by most of the people who have had the doubtful pleasure of coming into contact with them.

What really gave the Gestapo their tremendous power after a couple of years of National Socialism was their systematic compilation and analysis of all the information they could lay their hands on, and they had incomparably rich sources.

Every item, every report, every denunciation is put into a file. A synopsis of all the available information about every conceivable "enemy of the state" is noted on a card and filed away in a giant card index. In the card index you may find all you need to know about any individual, facts about his past, his occupation, his places of employment, about his temperament and about his "sins" both political and personal. Nothing is unimportant for the Gestapo. If an "enemy" has a weakness, it is all the better for the Gestapo, if for no other reason than that they may some day be able to use him as an agent. The Gestapo can wait.

The Gestapo's card index is the nerve center of the terror apparatus. Every trend and every tendency in German society are registered in this center and from it are transmitted the impulses that reach into the most distant ramifications of the National Socialist organism.

This instrument of rule is not entirely the work of Himmler. There was a good foundation already there. From his birth to his death the German citizen is accompanied by a mass of documents. They are a vestige of the time of the old absolutism, and people living in countries that have gone through a genuine democratic revolution will find it hard to understand this kind of bureaucracy. In the old days, everyone in Germany had to be registered with the police; not only that, every time there was a change in his family or an alternation in his status he had to re-register. In addition, the complicated system of German social insurance and countless other official formalities required registration in a dozen different official and semi-official agencies.

The Third Reich added registration for the rolls of the army, the "work books" of the German Labor Front, the lists of tenants which the Nazi Party needed for its task of "socio-political comprehension" of the population. When Josef Terboven, now Reich Commissioner for Norway, was Gauleiter of the Ruhr District, he described the lists of tenants as "the organizational base in order fully to command and philosophically to comprehend the entire people."

In March, 1937, the Labor Front distributed special "house lists" on which the name of "every wage earner and unemployed" had to be entered, complete with personal data. In addition, the National Socialist Popular Welfare Organization has its own "house card" with no less than forty spaces to be filled in with detailed information about each person. Finally, some time before the outbreak of war, the Nazis began to compile a "People's Card Index" to include every soul in Germany.

The "black lists" which the Nazis prepared long before they took power formed the basis of the Gestapo's own card catalogue. The mass arrests of the first weeks and months were based on these lists. In 1933, the Nazis also got the complete lists of the police including those of Section 1A, the political police. The files of politically suspect persons, kept by the Weimar Republic's political police, were not destroyed. In addition the Nazis also confiscated the files of parties and trade unions and countless other organizations, including their membership records, the lists of their officers and organizational information of all kinds.

Of course, this was only the raw material. Organized enemies of Hitler in Germany before 1933 numbered millions. All of these could not be locked up in concentration camps. Nor did the Nazis want to lock them all up. Their concern was to be able to judge every Hans Schmidt, Kurt Lehmann or Willi Schulze correctly.

For example, the janitor of a large Berlin apartment house is the local Blockwart. He reports that a certain man, named Ernst Mittler, is a suspicious character. Mittler doesn't contribute enough to Winter Help and he has many visitors.

The card index reveals the following: Mittler, Ernst: Former member of the Social Democratic Party; active politically for a long time; chairman of the Workers' Turnverein known as *Freiheit*.

There is additional information: Mittler, Ludwig—younger brother, now interned at Oranienburg Concentration Camp.

Further investigation yields the fact that the treasurer of the Freiheit Turnverein is August Pernau, now in prison under investigation preliminary to trial. The Gestapo investigate both "cases." They are at liberty to call witnesses in for questioning. Pernau had denied that he knew the Mittler brothers. Now the Gestapo begin to take an interest in this Turnverein. Who were the members? They are called in and questioned. So, this crowd turns out to be the same that visits Ernst Mittler regularly? Just old friends? We'll search the apartment. Look, a mimeograph machine and leaflets. . . .

Another case:

Illegal leaflets are found in the X factory. What does the card catalogue tell about the workers there? Twenty of them used to be trade unionists. Three were dismissed from other factories in 1933 because they were not reliable politically. One of them seems to be of particular "interest." A letter from him, written late in 1932, was found in the files of his union. He had complained about the lack of a militant spirit in the union and proposed that a network of underground representatives be set up in the factories, in case Hitler should come to power. That may be the man we are after. Careful investigation and constant surveillance will show.

A man may be able to change the conditions of his life, his home, his occupation, his friends, but he cannot get rid of his past. The fact that he was a "Marxist" before 1933 is alone, even in the Third Reich, not sufficient grounds for punishment. Nevertheless, you may often read in the verdicts handed down at political trials such words as: "The case is aggravated by the fact that the accused had been a member of the Social Democratic Party since 1920 and held a high office in its ranks," or "The accused was formerly a member of the

Communist Party, from which we must assume that still today . . ."

After all, who can really burn all the bridges to his past? What of your family? What of your job—can you give it up and face insecurity? What of the neighborhood where you grew up? Most important of all, what of your old friends; are you willing to lie to them? Only a small and restricted group of men and women is capable of making such a break with the past, men and women who have determined to make underground activity their life-work, men and women who are prepared to let conspiracy become second nature to them.

It took the Gestapo years to complete their card index of potential enemies, their "Inventory of Enemies of the State." Years of systematic work, hearings and more hearings, observation and surveillance. One of our friends who completed a long prison term and then succeeded in leaving Germany described the Gestapo at work from his experience. His case was particularly "interesting" to the Gestapo for a number of reasons, so he was cross-examined repeatedly. He told this story:

"At the beginning of 1937—many months after the completion of my own trial—I was once more taken from the Z Prison to Berlin. My travel order stated: 'wanted for questioning by the Secret State Police.'

"I was sent to the Berlin Police Headquarters to a division where I had not been before, nor did I know the officials who questioned me.

"After the customary formalities, the usual personal

197

data, I was told: 'This questioning has nothing to do with your own punishment—its purpose is simply to complete our own information. However, in your own best interests, you are requested to tell the whole truth.'

"The official placed about two dozen photographs on the table before me. I knew nearly half the people, colleagues of mine when I was a university student, acquaintances, some of them, of a decade ago. But no matter how long ago it was, I could not simply deny those acquaintances. Some of the pictures I knew were police photos—three views, front face and profiles from each side. Those people were certainly under arrest and I might be brought face to face with them at any time.

"You may get the most disagreeable surprises on being suddenly confronted with someone. I could not even be sure that the people who had ordinary photographs were not in the hands of the police or might not be taken at any time. Moreover, if dozens of people, acting on good faith, should state that I had known Mr. A. or Miss B. for years, it would be foolish for me to insist the contrary. In hearings of this sort, one's problem is not only to refuse to give information useful to the Gestapo; one has also always to be on guard not to deny completely innocent facts, not to lie about an innocent friendship. If one did, the Gestapo would probably consider the person in question under suspicion and subject him or her to hours of questioning, which in turn might lead to really dangerous revelations, perhaps because of the very fact of the victim's ignorance of the purpose of the inquisition.

"My hearing began quite innocently.

" 'You certainly know some of these people,' said the Gestapo Commissar; 'old friends, aren't they? We know that they were formerly Communist and Socialist students—there wasn't any law against it then, anyway. You were a member of the executive committee of the Socialist Student group, weren't you?'

" 'Yes.'

" 'Here is Robert Wendler. He was a member of your group, wasn't he?' He indicated one of the pictures.

"There was no point in denying it. 'Yes.'

" 'Where is Wendler now?'

" 'As far as I know, he left Germany in 1933.'

" 'Did you know that Wendler was married?'

" 'I heard something about it.'

"Then he asked about Wendler's wife, Frida Simon. Wasn't she a member of the Communist student group; did she hold office in the group; if so, what office?

"It went on like that for a time. Klaus Terner, member of the Socialist student group until 1931; Erich Bach, Communist student; Ann Ortner, leader of the student group at Frankfort University. Always the same questions: membership, offices held in political organizations, occupations entered after graduation. Where are they today? Did I, by chance, know that such and such a person had carried on political activity after 1933?

The Gestapo were astonishingly well-informed about some of these people, less informed about others.

"I tried to be as vague as I could in my answers, constantly reiterating that it had been a long time since I had seen the people, and besides, I had been in prison nearly two years. In the meanwhile, I was racking my brains; what was behind this questioning? Could the Gestapo have brought me on such a long journey to Berlin only to question me about such an old story, a story that seemed to have nothing whatever to do with the present?

"There was no limit to the Commissar's curiosity.

" 'So, around 1930, Fred Lerner was an assistant at the Chemical Institute? Pretty good job, wasn't it? Do you know whether he continued to attend the meetings of the technicians' group? The group was still in existence in 1933, wasn't it? There were groups of chemists and of engineers, weren't there?'

"I had a vague feeling that there was some system behind these questions, that they were leading to something, but what was it?

" 'The technicians' groups were organized by the trade unions,' I said. The Gestapo considered trade unions less dangerous than political parties, but the Commissar refused to be led off the track.

" 'There were special groups of Socialist and Communist technicians, chemists and statisticians at the universities and technical institutes—yes or no?'

" 'Yes.'

" 'Did the members keep up their connections after they had graduated and were working?'

" 'When you left the university, you also left the student organization; professional interests were taken care of in the trade unions.'

" 'We're not talking about trade unions. Answer my question—was there an organizational relation between the Social Democrats and Communists in technical professions?—answer yes or no.'

" 'No, not in the form of a political organization and there was absolutely no relation between Social Democrats and Communists.'

" 'But the people knew each other from the so-called technicians' groups?'

" 'Yes.'

" 'And they still came together after they had taken jobs?'

" 'I know nothing about that.'

" 'You know nothing about that,' the official repeated musingly and then, suddenly, 'Do you know this man?'

"I looked at the new picture and then I understood the point of the hearing. No, indeed, it wasn't a matter of rehashing harmless stories of the past.

"I knew his name. I had seen him in the notorious Columbia House during the first week of my arrest. I probably should not have seen him—he was being held in strict isolation. Because of an oversight on the part of an S.S. man, we once had stood next each other for an hour in the corridor, faces to the wall—waiting to be called in for questioning by the Gestapo. We were only able to exchange a few words in whispers. Later I found out who this man was and what was in store for him, the death penalty.

"Albert Eder was a radio engineer and he had built an illegal broadcasting station which had broadcast inside Germany. He was part owner of a small electro-technical factory and that was how he had been able to get the materials and the technical facilities he needed. The other owners of the factory were young technicians from the Communist and Socialist movements. The trial took place in complete secrecy at the end of 1936. Eder and two other accused were sentenced to death. The others were sentenced to from five to fifteen years. One of them, a former assistant in the Physics Institute of Berlin University, committed suicide while being held for investigation. The underground radio had operated for barely two months. It cost the lives of four men.

"Perhaps the Gestapo assumed that they had not yet arrested all the participants. Perhaps another radio station was broadcasting. In any event, the case had been reopened. Their concern now was to find other suspects and by investigating their pasts uncover other connections leading to the present.

" 'Do you know this man?'

"I felt hot and cold all over.

" 'No, Herr Commissar.'

" 'He was not a member of your student group?'

" 'Not in my time, anyway.'

" 'Was he a member of the Communist student organization?'

" 'I don't know that.'

"The Commissar put the picture aside. The case seemed to him to be closed.

" 'To come back to your technicians' group—did your group have anything to do with the Workers' Radio Association?'

"If it had not been that two minutes before he had shown me the picture, and if I had not known that it was Albert Eder, I would certainly have answered yes. What could have been more harmless or more natural than that ten years before students of physics and electrical engineering had helped amateur radio fans who belonged to a political organization with which they were sympathetic?

" 'I never knew of any such connection.'

"The hearing took more than four hours altogether. Two or three times the Commissar came back to the technicians' groups. But I knew what he was driving at. He learned nothing from me."

Even the most complicated filing system is not, in the long run, a sufficient means to control living human beings. It might be adequate if people acted in accordance with the Nazi philosophy, if they were not individuals, but tiny cogs in a giant machine. In that case, a complete filing system could be the basis for rule. Just as soon as Germany had been thoroughly organized in the Nazi way, the "enemies of the people" eliminated, every person lined up as a *Volksgenosse* (comrade of the people), the system would function totally and without friction.

But it wasn't quite so simple as that. No less a person than Reinhard Heydrich, who was chiefly responsible for the smooth functioning of the Nazis' police system, recognized that fact relatively early.

In 1936, the *Schwarzen Korps*, organ of the S.S., carried a series of articles, entitled *The Transformation of Our Struggle*. These articles were subsequently published in pamphlet form by the Nazi Party publisher, Eher. Heydrich wrote the following about the enemies of the Nazi system:

"A network of contacts penetrates into almost every branch of the state apparatus, of our public life and of our movement. Through this network or canal system the enemy is informed of the danger facing him. Through it he learns in time of all the projected state measures, decrees and laws. And at the same time the canal system fulfills the task of preparing those counteractions which are so vital to the enemy. Some of the parts of the canal system are working consciously as traitors; for others it is merely a matter of personal weaknesses which are consciously taken advantage of. . . ." Heydrich maintained that it was not only the handful of "unteachable reactionaries," the small minority of "Jewish-Bolshevik sub-humans," who participated in this activity against the state. No, indeed, the second highest official of the Gestapo recognized that "the ramifications of this network are tremendous." "Every party member must help in the fight," he exhorted. "The state police cannot carry on the battle alone. . . . It is necessary that we recognize that the battle has penetrated more deeply —it cannot be carried on with technical means alone."

This is a remarkable admission, even when one realizes that Heydrich exaggerated on purpose. The appeal for help from the party comrades was, of course, neither more nor less than a demand for unrestrained denunciations.

Such a system necessarily creates hatred. The Nazis know that. They do not fool themselves about the attitude of a large part of the German people towards their methods of rule. The S.S., the so-called elite of the "Master Race," are particularly well aware of the hatred and scorn by which they are surrounded. As early as 1936, Heinrich Himmler, Reich Fuehrer of the S.S. and Chief of Police, in a pamphlet entitled *The Schutz-staffel as a Fighting Organization against the Bolsheviks*, wrote with the cynicism so characteristic of leading Nazis:

"I know that there are millions in Germany who feel sick at their stomachs every time they see the black uniform of the S.S. We understand that; we do not expect to be loved by too many. Those who love Germany will respect us, but those who have a bad conscience should fear us."

It was the inner enemy—the German people—that Heydrich had in mind when he appealed to his S.S.: "If we want to maintain our hold on the people, then we must be hard with the enemy, though we may sometimes injure the individual enemy and eventually we shall certainly be decried by many well-meaning people as uncontrolled brutes."

The Gestapo left nothing to chance. They prepared for war with methodical thoroughness. In his famous 1937 speech on the *Inner German Battlefront*, Heinrich Himmler said:

"In complete understanding with the Fuehrer, I have come to the conclusion that a larger part of the functionaries [of the democratic movements] will have to be arrested. . . . We shall increase that number until we have reached a point where we can really guarantee that the creation of new underground organizations will be impossible simply for lack of officials and leaders. . . .

"As for the concentration camps, permit me to say at this time that I do not believe that there will be fewer of them. I am convinced that in certain events there will have to be more."

And there are more.

How many political prisoners are there in the Third Reich?

This question has been asked many times. It is a topic of frequent and heated discussions, particularly in the prisons and concentration camps of Germany. Estimates range from 300,000 to the quite fantastic figure of 2,000,000. We know people with long experience behind the bars themselves, who have attempted to calculate the number. They knew about the larger prisons and had a pretty good idea of the number of inmates. By consulting prison mates whose experience had made them experts, they could judge the approximate proportion of political prisoners.

But it is hard, even in this way, to arrive at definitive conclusions. For example, take the judicial district of Berlin. At the end of 1936, there were, in the large Brandenburg-Goerden Prison, 1,000 enemies of the Nazi regime serving sentence. But the number was growing all the time. Transports of prisoners arrived from Berlin twice each week and there were always twenty-five to forty political prisoners among them. The prison became so crowded that, in the summer of 1937, hundreds of political prisoners had to be transferred from Brandenburg. They were so-called mild cases, whose sentences did not exceed five years. Thus prisoners originally sentenced in the Berlin judicial district came to Luckau, to Ploetzensee and Sonnenburg. The mildest cases were also transferred to Tegel and Brandenburg Altstadt. Women were sent to Jauer, Luebeck or Waldheim, and young prisoners went to Kuestrin. The great Berlin-Moabit Prison, where prisoners are under investigation prior to trial, has a capacity of 2,000, but proved too small and two other institutions for prisoners under investigation had to be established, Lehrterstrasse and Charlottenburg. And how many political prisoners were there whose cases never came to trial? The giant concentration camp of Sachsenhausen near Oranienburg was not big enough to hold them. Then there were the many thousands of prisoners under sentence or in protective custody who worked in the marshes at drainage projects and were known as "peat-bog soldiers" (*Moorsoldaten*). Too, there was the great police prison on the Alexanderplatz, known as "Alex," and half a dozen smaller police prisons in Berlin.

It was just the same in all the other judicial districts, Hamburg, Dresden, Munich, Cologne.

The most difficult thing was to estimate the number of prisoners in the concentration camps and the camps for peat-bog soldiers. The numbers fluctuated constantly. For example, at one time there were 8,000 people in the big Buchenwald concentration camp and a short time afterwards there were reports of 20,000. At least twice a year "something happened" and tens of thousands of people were arrested or taken into protective custody. It was completely impossible even to guess what was happening in the prisons in the small and medium-sized cities. Suddenly you heard that in the local jail of Genthi, with a normal capacity of 30, there were 160 prisoners. Or, you heard that a "labor commando" of about 300 men had been sent to Willstock in Mecklenburg. How many auxiliary prisons of this sort were there really?

Several careful estimates, arrived at independently in Germany during the years from 1936-1940, placed the number of political prisoners between 500,000 and 600,000. The largest group consisted of men between the ages of twenty and sixty. That means that for every forty to fifty grown men in the Third Reich, one was behind iron bars as an enemy of the regime.

Who were the political prisoners?

This question is not easy to answer either. The rule of terror of the regime ran afoul of the most heterogeneous elements, although members and officials of the labor movement were by far the largest group. The great mass trials carried out by the People's Courts, the criminal courts, the Provincial Courts and countless special courts were all of members of the labor movement. There was a mass trial of 200 labor functionaries in District A of Berlin; other trials were of 250 accused who were members of the "Anti-Fascist Fighters League" of Z, of twenty-five former leading trade-union officials of District F, of the leaders of the illegal Communist youth group, of a group guilty of "continuation of the Social Democratic Party" in the provinces of X and Y, of others accused of the rebuilding of the Communist Party in District L. The record is endless. There were trials of couriers of the underground movement. There were two large trials of so-called "specialists," technicians and chemists, accused of volunteering their technical skills for Communist aims. Three persons were sentenced to death in the "specialists" trial and the other accused received sentences of from four to fifteen years. The verdict was generally death when there was only a shadow of suspicion that the accused had had some connection with the death of a Nazi killed in a brawl or some nocturnal shooting during the "fourteen-year battle for liberation" that preceded Hitler's taking power. A death sentence could also be given for "underground work in contact with some group abroad." Persons suspected of having "contemplated the divulgence of military secrets" were also condemned to death. Interpretation could make anyone, who had passed on a report about rearmament or conditions in a munitions plant, guilty of this crime.

The German courts developed a system of fixed punishments. The minimum punishment provided for in the so-called "High Treason" paragraph ("whoever attempts alone or with others, to change the German constitution by violence . . .") is two years in the penitentiary. This light punishment is reserved for those people who have somehow or other been involved in a large trial, but against whom nothing can be proved except, at the worst, possession of a single leaflet. Membership in the lowest organizational unit of underground work (a *fuenfergruppe* or unit of five) means three to three and a half years, leadership in such a group, three and a half to four and a half years. A courier for the underground movement or the treasurer of a city district of an organization gets four to five years; a member of the leading committee for a city district gets six to eight years; but a member of such a committee for an entire city or district gets ten to twelve years. A member of the central committee can count on from fifteen years to life. However, higher officials of the underground movement very often receive death sentences. Though

Social Democrats and especially trade union leaders sometimes get milder sentences than Communists, nevertheless, unionists have often been sentenced to as much as fifteen years. Members and officials of the Reichsbanner have been treated exactly like the Communists. Members of Otto Strasser's "Black Front" organization have always been punished with special severity because they are renegades from the Nazi Party. Members of "bourgeois" organizations, particularly Catholic political organizations, have seldom been accused of high treason. The only such trial generally known about was that of the Cologne chaplain, who was sentenced to eleven years in the penetentiary. In relatively "harmless" cases, especially of young people accused of underground work, sometimes the charge is not high treason, but simply "continuation of a forbidden organization," usually carrying a punishment of only a few months in prison.

In addition, there are countless sentences for *Heimtuecke* (underhandedness), on the basis of the "law against underhanded attacks on the party and the state." For example, telling political jokes is underhanded and may bring eight to twelve months' imprisonment. This paragraph is extremely flexible in application. There often seems to be no misdeed at all, and a person can be sentenced for underhandedness just for being a Jew.

After the war started, secret listening to the foreign radio became an important category of crime. Whether the many thousands who have been arrested for violating foreign exchange regulations or for *Rassenschande*

(violation of laws restricting Jewish-Aryan relation-
ships) should be counted as political prisoners is a moot
point. The motives of this type of offender are apt to be
personal or they may be more complex. Thousands and
tens of thousands of Germans have landed in concentration camps for a period of weeks or months for failure
to observe some petty "special regulation." Any large-
scale persecution of the Jews has always meant that
hundreds and thousands were thrown into concentration
camps.

It is evident that one cannot speak of "average" political prisoners. There are always important differences
in the degree of political motivation. A former deputy
of the Reichstag or an editor, who has spent his entire
life in a leading position in the service of the labor movement, naturally has a different reaction to arrest and imprisonment than an average worker who has gotten in
trouble simply because he could not resist the temptation
to read an illegal leaflet and pass it on to a "good friend."
A dyed-in-the-wool Communist has even less in common
with a middle-class Jewish business man who was overheard telling the latest joke about Goering's uniforms to
an acquaintance in a coffee house.

If we wish to find out how this heterogeneous mass of
enemies of the regime gets on in prison, we have to take
certain facts into consideration.

The prison regime of the Third Reich bears little re-
semblance to the picture of prison life that we may
know from the memoirs of Russian revolutionists im-

prisoned by the Czar. Siberia has been called "the university of revolutionaries." There, inhumane as their living conditions may have been, the political prisoners did have an opportunity to complete their education. They could study and they could carry on discussion with their fellows of similar political convictions.

In Nazi Germany's prisons, political prisoners are liable to new criminal charges if they so much as engage in political discussion. Care is taken that political prisoners should not be seated together and that they should not be placed near each other in their work, if it can be avoided. One of the reasons why political prisoners are not placed in special departments by themselves is in order to keep them from making friends. When political prisoners and criminals are together, the guards have strict orders to see that the criminals are not corrupted by their contact with "subversive elements."

Under these circumstances and under an extremely severe regime which specializes in exact and petty surveillance and has unlimited possibilities for punishment, there is, of course, no chance for large-scale organized activity among those in prison for political offenses. There have been instances, though, when persons, already sentenced once, have been brought to trial again, charged with high treason, "creation of political units within the prison." For example, in 1938 in the W. Prison a political prisoner was tried, charged with having prepared a political information bulletin which he passed around to the neighboring cells. The trial lasted several days. Dozens of prisoners were called as witnesses. The verdict of the court was that the accused should have five years added to his previous sentence of seven years.

An incautious letter, which a peat-bog soldier tried to smuggle out of the infamous camp at Esterwege in 1936, added two and a half years to his seven-and-a-half-year sentence.

But all of this does not suffocate the spirit of resistance, even in the prisons. The following incident took place in a German prison in 1935, although affairs on such a large scale are unusual.

At that time, there was in the R. Prison a division where, contrary to general procedure, a large number of political prisoners all had their work benches on one side of the hall. They determined that they would observe the anniversary of the murder of Karl Liebknecht and Rosa Luxemburg on January 15th. At three o'clock in the afternoon, they would all lay down their work and sit silently for one hour.

There may be differences of opinion as to whether an action of this sort served any constructive purpose. But you must know the atmosphere in a German prison, you must know that the basic principle behind Nazi penology is that every spark of individual initiative must be extinguished, to understand why it meant so much to these men to give this demonstration of loyalty to their old convictions.

The day and the hour arrived and the men laid down their tools. No one abstained, although several had been against the plan. After a few minutes the guard was completely baffled. What was wrong? No answer. "Pick up your work at once!" No answer. The guard from the neighboring division was called; the warden's office was informed. A few minutes later the prison director, Herr K., arrived, an old-time Nazi and a brutal slave driver. There was still no answer. Meanwhile the criminals had also stopped work and waited in suspense to see what would happen. K. drew his revolver and told the prisoners that he had ways enough of bringing them to reason; he expected an immediate explanation of what was going on. The general alarm had been sounded and the special guard arrived; twelve men with rubber truncheons and shotguns entered the hall. Finally, a trusty, one of the criminals, admitted that the day before he had by chance overheard a conversation in the latrine and knew that this demonstration was planned.

The result was that ten people, who were picked out for one reason or another as ring leaders, were put in solitary confinement on bread and water for four weeks each. Among them was the trusty, who should have reported the plan in advance. This special division was dissolved, and since that time the greatest care has been taken by prison authorities to keep the political prisoners from sitting together. Everyone who had taken part in the demonstration was reported to the Gestapo. On each of their records was added a notation: "To be kept in protective custody upon completion of sentence."

In other words, because of ten minutes' participation

in a demonstration within the prison walls, each of these men could expect an indefinite term of years or life in a concentration camp.

In prison, you are concerned not only in maintaining solidarity with your fellow political prisoners; you are particularly anxious to maintain some contact with the outer world. Even worse than the chicanery and brutality of the prison guards, worse than the stupidity of the work, worse than the hunger and hardships, is the feeling of isolation, of being cut off completely from the world. That is not changed by the fact that certain categories of prisoners are allowed to read newspapers. The things that political prisoners want to know are not in the Nazi papers. The desire for political information, the craving for knowledge, is always strong, especially among younger political prisoners. Workers, who for years have devoted all their leisure time to organizational work in the labor movement, are bitter because their long period of imprisonment has to be completely wasted. The few books in the library are read over and over again, and do not answer the questions in their hearts. If the more highly educated and well-informed men among the political prisoners were allowed to use the long months and years in giving courses, holding lectures—not necessarily on political subjects, but on science, medicine, philosophy—what a useful job of education could be accomplished. But that is exactly what the keepers have wanted to prevent at all costs. "Yes, they want us to go crazy!" the prisoners say.

Knowing that the entire Socialist movement has suffered a grave defeat, political prisoners feel a great need for serious discussion. But to have discussion it is necessary, first of all, to have the right people together, and secondly, to have some knowledge of events and ideas in the movement "outside," especially in other countries.

How frustrating it is! The great cell block in which the few political prisoners are swallowed up among the many criminals, the constant surveillance, the prohibition against talking, the impossibility even of changing one's place, the constant danger of denunciation by the criminals—what can one do?

A friend recently released from prison wrote: "We did all that was in our power. For some time we were lucky; a half-way decent guard tolerated the interest of one of my prison mates in scientific problems. So, during our free time on Sunday afternoons we sat together, a physics textbook open before us. Not speaking above a whisper, looking around us all the time, we spent an hour discussing the probable outcome of the Popular Front in France. Once during my prison term, after many weeks of finagling, I succeeded in getting a 'good corner' in the dormitory. It was hard work, but I actually was able, for a few weeks, to give a lecture every evening. First I reported on the news in the papers and attempted to analyze events. Then we had a general discussion of the problems of the labor movement. We had thirty to forty minutes for this and could only whisper since it was forbidden to speak in the dormitory. However, all too soon I was transferred to another division."

Another of our friends told his story:

"Early in 1937, when I was being held at the Berlin Police Headquarters, I had a chance to talk with a leading official of the Communist Party. He had just been sentenced to fifteen years; the prosecutor had asked for the death penalty. He had been in prison 'only' eight months, so he had news. He had been abroad early in 1936 to attend an important party conference. From him I learned for the first time what had happened at the Seventh World Congress of the Communist International, in 1936. He told me about the change in Russian foreign policy, about the Communists' new popular front 'line,' the decision of the Comintern to defend democracy.

"Most of the other political prisoners in the big cell at Police Headquarters at that time had been in prison since 1933 or 1934. Many of them were Communists who had been arrested at a time when the Communists considered every Socialist a 'Social-Fascist' and a deadly enemy. It was hard for them to adjust to the new policy, but they looked upon it as a step towards unity and everyone was in favor of that.

"We were all transferred later to other prisons, to Brandenburg, to Luckau, Sonnenburg or the camps for peat-bog soldiers. All agreed to inform the comrades in the other prisons of the news. The news was a year old by the time I got to Brandenburg, but for days, when we walked in a circle in the courtyard, the other prisoners took turns walking just ahead of me so that, in snatches, always interrupted by the guards, I could report to them what Moscow had decided."

It isn't only that they want political information; even more important for the men behind the prison walls is reassurance that the people "out there" are still alive, that they are still working, that they have not forgotten their imprisoned colleagues. There is the question of wives and children. The arrest of the father of a family has terrible consequences. It is punishable by law in Nazi Germany to support the relatives of a political prisoner. Whether or not his family is provided for determines largely how a prisoner holds out during the long years in prison. If his family is taken care of, it is proof for him that the movement still exists. Nothing is worse than the question: "Was it worth it?"

While unknown fighters were suffering the vengeance of the Nazis in the concentration camps or found themselves faced with endless years in prison, Hitler celebrated one triumph after the other. He introduced compulsory military service—he sent his troops into the Rhineland and nothing happened. Even a man who had been in solitary confinement for years knew what a comedy the policy of Non-Intervention in Spain was, the policy which allowed the vanguard of the fight against world Fascism to battle unaided.

Hitler occupied Austria. "For two days," a friend told us later, who at that time was in a prison in Saxony near the Czech border, "we heard trucks and tanks roll by our walls. We were not allowed to look out of the windows; we could only hear Hitler's troops marching to support his 'peaceful' conquest. Actually this military measure on the Czech frontier turned out to be superfluous. A few days later we found out that the people 'out there' had confined themselves to paper protests. Newspaper reports about the 'joyous welcome' did not fool us any more than the 99 percent 'Ja' vote in the popular referendum. We knew Hitler's methods, we knew what it meant to be 'liberated' by Hitler. When, after some time, Austrians came to our prison from Dachau and from the new concentration camp at Buchenwald, they only confirmed what we had already known, the same murders, mass arrests, a repetition of what we had first learned five years before. The world was silent or spoke of the 'right of self-determination of national groups.' But we knew that the cause for which we had fought had suffered another serious defeat.

"Nor was it the last. Two months later the Czech crisis began. We breathed easier—we said: Czechoslovakia is a different matter, Czechoslovakia will not be presented to Hitler as a gift. The Czechs will fight. The Czechs have firm alliances with France and Russia; France has an alliance with England. Hitler would be powerless against England, France and Russia. It may not even come to war, for Hitler will not dare a war against a world coalition. If he doesn't, then his end will be nearer. Prisoners who had been in Czechoslovakia told us of the free life there, of the Czech labor movement, of the Czech army. Half joking and half seriously we told men who were to be released from prison at that time that they should tell the Czechs that, in case war came, they should send us weapons and a truck with food and supplies—we'd take care of the Nazis at last.

"From the reports in the papers about the Runciman Mission in Prague, we couldn't make out what was happening, nor from Chamberlain's visit to Godesberg. The Nazi papers must be lying. Certainly the British had a trump card which they would play at the last minute— that is what we thought in prison.

"Again we heard the troops march by, day after day. Some of our guards were mobilized. The others were obviously nervous. Their behavior showed how much the German people feared war. The wildest rumors were told and believed. A blackout was announced; the night guard was reinforced and equipped with machine-guns.

"Then came Munich. Czechoslovakia had been sold out. The anti-Hitler front had collapsed. Chamberlain's slogan—'peace in our time'—peace with Hitler!

"We didn't understand, we knew only that Hitler had won another victory. And our prison guards, who the day before were whispering anxiously in the corridors, held their heads high once more and plagued us more than ever.

" 'You are the fools!' one of them said to us.

"Wasn't he right? We were the ones who were dumb. It was no consolation to know that we were not alone, that everywhere in the world those who were fighting against the common enemy had also to be resigned. They too were disgusted, felt that they had been betrayed and had to ask themselves whether there was any sense in fighting for freedom and justice. Who—we used to ask each other—will ever again have the courage to resist if he has to admit that it was all in vain? In this world of cowardice and betrayal, right is on the side of the strongest.

"Nevertheless, we didn't want to believe it. It couldn't be that the world had really and finally capitulated before Hitler. A few weeks after Munich our conclusions were confirmed in a surprising way. I got a message from my wife in Paris. She had been able to escape arrest and had got away from Germany. Every few months, through devious channels, I received a few harmless-sounding lines from her. She wrote: 'Hilda is here now too with the children. We are so happy to be together again.' Translated, that meant: the headquarters abroad of our organization has been transferred to Paris from Prague (for years we had called our executive committee Hilda). I could draw the obvious conclusions —the peace made in Munich was not expected to last long.

"During the next few days I made every effort to pass this message on to as many other political prisoners as possible. I told them: We can know now that Prague is not considered safe. Munich does not mean 'peace in our time.' They 'out there' expect that there will be war and they are preparing for it! The effect of this message is hard to describe. For every prisoner there was a conflict between his hopes and his disbelief.

"Barcelona and Madrid fell. Hitler entered Prague. Chamberlain made his famous confession that he had been mistaken. While the endless negotiations in Moscow baffled us anew every day, Hitler began the preparations for his next conquest. The allegations of Polish atrocities against the German minority were an omen which no one could mistake.

"Is it going to be war this time? we asked ourselves over and over. After everything that had already happened, only war and a military defeat could furnish the prerequisites of Hitler's downfall. Had they 'out there' finally realized that?

"But first came a bitter disappointment. For many of the men who had already spent years in prison it was the worst blow of all—the Russian Pact. Here again we couldn't fit the pieces together. Here again it was impossible to understand. Some of the political prisoners tried to find complicated theories to explain it. But from the cell block where Communists sentenced to life imprisonment were held in solitary confinement, we heard reports of suicides. . . . A Communist serving fifteen years pondered the unbelievable fact silently for several days and then he said to me: 'They are our leaders—we can't do anything about it. I guess all leaders betray you; but that does not change anything, we were right and we did our duty.'

"Then came the war. 'At last!' the political prisoners said, 'now the Hitler regime must collapse.' Most of them believed that Germany's defeat would come soon.

"Externally, prison life did not change much. The penal screws were already screwed so tight that it couldn't be worse. Working time was increased by one hour. They couldn't give us poorer food. But there was a new reason for all kinds of annoyances, curtailment of letters, withdrawal of visiting privileges, etc. War!

"Half a year after the war began I was released. It was almost a miracle. I could thank the fact that I had been expatriated and was technically a foreigner for that. Instead of sending me to a concentration camp, the usual procedure upon completion of a sentence, the Gestapo expelled me from Germany. During the last night the political prisoners came, one after another, to my bed. They wanted to shake my hand once more and wish me luck.

"Good luck! Do right by us out there, comrade. Tell the people how it is here; tell them that we are waiting for them, that we haven't given up!"

7

Between Despair and Hope

Underground organizations cannot exist in a vacuum, not even when they are reduced to tiny groups of the most carefully selected people, and when it is a part of their design to cut themselves off almost entirely from Fascist society. Their activity, their satisfaction in the struggle, yes, their very existence is largely dependent on whether, and in what degree, they are able to move within a group sympathetic to their aims. There is the closest relation between underground anti-Nazi *organizations* and the current strength of anti-Nazi *opposition*.

Opposition under Fascism is only in the rarest cases an organized opposition. The regime cannot prevent each individual from feeling opposition to it, but the regime can go far in preventing its enemies from joining together in an organization. The general concept of opposition may embrace all shades of activism, from merely grumbling within your own four walls to belonging to an underground group. The opposition in Germany includes every variety of opinion—from Storm Troopers who consider themselves potential "avengers of Roehm," civil servants and officers who have grown old in the service and are baffled by the Nazis' methods, Catholics whose religious feelings have been outraged, Jews who have been robbed of any possibility of existence, to members of the democratic political parties who have remained true to their old convictions. There were people who rejected National Socialism in every age group and in every occupation, from under-secretary of a ministry to street-sweeper, from university professor to servant girl. But the conceptions of this opposition and the aims which motivated it were just as varied as was its composition.

This wavering, unstable group, with all its contradictions, was the soil in which the organized anti-Nazi opposition had to grow, including the genuine underground organizations. It was in this milieu that the underground groups lived, here they had to find their strength—and this milieu was also responsible for their weakness.

The underground organizations were the backbone of the anti-Nazi opposition, its potential leadership. But the ebb and flow in popular opinion, every change in the attitude of the masses toward the Hitler regime, determined the radius of activity and the stability of the essential core of the underground.

The attitude of the broad masses of the German people towards the Hitler regime fluctuated constantly. During the "national uprising," the Nazi Party did not yet have the majority of the people behind it. Desperation, born of the post-war crisis and the depression, the failures of the Weimar Republic and its unresisting capitulation, the skilful social propaganda of the Nazis together with their terror against their enemies undoubtedly drove large sections of the populace during the first months either directly into the Hitler camp or into indifference. The indifferent people said "give Hitler a chance." However, this development was halted and complicated by the crises the Nazi system went through during the first period of its existence, the most critical point being reached in the bloody "German night of St. Bartholomew," on June 30, 1934.

It is understandable that enemies of Hitler, both inside the country and outside, looked upon that event, when the Nazis' own Storm Troopers were disarmed and their leaders murdered, as the beginning of the end.

What should a person think who, like one of our friends, witnessed the following incident on a peaceful summer evening.

"I was standing with a friend on a corner of the Kurfuerstendamm [the busiest street in the western part of Berlin]. During the afternoon we had heard rumors throughout the city that something was wrong, but the streets looked completely normal, with the coffee houses filled and thousands of people strolling on the sidewalks.

"We heard military music and the sound of marching feet. A Storm Troop column marched down the Kurfuerstendamm, swastika flags flying, the Storm Leader at the head with his adjutants by him, the leader of each

227

troop marching before his division. The people on the sidewalk stood at attention and their arms raised up in the Hitler salute. [Saluting the flag is required by law.]

" 'Halt, do not move or you will be shot!'

"A hundred policemen swarmed over the street, their machine-guns ready. Before thousands of people who could not believe their eyes, the Storm Troop leaders were taken out from the ranks, arrested and carried off, the column dispersed."

If such a thing could happen, the end of the Hitler regime must be at hand. Our executive committee in Berlin thought otherwise. They prepared an analysis of the events of June 30th and sent it abroad. Their report was published in Prague in the middle of July:

"It was first judged to be a symptom of complete panic within the Nazi ranks. Apparently they had shed their own blood, insanely murdering their own high officials. At the same time they wiped out leaders of groups in German society which seemed long to have belonged to the past. In reality this drastic, brutal action, in spite of the confusion, was a planned and considered action in the interests of the Fascist Party. Though at first it may seem incredible that this mass murder, this blow from Olympus which sent hundreds of the founders and heroes of the Third Reich before the firing squads, will reinforce the power of the murder band, we must not forget that Fascist dictators observe laws quite different than those observed in non-Fascist countries. . . . What June 30th really accomplished for the

Nazi Party was to remove the leaders and the spokesmen of all anti-centralist forces in Germany. The Storm Troops had become a rebellious organization. Now its leaders are dead. In the same purge Hitler took care of leaders of the Catholic Action and of the old Hindenburg clique in the state administrative machinery and the army and the leaders of the separatist tendencies in Bavaria. Thus every possible point of crystallization for the varied and scattered opposition in Germany has been liquidated."

In July, 1934, no one credited this realistic picture. In the centers of the German political emigration abroad, hopeful exiles were packing their suitcases. But soon it became evident that on June 30th a blow had been delivered against all conceivable enemies of the Hitler regime. In enumerating the victims in the report you find scarcely a single political group hostile to the regime missing, except the labor movement and the Jews, who already enjoyed the position of enemies of the state.

It was only some time later that the new consolidation of the regime, made possible by June 30th, became visible. In the plebiscite of August, 1934, when Hitler was "elected" as Hindenburg's successor, even official returns showed the astonishingly high rate of 20 to 25 percent "No" votes in many districts. An analysis of the election returns shows, however, the almost complete disappearance of the opposition in all districts which, prior to 1933, were not strongholds of either the labor parties or the Catholic Centrists.

The real stabilization of the Nazi regime and, with it, the numerical decline and demoralization of the opposition did not come until Hitler's first great political successes within the country and abroad—the return of the Saar District to the Reich in January, 1935, the introduction of compulsory military service, open rearmament, the Naval Treaty with England, the remilitarization of the Rhineland, the failure of sanctions against Italy. Much as people might criticize Hitler as an adventurer, his economic policies, particularly the creation of work, began to show results. The frightful nightmare of the depression almost vanished. Schacht's complicated system of trade treaties also bore fruit.

Hitler had finally entrenched himself. His regime of adventurers was now recognized as an indisputable fact. The period of initial crises had passed. The gloomy reality of everyday life under National Socialism had begun.

The Nazis succeeded in overcoming many difficulties which, it had been assumed, would cause Hitler to fail and his regime to collapse. These problems had been solved in the National Socialist way.

Unemployment had been liquidated, though only to make room for the Nazis' own labor regime. Wages were cut down to the level of the old unemployment benefits, hours of work lengthened, the workers' freedom in changing jobs removed, "military discipline" introduced in the factories, men shipped off to work on the new highways and fortifications, compulsory deductions instituted for the Labor Front, for Winter Help and other Nazi organizations.

The peasants were made the "nobility of the nation." But the law governing inheritance of farms and the new market regulations for farm products practically turned the independent farmer into an overseer on his own farm.

The Nazis had promised to "save" the middle class. It was the class that had contributed most to bringing Hitler to power—only perhaps to be betrayed more completely than any other. Small shopkeepers and independent artisans saw their businesses expropriated under any convenient pretext. They cracked under the burden of taxes and were drowned in a flood of regulations.

The Nazis had played themselves up as "the liberators of Christian culture from materialistic and atheistic Bolshevism." But, in the first months of their rule, they tried to bring the Protestant Church under their complete domination. Soon they began the great campaigns against the Catholic Church and its organizations, alleging that the priests were "immoral" and that the Church officials were "smuggling foreign exchange." The Nazis' real motive was to break the influence of the Church on the youth.

They assured young people that National Socialism was a "revolution of the youth" against their "degenerate elders," that the Third Reich would be the "State of Young People." Instead, however, came the Reich Law Governing Youth, labor service, service on the land, military service, which subjected every German boy to a dozen years of uninterrupted drilling, and in place of initiative and freedom for young people gave them the parade-ground.

The Nazis promised that they would bring back "the honor of the profession of civil servants," that they would do away with the "corrupt party office holders." What happened was that, in questions of appointment and advancement in public office, the Nazi Party played the only role. Corruption and graft reached an extent hitherto unknown, an extent that had been believed impossible in Germany. Experiments with a "new German justice" brought only insecurity in all branches of the law, civil, criminal or administrative.

The Nazis promised a renaissance of Germany's spiritual and intellectual life. But the public burning of books was followed by the compulsory exile of the best minds and talents in German science, art and literature. Membership in the Reich Chamber of Culture was a substitute for genuine ability. Drilling with the Hitler Youth and in the army was more important than attending school or studying in the universities. A total inquisition, such as Loyola and Torquemada never dreamed of, removed the "Country of Poets and Thinkers" from the ranks of cultured nations.

And this everyday life in the Third Reich was shadowed by an ever-present fear. Fear of the Blockwart, fear of the Gestapo, fear of this regime from which no escape was possible and against which there was no opportunity to fight—and, finally, fear of the inevitable war, the end goal of Hitler's policies.

It was not, however, fear alone which prevented the people in Germany from even raising their voices. The Hitler regime, although it had broken its promises to almost every group in the society, knew how to chain millions of men to it. There were the party members, the Storm Troopers and members of the S.S., officials of the Labor Front and the Labor Service, of the Reich Farm Estate and the National Socialist Welfare, the Hitler Youth and countless other organizations which had sprung from the ground like mushrooms. In addition, Hitler had the greatly swollen government apparatus of officials and state employees of all sorts, the new army with tens of thousands of officers and hundreds of thousands of non-commissioned officers. There were uncounted persons whose daily bread was directly or indirectly dependent on the fact that they were National Socialists, or pretended to be. And there was something else. There were hundreds of thousands, perhaps millions, whose material situation had been worsened by the Nazis, who suffered just like everybody else from the regime, but who had become "somebody." They were permitted to wear a uniform. A man was no longer just Meier, the janitor; he had a title, Blockwart Meier; it was no longer Schulze, the postman, but "party official" Schulze. These people belonged "to the movement," the movement which would win a place in the sun for Germany.

233

They were conscious that they had a power over their neighbors, even if they had no more to eat than anyone else and trembled like the rest at the thought of the Gestapo. The relentless hammering of Nazi propaganda did not succeed in convincing the average German that he belonged to the "master race," but Hitler's triumphs in foreign policy created a feeling that "now the world won't dare to treat us the way they did when we were a Republic."

However, the feeling of fear remained dominant and it was cultivated and utilized by the regime. Almost everybody knew someone who had made the acquaintance of the inside of a concentration camp or at least had heard of people who had. Everybody was familiar enough with the dread red notices posted by the People's Court, reading, "On such-and-such a day, so-and-so was executed for high treason." Even more demoralizing were the vague rumors that were always being repeated, telling of large-scale purges and mass executions. Sometimes the persons purged were reputed to be army officers discovered planning a revolt; sometimes the story was of a strike in a munitions factory. The Nazis themselves put many of these rumors into circulation. You could almost never distinguish between truth and fiction; you never knew whether rumored attempts on the lives of Nazi leaders had really taken place. A bomb was said to have exploded in the Air Ministry; General von Schleicher's daughter was said to have shot at Hitler; a bomb had been thrown from a new building in the center of Berlin at Goebbels' car. Such rumors were repeated all over Germany and always with an account of the subsequent measures of punishment against the supposed authors of the crimes. It was curious, though, how many leading Nazis were killed in automobile accidents, and then buried with the pomp and ceremony of the state. Sometimes it was a Gauleiter, sometimes a high officer of the Storm Troops. In one accident near Potsdam, no less than four attorneys from the Berlin People's Court lost their lives. In the years before the war, automobile accidents played a role similar to that played by airplane crashes in Germany in the last couple of years.

Were they really accidents? What was pure rumor and what was fact? If genuine acts of violence were behind these stories—how often could they be charged up to the Gestapo as the inevitable by-products of the never-ceasing rivalry between different groups in the regime?

Assassination, murder as a political weapon, had scarcely played any part in Germany before. There was no tradition to correspond with that of the Russian terrorists. Only one oppositional group in Germany had practised political murder: the "National Revolutionaries" and "Vehme murderers" of the first years after the World War. The National Socialist Party had grown up out of these groups. Murderers and terrorists had been the masters of Germany since 1933. They had made murder and terror instruments of their rule, first in Germany, later in the countries which they conquered.

The underground movement was profoundly convinced that individual terrorism could be used as an effective weapon against the totalitarian regime only within the framework of a rising revolutionary movement. A study of other revolutionary movements, especially the Russian, had shown that in the years when a movement is beaten and depressed, individual acts of terror are only an expression of desperation, that they more often lead to disruption in the ranks of the revolutionaries themselves than to the weakening of the regime.

Sabotage, too, can only be effective when practised on a mass scale; gains achieved by isolated individual acts of sabotage are in no relation to the sacrifices which they demand from the ranks of underground workers. It is a mistake to think that, in a period of depression for the opposition, the news of a successful act of sabotage is encouraging or inspiring. It is not, because it is always accompanied by the news that ten, twenty, a hundred people have been executed. It is only when the dissatisfaction of the masses of the people has been transformed into determination to resist, when not just a handful of members of underground organizations, but great numbers in the opposition are ready to risk their lives in the fight for freedom, that assassination and sabotage can become a weapon for the disorganization and the disruption of the Fascist regime. Even in the countries occupied by Hitler, the waves of terrorism and sabotage started up only after the Nazi armies in Russia had met their first serious setbacks. Then the masses of oppressed Europe became convinced that—if not today, then surely tomorrow—Hitler would be beaten and the slaves of today would become the masters of tomorrow. And it was just about the same time that the first reliable reports came from Germany of fires and explosions in the armament factories.

In 1936 and 1937, a sign "Down with Hitler," chalked on the walls of a factory, sufficed to bring trucks full of S.S. men rushing to the spot, and to set Gestapo agents to making handwriting tests of every worker. Irrespective of whether the "guilty" were discovered or not, a dozen of the workers known to be unfriendly to the regime were always arrested and taken to the concentration camp. People who made uncomplimentary remarks about a higher-up in the Nazi regime were arrested in restaurants. Women were arrested in the markets for grumbling about the lack of food or the high prices. In the face of this, scarcely a hand moved, scarcely a voice was raised in protest. What kind of action could be expected from the underground organizations in those years?

During that period, the only spark of encouragement that the German underground got was in events in western Europe: the Popular Front in France, the Spanish Republic's heroic struggle for its freedom. It seemed that the procession of victories of international Fascism would be halted. Also it seemed that, in spite of the barbarous Moscow trials, the Communists too had realized that all forces had to join in fighting the great common enemy. A Socialist Premier in France! Mussolini's troops beaten by anti-Fascist volunteers at Guadalajara! The underground workers eagerly studied the columns of the *Frankfurter Zeitung*, the only paper in Germany that reported events, at least in France, in some detail, even with some objectivity. Little groups of old-time political friends, which had declined to nothing more than *Skat* clubs, became the scenes of heated discussions about sit-down strikes in Paris, and of arguments about the best way to turn a revolutionary militia into an efficient army. The enthusiasm was not limited to discussion. From their miserable wages, German anti-Nazis made contributions to the anti-Fascists of Spain. In the pockets of a bicyclist, run down by a truck in the streets of Frankfurt-am-Main, the Gestapo found a collection list of forty names and more than 100 marks. Risking all kinds of dangers, some young German anti-Nazis managed to get to Switzerland or to France to volunteer for the International Brigade. The many who fell for freedom at Madrid and at Barcelona were spared the fate of waiting in a French internment camp to be delivered over to the Gestapo or to be sent to northern Africa to work as slaves for Laval and his masters.

The events in France and Spain posed the question whether a "popular front," uniting all anti-Fascist forces, would be feasible in Germany. At the time the underground movement in Germany adopted the term "Popular Front," it had not yet been discredited as it was subsequently by the failure of the Blum government in

France and by the Communists' ambiguous policy. To the underground workers a popular front was a convenient designation for their attempt to unite the split ranks of the anti-Nazi opposition.

Early in 1937 a document, entitled *The Basis for a German Popular Front Program,* was published in Prague. This statement was the result of a series of discussions inside Germany which had led to the uniting of a number of groups, all originating from the Social Democratic movement. The new united group was in contact with Communists and other oppositional factions. Representatives were chosen to go abroad to try to bring about unity in the split ranks of the German emigration. The statement which they brought with them read:

"A [German] popular front cannot be created by the decision of a few remnants of organizations abroad. It must live and grow within the country.

"The old social and political structure of Germany has been destroyed. What remains of the former political parties, reduced to tiny circles who maintain personal friendship, stand by each other, carry on discussions, and distribute illegal information, has no relation to the old organizations. No Social Democratic Party member, who is still active, thinks in terms of re-establishing the party of parliamentary and social reform. The Communists who are still active have had enough of fratricidal fighting and violence. . . . The popular front is the most suitable means of bringing these strivings for unity into realization. . . . How far middle-class groups would come into a German popular front is a question of practical politics.'

The authors of this program believed that a large part of the working class, sections of the peasants, certain groups among the middle class and the religious organizations and even groups within the army and among industrialists were emotionally opposed to the Nazis. However, emotional hostility is not the same thing as readiness to make active underground resistance.

"The strongest aspiration that all parts of the opposition have in common," the program stated, "is their desire for a lawful state which would create and guarantee freedom. . . . The second aspiration for which all are united is their desire to be saved from war. . . . The third is to be saved from economic and social chaos."

That provision must be made for just punishment for all the guilty was essential, "because among the broadest circles of the German people there is a lust for revenge."

The authors of the program advocated that the need for revenge be satisfied by orderly legal processes. In addition to members of the Nazi Party, those groups in the society which had cast their lot with the Nazis, for better or for worse, would also have to be dealt with and rendered harmless once and for all.

"Once the great land-owners are expropriated . . . and the banks and heavy industry, which paved Hitler's way to power, are socialized, the roots of dictatorship will have been torn out."

The program closed with the words:

"Whoever promises to the German people justice, freedom and work—and promises it in a way that it is convincing—will have the entire nation behind him."

To what sections of German society should the organized underground movement look for allies in their fight and partners in a German popular front?

From the early days, the churches were considered enemies of National Socialism. During the first two years, the Nazis concentrated on trying to coördinate the Protestant churches with the regime and to destroy their independent existence. Later they directed their anti-religious persecutions primarily against the Catholic Church, and the whole world learned of Catholic resistance to Hitler.

The Church was forced into opposition because National Socialist ideology was inherently anti-Christian. Even more important in the eyes of German Catholics was the regime's uncompromising stand in all matters, particularly in the vital question of the education of youth.

In spite of these obvious conflicts, there has never been a concerted religious opposition and certainly no underground activity of consequence. Until recently, there were only courageous individuals who dared to raise their voices in protest.

The reasons are not hard to find. The Protestant Church in Germany was split into regional and denominational groups. Since the time of the Reformation, all

German Protestants had observed the principle *"cuius regio-eius religio"*—the faith of the ruler determines that of the subjects. Moreover, throughout their history the Protestant churches, particularly the Lutheran branch, had identified themselves closely with the ruling state power. During the time of the Republic, most pastors and elders of the church had belonged to the Nationalist-Monarchist opposition. The progressive clergy that is so influential in England and the United States had, except in rare cases, no counterpart in Germany.

These conditions contributed to the Nazis' success in convincing religious-minded people that the Party was to be the saviour of Christian culture from the threat of atheist Bolshevism.

It is well known how extensively the Nazis were able to influence the Catholic clergy, both in Germany and abroad, with this propaganda, particularly during the Spanish Civil War. The Nazis had also been clever enough to direct their attacks mainly against "political Catholicism," against the Catholic Center Party and its peripheral organizations, and not against the Church as such.

The masses of German people felt that the Catholic Center Party shared with other democratic parties the responsibility for the failure of the Republic. Its representatives had been in every government since 1918, and Reich Chancellor Bruening was blamed for all the disagreeable measures passed during the economic crisis. This discrediting of the democratic political organs of the Church naturally weakened the Catholic opposition during the first years.

Potential church opposition was also thwarted by the Concordat which Hitler concluded with the Catholic Church in 1933. Though he has violated many of the provisions of that treaty, he has kept one to this very day—the agreement to pay many millions of marks each year to the Catholic Church. This arrangement made the Catholic clergy practically state employees. In Germany the churches have always been supported primarily by church taxes from the members paid into the treasury of the state. Hitler not only continued but increased the financial dependence of the churches on the state.

Among the Protestants, the heroism of Martin Niemoeller and some of his colleagues of the *Bekenntnis* or Confessional Church, during the first years of the Third Reich, was an exception. Later, the opposition of the Confessional Synod was more organized. Some of it has been purely religious without political consciousness, but some of it has had fairly clear-eyed political convictions. Niemoeller happens to be politically a nationalist, and from the standpoint of thought is certainly not the most significant leader in the group. Less well-known members of the Confessional clergy were much more influenced by the progressive teachings of Karl Barth, the famous Swiss theologian who was expelled from the University of Bonn by the Nazis. The Confessional pastors made up only a small minority of the Protestant clergy, but their influence among middle and lower middle-class groups was out of all proportion to their number. This influence has grown with the increasing disillusionment of the *Kleinburgertum* (lower middle class) with Nazism. The recent courageous statement of Bishop Wurm of Wuerttemberg is a symptom that opposition among Protestants has increased.

Only seldom have the "political" Catholic organizations, the trade unions and youth groups, dared to carry on real underground activities.

The attitude of the clergy has never been uniform. Some priests protested openly against the Nazis from the beginning. Foremost among them is the Archbishop of Munich, Cardinal Faulhaber. His four "Advent Sermons" in 1933, in which he spoke out for freedom of scholarship and against the distortion of history, have become famous. In the last year, the Bishop of Muenster, Count von Galen, and the Bishop of Berlin, Von Preysing, have boldly criticized the Nazis' treatment of religion. The latest Conference of Catholic Bishops, at Fulda, sharply attacked measures of the Nazi regime and in an official statement, for the first time, asked for freedom and justice for the individual. But this was in the summer of 1942, long after the Nazis had committed unspeakable atrocities against the Catholic Church in Poland and other occupied countries, and under pressure from a growing anti-Nazi opinion in all Germany.

This widespread spirit of opposition has sent the people into the churches as the only legal organizations in all of Germany which are not National Socialist. The churches are crowded, not only in rural areas, but also in industrial cities, in former strongholds of the labor movement which, in Germany, is traditionally anti-clerical. Undoubtedly, suffering and the gravity of the times have led to a reawakening of religious feeling, but the churches are not filled from purely religious motives. Attendance at church has become a political demonstration, at least, of a desire to hear one speech a week that is not about the Fuehrer and National Socialism. Pressure from the laity has reinforced the anti-Nazism of the clergy. Bishop von Galen's stern letter to Hitler, in which he objects to interference in the private lives of the people by the Gestapo and the S.S., has been circulated as a "chain-letter" among both Catholics and Protestants. It has probably been more widely read than any previous underground document.

The underground movement has always considered the church as a potential ally, but has recognized the decisive difference between its own aims and those of the religious groups. The churches have protested against Nazi intervention in matters of conscience. Their main concern is to retain freedom of worship, not to overthrow Hitler. Only under the terrible pressure of war has this attitude been changed to a general enmity toward National Socialism.

Therefore, it is not by chance that, aside from the International Bible Students or Jehovah's Witness group, there has been only one religious body in Germany which has been unwavering and militant in its anti-Nazism and has tried to carry on underground activity. This is the small group of the "Religious Socialists," whose most important leader is Dr. Paul Tillich, now in the United States. The Religious Socialists consider Nazism their enemy not only because it is irreconcilable with their religious beliefs, but also because it is contrary to their concepts of social justice. This small group, whose influence was greatest in university circles, has much in common with progressive church groups in America and England.

The underground labor organizations have maintained close association with the Religious Socialists because of the similarity of their aims, whereas contacts with the other parts of the religious opposition have been loose and incidental. However, the deepening of the church opposition during the last year or two has brought the possibility of closer contact.

The story of coöperation between the underground organizations and oppositional intellectual groups has been rather similar. Contacts have been close with certain progressive circles that were working for the overthrow of the Hitler regime, less close with those who were concerned only about Nazi restrictions in intellectual and academic spheres.

The process of *Gleichschaltung*, or coördination, of intellectual life has caused more trouble for the Nazis than is generally known. Time after time they have had to purge universities, scholarly societies, theaters, editorial offices and bookstores in their efforts to keep art and scholarship fully in accord with Nazi barrackroom ideology. There have been many cases like that of the professor at Berlin University, a Nobel Prize winner with a worldwide reputation, who, in addressing a public assembly of scholars, repeated Galileo's last words—"the world does move anyway"—and then turned to a consideration of Einstein's most recent work. This man was an "Aryan" who, like hundreds and thousands of others, could not reconcile it with their conscience and their convictions that Goebbels should prescribe for them what "truth" was. For most anti-Nazi scholars there was no possibility of protest except to emigrate. The political weakness of the German middle class, the capitulation of its intellectual leaders in the decades after the 1848 revolution, still had their effect after 1933.

Those intellectuals, who rejected the barbarism of the National Socialists but could not leave the country, found their only salvation in a kind of "internal emigration." They tried to retire as much as possible from public life and privately to preserve the cultural heritage of the past. Nazi society brings terrific pressure to bear on every individual to give constant expression to his National Socialist beliefs, and it isolates whoever does not conform totally to official attitudes. It requires tremendous inner strength for anyone, and particularly a man in public position, to maintain his inner freedom and to keep from being broken by the conflict between his private convictions and his outward conformity. As

long as they could, the anti-Nazi intellectuals got "undesirable" books from the libraries and bookstores. They
eagerly read and secretly passed around the famous declaration made by Thomas Mann when Bonn University
recalled his honorary doctorate. They formed small private circles in which they could discuss philosophical,
religious and scientific problems. These half-clandestine
groups are the catacombs to which the German spirit
has fled.

From time to time the intellectual darkness of the
Third Reich has been pierced by rays of light that have
emanated from these catacombs, signs that under the
pompous buildings of Nazi anti-culture some remnants
of the past are still at work.

Noted scholars have published historical studies concerning Cromwell, Machiavelli, the ancient Romans or,
for example, the "Chilean Revolution of the Nineteenth
Century." Blending appropriately with the historical
analysis of the given subject we may read a carefully
formulated, but unmistakable, criticism of National Socialism. German scientists have cautiously, but definitely,
rejected the Nazi conceptions of "Aryan physics." Military scientists in discussing the theories of Clausewitz
have attacked the Nazi doctrines of total war. Goebbels
has, on many occasions, had to attack the unprecedented
number of translations from foreign languages which
have flooded the book market. Apparently people were
not satified to limit their reading to the mystical *Blut
und Boden* literature favored by Hitler's litterateurs.

Even during the war, such an amazing book as Ernst Juenger's *Marble Cliffs* could become a best-seller. Juenger is a famous German writer and intellectual leader of the super-nationalist group of younger veterans of the World War. When his book was published he was an officer in the new German army. This controversial and magnificently written book is a bitter criticism of the Third Reich only lightly disguised. But more important than that such a book could be published is the fact that the author, who has for two decades been an outstanding spokesman for nationalism and militarism, now rejects the idealization of force and turns to cultural and spiritual values.

Only later shall we see how far the intellectual forces in the Third Reich have developed and to what extent they will be able to become the representatives of the "other Germany."

There is one group which has been completely excluded from German society, namely, the Jews. The nature and extent of the persecution of Jews have varied greatly. But, irrespective of whether the Nazis happened to be giving strong or slight expression to their anti-Semitism at the moment, the Jew in the Third Reich has always been a Pariah. Almost a million people, including those of mixed ancestry, were declared the deadly enemy of the Reich.

Under the circumstances, of course, the Jews were all oppositional. But their active participation in the underground movement, or even their support of the underground movement through financial contribution, has been very limited. There has been a kind of nationalist renaissance among younger German Jews, linked with Zionism and emigration to Palestine. In any case, emigration seemed the only possibility for most of the well-to-do Jews in Germany. Those who could not leave the country lived in constant fear as the persecutions got worse and worse. There was little that they could do except try to create some kind of life for themselves.

Nevertheless, there were a good many Jews in the underground movement, mostly people who had formerly been in the labor movement and wanted to continue the fight against Hitler, not as Jews, but as Socialists. They shared all of the dangers of underground work with their "Aryan" colleagues, but at greater personal risk because they were Jews. They awaited a worse fate if they were arrested, as concentration camp guards would treat them more brutally and judges would give them more severe sentences. The fact that they were Jews laid them more open to suspicion and exposed them the more readily to the danger of denunciation. After the Nuernberg Laws were put into effect in September, 1935, the danger for all Jews became so great that most underground groups felt it advisable to exclude their Jewish members from active participation in underground activities.

The underground movement's weakest contacts were with the peasants. The labor movement had never been strong in the farming sections of Germany. The large farmers' organizations, especially in the north, were mostly under reactionary leadership. Conditions were more favorable in the southwest, where the traditions of a democratic peasant movement had survived since 1848.

But only rarely could the traditional rift between urban working class and farmers be overcome in underground conditions. In the period before the war, there was little expression of opposition by the peasants except in individual attempts to sabotage the countless Nazi regulations that irritated them. In the last two years this hidden kind of sabotage has developed on a mass scale. The most recent reports from southern Germany indicate that certain underground groups in the cities have established regular coöperation with opposition farmers.

It has been a very long time since German peasants have exerted an independent political influence. Their opposition in the future can contribute greatly to the overthrow of the Nazi regime. Also, the attitude of the peasants will influence both the Catholic and the Protestant Churches, and a growth in peasant opposition, like a growth in any opposition, indirectly strengthens the real underground movement.

What is true of the peasants is also true of Germany's important *Kleinburgertum* in so far as any generalization is possible. This class is the one that has been most bitterly disappointed by the Nazi regime, but it is the class that Goebbels for years has decried as the grumblers and the bleaters. Members of the lower middle class have objected strongly to Goering's castles and uniforms, to Goebbels' mistresses and to the corruption of local Nazi leaders. They believe every rumor and tall story they hear and eagerly pass it on, only to land in prisons and concentration camps for their indiscretion. Often during past years the grumbling lower middle class has been lauded by the uninformed as the most active opposition, because the working class remained silent. But all the fussing and complaining of this economically impotent and moribund class could never seriously threaten the Nazi regime. The less so, since every success that Hitler celebrated has brought them "back to their senses again," and every appeal to their patriotism has found a ready ear. However, the war, with its horrors and suffering, has finally deepened the feeling of opposition within the lower middle class.

At the end of 1941 a curious thing happened in Germany and its significance has not been recognized. Hitler reduced the Storm Troops to a feeble skeleton organization. The newspaper, the *S.A. Mann*, was banned; S.A. parades and meetings of rank and file members were forbidden. This group is made up exclusively of members of the lower middle class and peasants, all of whom were formerly 100 percent Nazis. Hitler would not have done this to the Storm Troops unless discontent had penetrated deeply in their ranks.

There has been a division into Nazis and non-Nazis in every class in German society, with the balance of strength in either enthusiasm for, or hostility to, the regime depending on the social structure of the class and fluctuating with the situation. As, in the course of the years, the machinery of the Nazi rule constantly increased in strength, its mass basis became constantly weaker—a paradox characteristic of totalitarian dictatorships.

The charge that has to be made against the German people is not that they never rose up against the Hitler dictatorship in the years following 1933; that would have been expecting the impossible. A revolution cannot be "made" at whatever moment you want it. It depends on the existence of a number of objective conditions. The tragedy for Germany and the world is that the German people and especially the leaders of the Weimar Republic were not politically mature enough to recognize in time what National Socialism really meant and where Hitler was leading Germany. Nor is it an excuse for the Germans that for a long time leading people in the democratic countries did not understand the real nature of National Socialism either and believed that they could do business with Hitler.

The German people have already paid a frightful price for their political immaturity and the account is not yet paid up. Even if there is a progressive post-war settlement, the German people and particularly the youth will, for a long time to come, have to expiate the failures and the guilt of 1933.

There is a special question that has always disturbed

the underground organizations. The same question has been asked by people all over the world as they felt its answer would be decisive in determining the chances of National Socialism for survival. What about the youth? Had Hitler succeeded, as he boasted, in completely capturing the younger generation? Would the boys and girls who had grown up under National Socialism, who had been taught in its schools and trained in its organizations, give their unqualified allegiance to the regime to the bitter end? And, after the collapse of the regime, would they be incapable of taking their place in a new and free world? Was this to be a lost generation?

This problem has a very specific importance for the underground movement: Who is to carry on the work in the future? When Hitler came to power, the underground organizations could say, with justification, that they represented the younger generation of the labor movement. For a long time they had a reservoir from which they could draw new strength—the youth organizations of the democratic era. However, a movement which looked upon itself as the vanguard of the future could not continue, during the indefinite period of Nazi rule, to depend on forces all of whose political convictions had come from the past.

Could the underground movement have any influence on the young people who went into the Jungvolk as children, then on to the Hitler Youth, the Labor Service and finally the army? Could it bridge the gap to a generation whose youth had been spent in uniforms, marching on the parade-grounds and singing military songs?

One of our friends, who served several years in a Hitler prison, told us a story. "One of the most exciting experiences of all my years in prison came during the summer of 1939. A new prisoner, a boy of seventeen, was brought into my division, sentenced to three years for high treason. He was only one of a group of eighty-eight boys and girls from fifteen to twenty-three years of age, all from the same city, who had been tried in a mass trial.

"Ernst was an average boy from a working-class family. He didn't know whether his father had ever been a trade unionist or member of a political party. He had an older brother who used to belong to a labor youth organization; Ernst didn't know what kind of group it was. The brother had had nothing to do with the affair that led to Ernst's arrest. The central figure in the trial at which he was sentenced was a boy of twenty-one who got eight years in prison. This boy, according to Ernst, had once been in an organization 'of some kind.' During the trial, the judge had spoken repeatedly of the *Buendische Jugend*, the famous pre-Hitler youth movement. Ernst had not understood what he was talking about.

" 'What were your activities?' I asked him, and got the amazing answer: 'We fought against the Hitler Youth.' 'What are you fellows anyway?' 'We are the Pack.'

"This is the story:

"Ernst, along with thirteen or fourteen other boys, had joined a football club that was a kind of carry-over from an old workers' sports society. That was several years ago, and when all sport clubs were incorporated in the Hitler Youth, Ernst and most of the other boys resigned. They didn't want to be in the Hitler Youth.

" 'Why not?'

" 'Who the hell wants to spend all his time in marching, drilling, doing service and the rest of the damn foolishness? That's no life.'

"The boys who left the football club stuck together. They used to meet in the evenings, go on hikes on Sundays and camping trips in the summer. They wanted, under no circumstances, to be confused with the Hitler Youth so they got their own uniform, short black trousers and what Ernst called a 'pirate's necktie,' meaning a bright-colored neckerchief. On their camping trips they had met other groups of boys who also weren't in the Hitler Youth or, at least, tried to get out of participating in their activities and go off by themselves. There were groups from the Rhineland, from Saxony, from northern Germany and Bavaria. Many of the others adopted the short black pants and the pirate's tie. Somewhere or other they picked up the name, the Pack. Friendships were formed between the different groups; they made arrangements to meet again. 'Next vacation we'll be in the Fichtelberg or the Harz.' Ernst told me proudly that they had held a regular Congress of the

Pack at the same time that a big Nazi Congress was going on.

"What did these boys think and what did they do?

"Ernst assured me that there were Pack members who read books, but when I asked him what kind, he didn't know for sure—'about Russia and things like that.' It was obvious that Ernst had never even had a political book in his hand, but that was not the important thing.

"What kept the Pack together was their hatred of the Nazi regime because it took away their chances to have a good time while they were young. They hated the compulsory aspect; they hated the drilling, the hypocritical speeches; they hated the war which they knew was coming. They wanted to be free. They wanted to live their own lives.

"The practical result of their feelings was that they carried on unceasing warfare against the Hitler Youth. At night they used to stone Hitler Youth clubs; one time there was a fight in which knives were used and a sixteen-year-old Hitler Youth functionary was stabbed to death. It is an amazing commentary on moral conditions within the Hitler Youth that the police hushed up this killing. They assumed that the boy was killed in a fight over a girl and didn't want to order too thorough an investigation because of the shocking things they were afraid would be uncovered.

"Ernst told me that, the year before, he had been arrested along with some of his friends, at the request of a Hitler Youth leader. They had been released after two weeks. However, in the spring of 1939 the S.S. asked to have a special Gestapo division appointed to combat the Pack. In the trial a Gestapo commissar testified that there were at least two thousand boys and girls organized in this opposition movement throughout the Reich."

The story of Ernst came from the period just before the war. This story can be supplemented by reports of conversations with other young Germans who used to go abroad on camping trips in the summers before the war. Most of them came from middle-class families and were elementary-school and university students. They were all members of the Hitler Youth, but they tried as hard as they could to get out of the service required of members. They went through all kinds of complicated business to get permission to make trips outside Germany. Most of these boys, like Ernst, were completely "unpolitical." At least, old political terms, such as democracy, Socialism, parliamentarianism, had no clear meaning for them. But in talking to them one found that the chief reason for misunderstanding was that they talked another language and associated the words you used with entirely different meanings. For example, one boy described his friend, Hans. Hans had been an enthusiastic Hitler Youth until after he finished his labor service duty; then he was "fed up" and began to bring a group of oppositional Hitler Youth members together. "Some people think Hans is a Communist; he isn't, but he is a dependable reactionary." He meant that Hans was a dependable anti-Nazi. In the Hitler Youth they

258

always described the old youth movement and all opponents of Hitler as reactionaries.

Why were these boys opposed to Nazism? They, too, hated the Nazis because they didn't give them a chance to enjoy their youth and freedom. Also they rebelled instinctively against the brutality and the lack of spiritual and cultural values in the Nazi system. Perhaps the most important reason for their bitterness was that they could see through the hypocritical Hitler Youth leaders. They knew that most of the "rah rah" boys were only interested in getting ahead and put on their enthusiasm for the movement in order to get nice soft jobs. They had observed that it was the cynical careerist who got promoted in the Hitler Youth. "If you're really a sincere Nazi and believe all the rot they tell you, you haven't a chance to get ahead," one of the boys explained.

Hitler won great numbers of young people to his cause before he came to power. What had the post-war period and the economic depression to offer them? Neither prospects of security nor, and this was very important, ideas that caught their imaginations. The way the Weimar Republic talked about democracy and Socialism and the way it went about achieving its aims were hardly calculated to inspire youth. The sterility of youth. The Nazi movement, never wearying of pro-the German Communist movement was shown, among other ways, in its failure to attract large sectors of the claiming itself the "movement of youth against the rotting society of the old," had many attributes which must make an impression on young people. It talked about a national reawakening, about a revolution; it romantically glorified the past and professed a religious devotion to the wonders of modern technology.

During the great crisis that accompanied their seizure of power, the Nazis were very clever in utilizing the conflict between the generations for their own purposes. It did not matter that the system of discipline and service into which they forced the young people in the following years was as unyouthful as could be imagined. The law of January 12, 1936, providing that every young person in Germany enter Hitler Youth service, begins with the following statement:

"The future of the German people depends on its youth. The entire German youth must therefore be prepared for its future duties."

In effect, this law binds the entire younger generation of a nation in the service of an all-powerful dictatorship. For the Hitler Youth, it is: "Service, Service and always Service." In place of the revolutionary romance they used to talk about, the Nazis have substituted drilling. Instead of a national reawakening this youth has lived through the grim reality of the Third Reich and three years of a war whose end is still not in sight.

For a boy or girl who is seventeen or eighteen today, National Socialism is not new; it is what their fathers believed in. They went into the Jungvolk and the Hitler Youth, not as fighting organizations, but as organizations you had to belong to, just like school, a duty prescribed by the government. Children go willingly to a good school; they would also go gladly to a good youth organization. But the bureaucratized youth organizations have none of the qualities that are associated with sound training of the young.

Baldur von Schirach, Reich Leader of Youth, a man of nearly forty, said in 1938:

"The generation conflict has been overcome. . . . The only justification for the youth movement lies in its ability to render a positive service to the state and thus to all generations. There is no place for a youth movement as an organization of immature forces of opposition."

But, of course, these "immature forces of opposition" exist in the Third Reich despite Von Schirach, the eternal opposition of the growing to the world of the grown-up. The world of the grown-up is represented for the youngest groups in Germany today by National Socialism. Today, after almost ten years, the "generation conflict" is beginning to work out against the Nazis.

A transformation is taking place among young Nazis. Evidence of this and something of the desperation that has implemented it can be seen in the letter of a young German soldier on the Russian Front, which somehow found its way into the Nazi press.

"I am on guard duty," he wrote. "I can hear my drunken comrades inside making a great row. But what of it? If I weren't on duty I'd be drunk too. Why

261

shouldn't I? You don't get schnapps very often out here.

"I am thinking about home. I remember, as clearly as if it were yesterday, one night when I was in the hills with the Hitler Youth. We were happy and full of hope as we sat around our camp-fire and sang songs, songs about freedom and honor, about faith and victory. We all looked forward to a better future.

"The boys whose laughter used to ring out in the hills in those days have grown up since. Today we know what duty demands of us. We know what it is to die. We haven't time to light camp-fires in the hills.

"What we want to know is whether the fires that meant so much to us are still burning at home. Do they still burn in men's hearts, or were they only lit for a short moment and now are gone and with them courage and hope?"

A "lost generation"?

Stephen Laird, who was Berlin correspondent for *Time* and knew Germany well, gives the answer in his book, *Conversation in London:*

"They're a lost generation. . . . But they would like to be found. They'd like to have something and they can't find it. They are not looking to the future—because in the future they see nothing."

There is no doubt that tens of thousands of young Germans have gone willingly to their deaths, "Heil Hitler" on their lips. Certainly there are still many of them. But it is just as certain that desperation and hopelessness are leading the young generation in the Third Reich to cynicism and demoralization.

How will a generation which has been taught to idolize force and success, achieved at whatever cost, react when their gods are overthrown by a greater power, when they see, not mastery of the world, but the frightful catastrophe of defeat? No one can predict with certainty now. But a great deal, perhaps everything, will depend on what new ideals, what chances for the future those who overthrow Hitler can offer to these young people.

8

The German Underground Prepares for War

While he was preparing for war, one of Hitler's greatest accomplishments was to fool the world about his real aims. He would not have dared to go to war had he not already won some of the decisively important positions without battle. In modern history we can find no parallel for the passive acceptance of Hitler's strong-arm measures: the occupation of Austria was received as a simple *Anschluss* or annexation; Czechoslovakia was handed over to the Nazis for the sake of the "oppressed" Sudeten Germans. There is no comparison for the blindness of the other players in the game of international politics except the blindness of the German political parties before 1933. The way Hitler played his inner political enemies one against the other and his external enemies one against the other, the way he outmaneuvered them, weakened them and finally dealt the finishing blow against each in succession, is one of the most amazing political accomplishments of all times. The political and psychological "impossibilities" of the year

1938 will present puzzles enough to the historians of future generations. The generation now living is paying a high price in blood, sweat and tears for the illusions, the wishful thinking and the mistakes of the rulers of Europe during that decisive year that paved the way for National Socialism's launching of the Second World War.

One of the most important tasks of the underground movement in Germany and its representatives abroad, in preparation for the war, was to inform the world about Hitler's true aims, to publicize reports about the little-known events in the Third Reich and to win sympathy and understanding for the German opposition. For a variety of reasons this activity met with little success. This is neither the time nor the place to go deeply into those reasons. But the principal one was that the world wanted to hear nothing about war. Goebbels put this general attitude to good use in his own propaganda even after the war had started. He maintained that the "real warmongers" were to be found in the ranks of German emigrants, and this argument won credence, especially in France.

The more imminent war became in Europe, the more important it was to win friends and understanding for the aims and the work of the German opposition, in the United States as well as on the other side of the Atlantic. One of the organizations that attempted to do this was the American Friends of German Freedom. A report this organization published in February, 1938, analyzed the "purge" in the German army which was to pave the way for the expansion of National Socialism as follows:

"Hitler's second conquest of power on February 4th means the end of an illusion. It is the end of the illusion that the army, the reasonable capitalists and the diplomats, in short the leaders of bourgeois society in Germany, would have the strength or the will to overthrow Hitler. The 4th of February is a kind of reversed 30th of June, 1934. In 1934 Hitler was forced to murder his own *party* generals in order to make his position in Germany secure. Now, in 1938, the Nazis have become strong enough to remove the *army* generals. Never before since there has been a Prussian army has there been a German government with enough power to deal arbitrarily with it as the Nazis have just done. The dethroned generals and colonels, the staff and subaltern officers, the recalled diplomats and economic leaders, who are the victims of this purge, were only the spokesmen of a growing opposition of the masses of people against autarchy and the brutal state control of economy with its preparations for war. Themselves personally bound up with the top of the regime and entangled in its policies, they were and are unfitted to break through the Nazi lines. A revolutionary leadership was needed. Today it is clearer than before the 4th of February that the coming revolution can only be a people's revolution, and it is the preparation for this alone that deserves the attention and the support of the progressive forces of the world."

266

This report, which had been prepared by the Auslandsburo of the New Beginning Group, went on to speak of the duration of Nazi rule and the purposes of the underground movement:

"We consider the 4th of February as a preparation for the plunge into an adventure that the Hitler regime can still dare to attempt. From the experiences of the Italian Fascist dictatorship, from the Bonaparte dictatorship of the past and even from the Russian party dictatorship—though that is a different matter—we have learned the lesson that such dictatorships have a tendency to last a long time. They have shown themselves stronger than the opposition tendencies that have collected under the Fascist rule. In the last hundred years, it has almost always been only a military defeat which gave the opposition forces a chance to break through. In spite of this long perspective, we have never felt that we should do nothing now. On the contrary, just this understanding of the prospects makes the patient, systematic, conscious preparation so much more significant."

The same report also told how the underground movement in Germany had developed following 1936, when the opposition reached the lowest point in its history.

"In the most important nuclear groups among the workers, the progressives forged on to new attempts at organization. Throughout the country there was a great increase in the little local groups numbering in the thousands. It is, of course, understood that we cannot report in detail about these developments. The majority of anti-

Fascists still refuse to make any but local contacts, and limit themselves to a narrow circle, avoiding particularly the dangerous contacts with the emigration, which cost so many casualties during the first years. Even under the best circumstances any single local organizational unit can know only a part of the entire organizational structure. Today we can say with certainty that there is hardly a town of any size in Germany in which there is not some sort of organization. In all of these places, varied groups of young activists, from the labor movement, have arrangements for discussions and for bringing new people into their groups. The solidarity of the workers in the factories, which has been on the decline in the last years, is growing again."

This was the kind of information the organized Socialist opposition in Germany could give and did give before the landslide of 1938 started. A few weeks later Hitler's armies marched into Austria. The "German brothers in the *Ostmark*" had scarcely been liberated when the preparations for the invasion of Czechoslovakia started. The German people were filled with fear of war, as they had never been before and have never been since. This fear strengthened discontent and opposition. The growing opposition gave the underground movement a powerful impetus. The underground workers began to concentrate all their forces on preparing their organizations for the war.

They became more and more convinced, not only that war was inevitable, but also that it would lead to Hitler's collapse. Many looked upon the war to come as a kind of release. Few anti-Nazis deceived themselves about the sacrifices that the war would demand, including sacrifices from the German opposition. But they knew that no fight for freedom can be won without sacrifice. The opposition was ready to make sacrifices for freedom in war, as it had in the years of preparation for war. One of the phrases heard repeatedly was: "Better a horrible end than horror without end."

At the same time, the more realistic observers were cognizant of the real obstacles that stood in the way of a determined resistance to Hitler's further advance. So, while the German Socialists were preparing for the war, they were also preparing themselves for more bloodless triumphs of Hitler. An article entitled *Blackmail or War*, which appeared in the *Social Democratic Information Letter*, Number 40, published in Paris on August 15, 1938, reflected the political thinking within the underground organizations.

"If the British fear of war is so strong," wrote the German Socialists, "that they advise Czechoslovakia to commit suicide, to make concessions dooming its existence as an independent power; if under this pressure the Czechoslovaks lose their present determination to resist and collapse; if in this way the Nazis can break down the strong Czech barrier in such a short time and without war, then we can expect that they will be able to control developments in all of southeastern Europe.

"That this danger exists is the result primarily of the

ambiguous policies of British upper classes. The French press often boasts that England has taken a firmer stand toward war than in 1914. But England's attitude towards Hitler's crucial diplomatic acts is more ambiguous. In trying to gain time, in pursuing the chimera of appeasement with the dictators, in trying to prevent the influence of the Soviet Union from becoming too strong, the British upper classes make concession after concession, which does not weaken Fascism, but strengthens it and at the same time strengthens the Fascists' determination to go to war. . . . Hitler's blackmail is the avenue leading to war."

In spite of their doubts about the preparedness of Chamberlain's government to resist, the underground organizations could not postpone their own concrete preparations for the war. The same number of the *Information Letter* had the following to say about organizational adaptation of the underground movement for war conditions: "It is absolutely essential that the organizations set themselves today in a position of readiness in which they can survive the war without being destroyed."

This was not easy to do. Already the Fascists were seeking out all the former functionaries in the labor movement and removing them from war industries as a preventive measure. Mobilization would destroy many contacts. But, just as the Fascists were preparing support behind their first line of offense, the underground could also prepare reserve functionaries and reserve contacts.

The fact that their organizations were decentralized, for reasons of safety, made these preparations the more necessary. Their decentralization meant that instead of a network of contacts within the country, there were many independent lines of communication directly to centers abroad. The tenseness of the situation even at that time made it hard to maintain contacts abroad, and the war would make their maintenance impossible in most cases, if not in all. Thus the creation of reserve contacts involved, first of all, increasing the number of contacts with foreign countries in the hope that one or the other of them might still be usable. It was still more important to create emergency-lines of communication within the country, wherever possible, which would come into operation when contacts abroad were cut off.

The *Information Letter* concluded: "The fight against Hitler's war policies and, in the event of war, the fight for the defeat of Fascism, is the common interest of all who really want to see Fascism defeated. This interest is not confined to a party, not confined to an underground organization, nor is it confined to the Socialist movement as such. Therefore, coöperation among all anti-Fascists must be the basis of our war policy."

The capitulation of England and France at Munich meant not only that an important bastion in the coming war was delivered over to Hitler; it meant not only that Russia was excluded from European diplomacy and driven into Hitler's arms; it meant not only that the confidence of the small states in England's readiness to defend democracy was destroyed. The Munich Pact was also a decisive blow against the German underground movement. Little attention has been given to this by-product of appeasement, and we understand why. The visible results of "peace in our time" were distressing enough in themselves. But, after three years of war during which we have been bombarded with impatient questions—What about the underground movement? Why doesn't it do anything?—it seems only fair to tell about the conditions under which the underground movement has had to develop.

By now it is accepted that factors of morale are just as important in a modern war as military factors. How can anyone expect a democratic opposition against totalitarian Nazi rule to develop if time after time it is slapped in the face by a new success of the Nazis? How could the German anti-Nazis convince a people who have a tendency to believe in power anyway that a rule built on power alone would be destroyed by a superior force, when through the very threat of violence Hitler had achieved all the things that the tame and peaceful Weimar Republic could never achieve and a great deal more? How could an underground opposition gain influence in the name of democracy, when the official representatives of British and French democracy had handed democratic Czechoslovakia, bound hand and foot, over to the power-drunk Nazis? With any understanding at all of the psychological conditions in which underground work is carried on, one must understand how demoralizing the Munich Conference was and that the question was often asked: Have all our sacrifices been in vain?

After Hitler had had such unprecedented success with blackmail, a good part of the opposition, which had developed in the summer, collapsed. Many anti-Nazis withdrew from the movement, some of them frightened, some of them disgusted. Many landed in the prisons, for when public opinion had loosened up during the summer months, many Germans had done things which seemed safe enough then, but in the new situation they were trapped. When people are obsessed with fear of war, as all Germany had been, they look upon opposition of any kind as a possible salvation from the thing they dread most. But when their fears of war turned out to be groundless, when Hitler proved to be right once again and all his critics and opponents wrong, there was a new wave of denunciations. During this period, some of the most careful and skilful underground leaders were arrested, men who had been able to keep out of the clutches of the Gestapo for more than five years. Because, before Munich, opposition had grown, especially among industrial workers, the underground organizations had to increase their activities, with the result that underground leaders were more exposed than ever. After the collapse in morale that followed Munich, they were easy prey for the Gestapo. The wave of arrests in September and October, 1938, was one of the most bitter blows that Germany's underground movement ever suffered.

Sacrifice is the daily bread of the underground movement and arrest is the occupational hazard of an underground functionary. The work must go on: broken contacts must be replaced, new functionaries must take the places of those arrested. There were three major tasks which had to be completed before the war came. First, arrangements had to be made so that contacts within the country and contacts abroad could continue to function in war time. Secondly, since the Socialist emigration was split up into many groups, every effort had to be made to unite it organizationally. And, thirdly, it was essential that a homogeneous opinion concerning the task of the German Socialist movement in the war should be arrived at within the Socialist opposition.

During the first phase of the war, more contacts between Germany and the outside world were maintained than had been hoped. But, after the collapse of France and the loss of almost all contact points in Europe, most of the outside connections with the movement within the country were destroyed, and inside information became almost entirely dependent on chance. We shall deal more fully with these problems in the next chapter.

The organizational unity was not achieved in the German Socialist emigration. The representatives of German parties and groups who emigrated abroad had clung to old conflicts, most of which had become meaningless in the Third Reich. Former Social Democrats, Communists, trade unionists and members of labor sports organizations were all faced with the same problems in their

274

daily battle to maintain even the most primitive organizational contacts. The techniques of conspiracy are the same for everyone. Moreover, those who had once supported "The Dictatorship of the Proletariat" without question had learned what that dictatorship really meant. And those who had once supported formal democracy without question had learned to understand the difference between democratic wishful thinking and democratic reality.

In the hunted atmosphere in which the emigrants lived, the old conflicts were kept alive synthetically. All attempts to resolve those old differences failed. All efforts towards a concentration of the forces of the democratic Socialists of Germany were futile.

The annexation of Austria by the Third Reich had given new impetus to the strivings for unification. The Social Democrats of Austria had not, like the Germans, been beaten without a struggle. Following the First World War they had been able to prevent a split in their labor movement. Up until Chancellor Dollfuss' coup d'état in 1934, the Communists never exerted any real influence in the Austrian Republic, and the Austrian Social Democrats had kept their unity after the heroic struggle in February, 1934. After they were forced underground the old leaders of the party, headed by Otto Bauer, understood that illegality under Fascist conditions demanded new methods and new people.

In his book *The Underground Party*, Otto Bauer wrote:

"The underground movement develops a new kind of Socialist; only a new leadership, the new type of Socialist, can win the confidence of the underground cadres. In every new phase in the development of the Socialist movement, natural selection among the party members produces a staff of leaders who are adapted to the existing conditions and to the tasks which those conditions impose on leadership. This staff of leaders is bound to fail as soon as it is faced with a new and different phase of development, involving changed conditions of struggle and different responsibilities. The legal mass party, fighting on democratic ground, needs orators who can move the masses; it needs writers who can influence them; it needs organizers who know how to unite the people; it needs industrious parliamentarians; it needs men who are able to administer cities, states and the nation. An underground party made up of small cadres has no use for men with these specific qualities. It has entirely different needs; it must have men with iron nerves, men who are tough enough to hold out under the continual threat of the police of the hostile government, men and women who combine the capacity for heroic self-sacrifice with the self-discipline which conspiratorial tactics require, organizers who can master the technique of creating small invisible cells, leaders who have that special sensitivity which enables them to recognize and to make use of the molecular mass processes which are hidden under the fog of illegality and invisible to the coarser eye. Thus, the underground party

276

needs a different type of leader from the legal party."

The old leaders of the Austrian Social Democrats had the courage of their convictions. In the first number of the *Arbeiterzeitung*, published on February 25, 1934, by the Auslandsburo of the Austrian Social Democrats, set up after the February defeat, they wrote:

"The Auslandsburo has no intention of being the new leadership of the party. As soon as the new organizations inside Austria have been sufficiently developed, the new leadership must be created from among the comrades who are active there. The Auslandsburo considers its task to be one of supporting the battle of the comrades in Austria by sending them newspapers, leaflets and pamphlets."

The Central Committee of the "Revolutionary Socialists," which was created within Austria, took over the leadership of the underground party.

The Austrian Social Democrats enjoyed widespread respect in the international labor movement. After the destruction of Austria, they took it for granted that the entire German Socialist movement should join together.

At the beginning of June, 1938, the leader of the underground movement of Austria presented a proposal for uniting all German Socialist forces. As the first step, he suggested that the most important Socialist groups of the German and Austrian emigration be called to a meeting to set up a joint committee. This committee should then organize a conference, which representatives of the underground organizations inside Germany could also attend. The proposal was accepted as the proper basis for further negotiations by all the invited groups except the *Sopade*. The latter, which represented the older generation of German Social Democrats, resented the proposal of the Austrian representative and declared that it was the only body that had authority to deal with questions of unity among German Social Democrats.

Although organizational unification or coöperation among all German Socialists was not achieved, efforts made during 1938 resulted in closer coöperation among the groups who wanted unity. Among other things they were able to arrive at a general agreement about the aims and purposes of German Socialists in the war.

A brochure, published in July, 1939, in Paris, under the title *The Coming World War*, set down the principle ideas on which these German Socialists agreed. In the introduction, its authors pointed out that the building of fronts for the Second World War had already reached the final stage, the stage of open military alliances. "A war that should break out with the present alignment of powers . . . would involve at least all of Europe, and in its course would necessarily lead to the involvement of the Soviet Union, the United States and Japan. We have reached a point where the danger of war is constantly with us and will become acute with each local conflict, a point where the armies of the important European countries are in a continuous state of mobilization. Of course, actual outbreak of war may still be delayed, but now we must expect that any conflict may bring it."

The attitude which a German Socialist has toward war is necessarily determined by the character of the war. His present attitude differs fundamentally from that of revolutionary Socialists in the First World War. Considering the historical role of the Fascist powers, the brochure says, "It follows that the primary interest of all Socialists lies in the military defeat of this bloc. The German Socialists will devote all their energies to aid in the military defeat of the Fascist bloc, the prerequisite for victory of the anti-Fascist revolution in Germany."

One month after the publication of *The Coming World War*, the bomb of the German-Russian Pact exploded, and then came the war.

The German-Russian Pact was a most terrible moral blow to the anti-Nazi opposition inside Germany. When the news of the pact was first announced in the German press and on the radio, no one believed it. One report said, "We all thought it was just another propaganda lie." At the same time, there was reason enough to be prepared for such a revolutionary change in Hitler's policy. Another report a few days after the conclusion of the pact said: "For months prior to the pact, the National Socialist Party had boasted, 'The Russians will come to an agreement with us,' but we had looked upon this as cheap propaganda."

The German anti-Fascist opposition generally did not want to believe that Russia would take such a step. Later reports indicated that Communists, who knew Moscow's kind of politics better, believed in the pact more readily than other anti-Nazis; they soon began to defend it.

279

But most of the underground workers, like all people who were opposed to the Nazi regime, were stricken dumb. They could understand the French and British Governments selling Czechoslovakia out. But that Bolshevik Russia should ally itself with its deadly enemy, National Socialism, seemed incredible.

It is not our task here to pass judgment on the political decisions made at Munich and Moscow; we are primarily concerned with the effect of these decisions on the German opposition. An underground report from Munich, dated August 25, 1939, said: "The Russian Pact was a great blow to the active members of our underground organizations. Depending on their former attitude to Russia, our friends felt more or less insecure in their whole political orientation. If Hitler succeeds in forcing Poland too to capitulate without war, it looks ominous for the morale of our underground friends. Most of us are, however, convinced that war now is inevitable."

Even at the opposite pole of German society, among the members of the Nazi Party, it was not altogether easy to adjust to the new situation. A report from Berlin told something of this. "They were just as dumfounded in Nazi circles, and the pact with the Bolsheviks found a rather cool reception. One Nazi wrote to a friend: 'The older party comrades have explained to me that it is not possible to comprehend the pact at once. One must simply believe the Fuehrer and have confidence in him, because he has always done the right thing before and he must know that it is right to make this pact. Since Litvinov is no longer in the government, Russia has changed so much, that in time, even there, the nationalist currents may predominate.' A young soldier who had fought in the Condor Legion against the Spanish Republic said to a friend, 'Now, I'll be damned if I know why we went to Spain.' "

Disorientation, confusion, doubt everywhere—that is just what the Nazis needed. The decisions of their leaders must surprise and confuse the people. It was necessary that the German people realize that they neither could nor should have any influence on decisions. The Fuehrer always does the correct thing. The Fuehrer is always right.

And hadn't Hitler always been right? Hadn't he brought the Rhineland and German Austria back to Germany without war? Hadn't he taken Czechoslovakia peacefully? And hadn't the Russians come to an agreement with the Third Reich?

The summer of 1939 showed very clearly what a blow the Munich Pact had been to the morale of the German people. In 1939 there seemed little doubt that Hitler would get what he wanted without war. Everybody had feared war in the summer of 1938, even a large section of the Nazi Party, but there was little anxiety in the summer of 1939. Nazi whispering propaganda passed the word from mouth to mouth: The British cannot make war and the Fuehrer doesn't want war. The masses of the German people were only too glad to believe this.

Even the fact that visible preparations for war had increased again, mobilization and movements of troops, had by no means the same effect on the people as a year before. A report from the middle of August said: "You are always seeing new evidences of war preparation, but we're so used to them that we don't give it a second thought. The conscious anti-Fascists among the workers recognize the danger but always think back to Munich and are inclined to believe that Chamberlain will make another compromise."

This lack of faith in resistance on the part of the British or the French was as crippling as it was justified. But in spite of this general tendency the better qualified underground observers missed no important trend in the development in Germany. They had learned of every coup the Nazis made in advance and had reported about them. As early as the beginning of May, 1939, they sent out a report concerning certain directives given in a course for officers of the army which gave some indication of a change in Nazi policy towards Russia. In the officers' course, Nazi leaders were saying: "Hitler is now pursuing a new line in his Eastern policy"—it would only be a continuation of Bismarck's *Realpolitik*. "The Russians have understood our attitude"—there need be no fear of an English-Russian alliance.

There were repeated reports from highly qualified underground sources during the next months about an imminent agreement between Russia and the Third Reich. A report from Munich on July 18th, five weeks before the conclusion of the pact and two months before the Russian troops marched into eastern Poland, spoke definitively: "The Nazis now declare at their party meetings that Germany has come to an agreement with the Russians, and therefore, there will be no alliance between Russia and the Western Powers. The price of the understanding is the fourth partition of Poland." The success of the Nazis in their preparations for war, as well as the effect of the Munich Pact, is clear from the following passage from the same report: "Most of the people are very much against Poland. Even enemies of Hitler say: 'It serves the Poles right, they betrayed the Czechs.' "

Hitler's peaceful victory at Munich thoroughly prepared the ground for the war against Poland. In the expectation of another "cheap success" the nationalism of the people became more aggressive, while the opposition stood on the sidelines, robbed of their arguments, disappointed, confused and bitter. Not only had the democratic Western Powers, England and France, betrayed their democratic principles. Even the Bolshevik Soviet Union had betrayed its principles and completely reversed its anti-Fascist line. In this unprincipled world, was there any use at all in standing up for principles, for democracy, for Socialism, for anything? Was there any use in risking one's life in the underground struggle against Hitler when his game was made so easy for him in the field of international politics?

In the days before the outbreak of the Second World War, the German opposition felt that it had been abandoned by all its friends and "allies."

9

The Battlefield Inside Germany

"If it should come to war with Poland, it will be nothing worse than a *Kraft durch Freude* [Strength through Joy] war." The Nazi leaders tried with this assurance to dispel the fears that had been reawakened among rank and file party members as the threat of war became more ominous during the summer of 1939. It was explained in party meetings: a *"Kraft durch Freude war"* would take only "about three weeks; casualties would be few and before they knew it they would be marching into Warsaw, with garlands of flowers around their necks."

The Polish war ended in eighteen days. Poland had got no help from France or England. Russia had joined with Germany in the fourth partition of that unfortunate country. All that the Nazis had predicted had happened more quickly, more efficiently and with more precision than even they had expected.

After England and France had declared war—a fact which the Nazis tried to suppress during the first days—anti-Nazis became hopeful again. War against England and France could only end in defeat for Germany. All too many people were convinced that Germany was not strong enough for war in earnest. "A war that begins with butter rations is already lost," they said. But when the Western Front was more quiet than even the Nazis had anticipated; when England and France, despite their declarations, still did not seem to take the war seriously; when Russia, not content to stand with its arms at rest, actually helped to destroy Poland, those hopes vanished as quickly as they had come. The most pessimistic anti-Nazis found their worst fears had not been half bad enough and the most optimistic Nazis found their wildest dreams had been exceeded. A report that came from Berlin early in October told what had happened to the German opposition: "Stalin's pact with Hitler and its consequences have added greatly to the confusion among our friends. The best people are asking: What sense does it all make? The combination of our own propaganda, the propaganda from Russia and from other countries—each contradicting the other—is about to drive us mad. The craziest rumors go around. Who is tricking whom? Which is the slyest? It's like following a picture on the screen. Young Nazis have complete faith in the Fuehrer's policies; the older people, especially in the middle class, are terrified that we'll get Bolshevism if Hitler has made a mistake. The workers just shrug their shoulders."

Like a motion picture—in these words one can sense the spirit of hopelessness in those weeks of disappointment.

But, during those same first weeks, we found that our

many years of preparation had not been wasted. We had been afraid that with the outbreak of war all of our contacts with the groups inside Germany would be cut off at one fell swoop. With the hope of re-establishing contacts as soon as possible, we had made friends among active and understanding members of the labor parties in those countries which were expected to remain neutral. They permitted us to use their addresses, they wrote and received letters. Sometimes we could bring our international friends into personal contact with individuals among the underground workers who could make such connections without too great danger.

Only a few days after troops marched into Poland our contacts in Denmark, in Sweden, in Norway, Holland, Belgium, Luxembourg and Switzerland began to receive letters and postcards from Germany, more than we had ever expected. Most of them contained no "special" messages, but they were important just the same. We could tell which of our friends in Germany were still at their old jobs and which had been mobilized or sent away from home. It was not long before we had received detailed reports describing the new conditions in the Third Reich, public reaction to the war, and telling of the thoughts and fears and hopes of the people in a Germany at war.

Our success in maintaining contacts during the first phase of the war was certainly not entirely due to our careful preparatory work. In great measure, we had to thank a rather paradoxical situation in the Nazis' own control methods. These are radical, direct and immediate. They concentrate on the source of opposition, not on the symptoms. They make certain that oppositional elements are deprived of any possibility of action. As a result, censorship in Germany can permit more freedom than can censorship in democratic countries. Postal, telegraph and telephone communications of neutral countries with war-time Germany functioned almost exactly as during peace time, while communications of those same neutral countries with France and England had to be carried on with the greatest difficulties and delays. In any case the representatives abroad of underground groups in Germany profited greatly and we were able to get an intimate view of developments on the inner front during the first year of the war.

Using codes and sometimes even invisible inks, we managed to keep in amazingly close touch with the Third Reich through the mails. Of course it was only makeshift, as nothing can take the place of direct personal contact. Our representatives abroad concentrated all their efforts on trying to find suitable people in the neutral countries who could make journeys to Germany. The plans for numerous journeys from various countries never went through because Berlin consistently refused permission for the applicants to enter the country. During that period 95 percent of all applications for visas were refused at the consulates, 5 percent were forwarded to Berlin and .05 percent were finally granted.

In December, 1939, we had a stroke of luck. A Swedish delegation was going to Berlin to negotiate a trade treaty. A number of Social Democrats were among the delegates, and we had connections with one of them whom we knew to be an ardent anti-Nazi and a trustworthy and cautious man. He agreed to take a pencil with him to Berlin and to deliver it to one of our best contact people—we shall call him Franz. In this pencil there was a tiny roll of film with a report of eight typewritten pages. For our friends inside, we had tried in the report to cover the following points: a brief survey of the war, an evaluation of the strength of the various fronts and of general perspectives, an outline on possibilities for action by the Socialist emigration abroad and, lastly, addresses abroad to which mail should no longer be sent. The last section of the report was written in code.

The Swedish friend carried out his mission and brought us a detailed report from Berlin in return. Our friends there gave a much more pessimistic evaluation of war prospects than most people outside the Third Reich would generally have believed at the time. "Don't fool yourselves," Franz wrote us, "for the time being the war is going according to Hitler's plans." He continued with a detailed description of the situation in Germany during the first three months of the war. He told of general confusion and disorganization in civilian life after the outbreak of the war, despair during the first two weeks, great relief after the victory in Poland and then an increase in chauvinism. He said that the workers had resisted the war economy decrees which, with one stroke, had taken away from them all limitations on working hours, their extra pay for overtime and their vacations. Lastly, he told of the great wave of arrests and executions. In the days immediately before and after the outbreak of war, many former members of labor organizations were arrested and taken to concentration camps. There was hardly a large factory from which dozens of workers did not disappear. No one dared to ask what had happened to them; no one needed to ask, because everyone knew why certain work benches were now empty. After a few weeks men who had been arrested began to come back, one after the other. All bore the well-known marks of their concentration camp treatment; the demonstrative exhibition of the results of "concentration camp courses" is a part and parcel of Himmler's terror propaganda. The other workers need only see what lay in store for them . . . and many had not come back.

The real wave of terror, however, did not come immediately at the start of the war as we had anticipated, but only in the middle of November. It was introduced by the mysterious bombing attempt on Hitler's life in the Munich Brown House cellar on November 9th, from which, in Goebbels' words, the Fuehrer was saved by "the hand of God." Franz's report said that people in Germany generally believed the bombing attempt to have been a provocation organized by Himmler as an excuse for thousands of arrests and executions. We quote a part of this section of the report which was published in the *Inside Germany Reports* of the American Friends of German Freedom in February, 1940: "Again all kinds of potential enemies were liquidated in a more quiet and efficient way than after the events of June, 1934, when Hitler executed a thousand of his supporters who were demanding a 'second revolution.' For days the firing squads could be heard around the famous Munich prison, Stadelheim. Not only did people disappear from the ranks of former democratic, labor and conservative parties, but, and this is the important fact, Gestapo officials and Nazi S.S. men disappeared as well."

Two of Franz's closest colleagues in Berlin were arrested early in September and one in the middle of November. He never found out what happened to the last. One of those arrested in September was released again after six weeks. The other was still in the concentration camp at Sachsenhausen at the time he sent his report. (He died in February, 1941, of pneumonia contracted at Sachsenhausen.) Two of Franz's other co-workers had been mobilized and a number of others had been sent from their factories to work in other parts of the Reich. Less than a third of the whole group was left. The groups in some cities had lost all their members.

Simultaneously with the November wave of arrests the Nazis began an intensive propaganda campaign. If it was the task of the Himmler terror to immobilize and destroy the centers of conscious opposition, it was the task of Goebbels' propaganda to disarm the underground ideologically. The new propaganda borrowed the terminology of the Socialist labor movement. The pact with Russia served as a basis for promises of a "Socialist Millennium." Goebbels began to popularize a new slogan, "Workers of the world, unite against English capitalism."

All through 1940 the Nazis continued this "Socialist" propaganda. Without let-up they hammered at the workers that this war was a war of liberation from capitalist and imperialist oppression. Dr. Ley, leader of the Labor Front, in his paper *Der Angriff*, appealed to the "invincible forces of the social revolution." At the end of his article, in bold face, were printed Karl Marx's words in the Communist Manifesto: "Workers of the world, unite."

This propaganda campaign reached its peak in Hitler's speech on December 10, 1940. He lauded the war of Socialist Germany against the plutocracies of the West, the have-nots against the haves, the war for the liberation of the common man. The country was flooded with pamphlets. A whole series was brought out under the title *England Unmasked*, the most ambitious and the cleverest of which was *The Hundred Families that Rule the Empire*. (This was subsequently published in book form by the Flanders Hall Press in this country, financed by the Nazis through George Sylvester Viereck.) Later they dealt with *The Sixty Families that Rule the United States*. In the book on Britain, one of the most astute ideologists of the Third Reich, Giselher Wirsing, proved that 181 conservative M.P.'s in Britain hold a total of 775 positions as directors and executives of important Empire firms, that they control all the key positions in banking and in the munitions industry. Wirsing used reports of Parliamentary Investigations, the magazine *Labour Research* and other organs of the British labor movement as evidence for this thesis. From an issue of *Punch* in 1900, he quoted the statement, "The more the Empire expands, the more the Chamberlains contract." Wirsing concluded, "A world empire is fighting a war for one hundred families," and he added that they would not continue long to exploit the world, that the true Socialism was on the march. Immature old-fashioned Socialist ideas had been replaced by more modern ones. "Even in the Soviet Union, something like a privileged class developed. The foolish Utopian Marxist theory of leveling all has lost its authority." Our interests now, he implied, are the same as those of the new Soviet Union.

This talk sounded pretty convincing. It was certainly far superior to England's half-hearted propaganda in 1939 and 1940. Of course, it did not affect the trained fighters in the underground movement. However, among the wavering masses of the people there were many who were influenced. The partial success of this new Nazi hypocrisy and the victories of 1940 brought the opposition once more to a new low. The Nazi whisper propaganda broadcast a statement of Hitler's which ran: "If we must have Socialization, then we shall socialize ourselves." Many former enemies of the Nazis who were uncertain and war-weary said, "Perhaps it's true, who knows? What good is it for us to resist when the Nazis win one victory after the other?"

During that first fall and winter of war, the Nazis were carrying on another propaganda campaign, terror propaganda aimed to intimidate those who still dared to work underground. Using whisper propaganda, rumors were started particularly about spying on, capturing and punishing enemies of the regime. During the very first weeks of the war, there were many stories about the arrest and shooting of persons caught listening to radio news from Strassburg and London. It was later proved that almost all of these reports were fictitious. But there were other rumors that sounded plausible: for example, the story that the Gestapo, not having enough men spies, had enlisted the thousands of women social workers from the National Socialist Welfare Organization to keep the people under surveillance. That this was pure terror propaganda was evident from the fact that Nazis often went out of their way to warn their neighbors against the new women spies. One rumor that cropped up during this period and revealed the purpose behind such propaganda was the warning that Gestapo agents would one day suddenly appear in every home with a new invention enabling them to determine what station had just been turned off the radio.

In many cases it was very difficult to tell where rumor stopped and truth began. For instance, there was a story heard over and over again about workmen who had laid down their tools and refused to work. They had been condemned to death and shot as "deserters." It was certainly suspicious that in one version the scene was Berlin, in another Leipzig, in another Munich. We never got the facts. A story of the same type was that told about the "Death Regiment." A special regiment was to be recruited exclusively from political enemies of the Third Reich. It would be sent into action on the front only in a situation where there was no chance of survival. During the first months of the war different versions of this story cropped up all over the Reich. Later nothing more was heard of it.

A report from western Germany in the middle of September, 1939, told that in order to frighten people the Bonn Gestapo had started rumors about the arrest of numerous persons who were still free. Actually such terror propaganda did intimidate many people.

Even more baffling for the German people during the first half year of the war than propaganda was the phenomenon of the *Sitzkrieg*, or phony war. Was it really a war? On the left bank of the Rhine, French soldiers were dancing to the tunes from microphones on the German bank. Were the Western Powers serious about the war? Hadn't the Nazis predicted that there would be no war in the West?

As a matter of fact before the war started, an officer of the German army, with whom one of our frontier secretaries was in touch, had foreseen this first inactive phase of the war. In a report, dated August 22, 1939, he wrote: "The version current among leading army circles is that Germany has nothing to fear from Poland. Holland and Belgium will not intervene, nor shall we take action against them. If France and England want to attack, let them come. It will not be dangerous, because this front can be held with small forces. Nor shall we have to go into the offensive here; from the first day on the front in the West will remain fixed."

At Christmas time, 1939, this same Socialist officer smuggled himself over the Swiss frontier and sought out one of the leaders of the local frontier organization of the underground movement. He said that an attack on Holland was planned for the early part of May, 1940. The frontier secretary told him how complacent most people in the democratic countries were about the safety of the Western democracies, a point of view also shared by many Socialist emigrants. The officer was very impatient. "I can't listen to such foolishness any more, this irresponsible way of dispensing with the whole Blitzkrieg theory. These methods were effective in Austria, in Sudeten Germany, in Czechoslovakia and Poland; you cannot allow yourselves to be taken in by such easy hopes. The very same thing could happen in the Netherlands. It would not mean the final victory, but it would give Hitler a springboard to attack England."

A month before his trip to Switzerland this officer had managed to get an outline of Nazi plans for attack on Holland to our representatives abroad. He predicted that the Dutch defense plan of opening the dikes and flooding the country would be of little value, for the German army had learned that most of the roads in the Netherlands were too high. He also reported that in leading circles of the army they doubted whether the Dutch would be able even to put this plan into effect, as the battle would be over so quickly.

This anti-Nazi officer of the German army asked that his report be sent on to the French and British governments. "Perhaps they will realize," he said, "that it is already five minutes before twelve."

His request was carried out.

This man lived to see his prophecies fulfilled; a year later, in the first weeks of war against the Russians, he fell in the service of a cause against which he had fought with all the means at his disposal.

The darkest hour for the opposition in the pre-war period had come after Munich; the collapse of the Western Front in 1940 ushered in the opposition's darkest hour in the war period. And, as the pulse of popular opposition against Hitler beat fast or slow, the underground movement was reinforced or weakened. In the summer and fall of 1940, men and women who for years had worked in the underground gave up their organizational connections. "You still believe in the overthrow of Hitler? You still believe in a social revolution?" a soldier of the German occupation army asked an old friend, a refugee whom he met in Norway. "All of us," said the soldier, a former underground leader, whom we shall call Karl, "have lost our faith." He had many secret meetings with his exiled friend and he told him how depressed anti-Nazis in Germany were. Most of the members of the group to which they had both belonged had given up the "hopeless struggle." Karl assured his friend, "Our attitude toward the Nazis and toward their regime has not changed one iota," but what was the use?

Another underground worker wrote from Saxony in September, 1940: "When the war began all of us assumed that Hitler would be beaten. Many anti-Nazis greeted it with a sigh of relief—'at last.' Now we have almost no basis to hope the Nazis will lose the war. Convinced enemies of Hitler are even saying: 'Perhaps it's better this way.' If Hitler wins, at least we'll have peace and quiet. Only the most stubborn among us are still holding the flag aloft."

In Germany, opponents of the regime thought up fantastic schemes that would afford them a personal solution. They made plans to escape from the Third Reich after the Nazi victory which they believed inevitable. A former trade union official wrote: "After Hitler wins the war, I can't stick it out here. I am going to try to be sent abroad somewhere as a machinist. There will certainly be great opportunities because Germany's heavy industry will control the entire European market."

Karl, the soldier, had started learning an African language. When his friend expressed surprise, he said: "You don't understand why I am doing this? That's easy. After Hitler's victory he'll get colonies; the Nazis have been preparing to take them over. When our lieutenant asked me if I wanted to take this course, I jumped at it. Do you suppose I want to stay in Berlin after *they* have won the war? Not on your life! I'd rather go to Africa, the farther away the better. Anyway, people like us will give the natives a better break than genuine representatives of the Third Reich."

Karl also told about life in the occupation army. "Don't think they let up on the discipline, just because we're not in the home barracks. The older N.C.O.'s are always telling us that we have it much easier than they did in the Kaiser's army. They may be right, but there's still more than enough drilling to suit us. Probably we wouldn't any of us make a fuss if we had a chance to say what we thought now and then. But just try once to open your mouth! There aren't many Nazis in our company, but there are quite enough. No matter where you are, one of them is always at your elbow. Under the circumstances, it's healthier to keep quiet. As a matter of fact, they don't often report on a soldier; but when they do, the 'black ones' [S.S.] carry him off, and you wouldn't wish that on your worst enemy.

"Of course, lots of us are against the Nazis. But we are all very careful and not only because of the Nazis and the danger of being reported. The kind of military discipline we have is practically enough by itself to keep the soldiers quiet. Before we went into action the company commander read us a warning to put the fear of God in us. Just before we got into the train and before we knew where we were going, he made us a speech:

'Cowardice in the face of the enemy will be punished by death before the firing squad. But worse than the cowards are those who display discontent, who criticize their officers and undermine the morale of the troops by their pessimism and their bad attitude. In the war of 1914-18 such disruptive elements were not treated with sufficient severity, and therefore our armies collapsed. This must not happen again, and any man who exhibits such an unsoldierly attitude will come up for court martial. The court martial makes only two decisions, acquittal or death before the firing squad.' "

When asked "Why don't you desert?" Karl answered: "Where should we go, to Sweden? Hitler will be there too."

Karl's attitude was typical of that of German soldiers at that time. We know of Danish Social Democrats who asked the same question of German soldiers who they knew had been members of the Social Democratic youth movement and they answered: "Can you name us a single country in Europe where the Nazis won't be able to catch up with us?" In the fall of 1940, this defeatist attitude began to change. When England did not capitulate as the Nazis had predicted and continued to resist, anti-Nazi Germans got new confidence and soldiers began to desert. In Norway, members of the labor youth groups used to fit them out with civilian clothes. Only a few weeks after Dunkirk, the Nazis were putting up posters in the cities of Norway forbidding the sale of civilian clothing to soldiers.

Norwegian underground organizations made contact among the anti-Nazi German soldiers, mostly with former members of German labor organizations, whom they were willing to trust. German soldiers working on fortifications and air bases used to put notes in the pockets of the Norwegians who were being forced to work for the Nazis. It happened all over Norway. An Oslo worker found a scrap of paper in his pocket on which was written: "Hold out, we're on your side," and a Trondhjem worker found a message: "We are for the defeat of Hitler too," and another, "Down with Quisling and Hitler." Often friendship grew up between the recipient and the sender of such a message. Once, young German soldiers warned Norwegian Socialists that they should keep away from the special troops who were to be sent into the neighborhood. "Do not try to get in touch with them; they are the S.S.!" That was only three weeks after the German invasion had started. The Norwegian workers and some anti-Nazi German soldiers who were working together on the construction of an air field in western Norway got to be such good friends that, in the summer of 1941, they even arranged a party together. During the party one German soldier got up and made a fiery anti-Nazi speech. A prominent member of the Norwegian Labor Party described the incident and told us that the Norwegians were astonished that the man dared to speak so openly with so many other Germans present.

A representative of the Norwegian underground

movement smuggled out a report in September, 1941, telling of the reaction of the German soldiers to the war with Russia.

"The morale of the German soldiers has become much worse. We know that several committed suicide after being told that they were to be sent to the Eastern Front. Their morale is not improved by the daily arrival of hospital trains in Oslo filled with wounded, and the wounded men tell hair-raising stories of what is happening in Russia. The hospital ships in Oslo harbor are over-crowded and the German army is constantly requisitioning local hospitals and schools for its wounded.

"The officers too seem to be depressed. A few weeks ago, the German harbor commander for Bodø and Sandnessjøen [in northern Norway] shot himself. Another high German officer shot himself in the street in Oslo.

"More than one German officer has indicated in conversation with Norwegians that he does not believe a German victory possible. Of course, if the officers feel this way, their men must realize it.

"The beginning of war with Russia brought a marked change in the behavior of officers toward their men; they try to be more comradely.

"In western Norway, the occupation authorities have ordered confiscation of all radios in coastal districts. There is a general belief that one of the reasons was to keep the occupation troops from illegal listening. German soldiers, singly and in groups, go regularly to Norwegian homes to listen to London, especially around those military bases where Norwegian workers are employed.

"There are more desertion attempts in western Norway than in other parts of the country. A notice was posted in the Norwegian police headquarters in Innvik [in Nordfjord, north of Bergen]: 'On orders from Commander von Stryn of this city, it is hereby announced: No one may aid Germans attempting to escape, by giving them lodging, food, clothes, etc., or assisting them in any other way. Any person who discovers a man attempting to flee must immediately inform the nearest police station. Any person who acts contrary to this order will be sentenced in accord with German war law.' "

Popular morale in Germany, too, shifted again during the winter of 1940-41. Great parts of the population had believed, immediately after the collapse of France, that the war would soon be over. "No one who witnessed the reception given the troops returning to the cities of Germany after France had laid down her arms," wrote the Berlin correspondent of a prominent Swedish newspaper, "could doubt that these people wanted only one thing, and that was peace." The troops who marched into Cologne carried posters with the words: "The sun shines bright in the East, the sun shines bright in the West, but we like the sunshine at home the best." This little rhyme tells the true story of what Germany's soldiers desired at the very peak of Hitler's victory and might.

When the promised capitulation of England and the hoped for peace did not come, only a second winter of war, discontent grew again. Opposition reawakened, affecting broader circles than before. A new theory became popular: "They are going to kill themselves with victories."

In a "great speech" in the Berlin Sports Palace on February 10, 1941, Dr. Goebbels said: "Long months of waiting are one of the specialities of this war. Nowadays, in contrast to the World War, a long time is spent in preparing for German offensives; then they are carried out swiftly and directly with a minimum of losses. Only one thing is important, our certain success. And that is why, since the very beginning of this war, I have consciously desisted from creating any kind of hurrah spirit or even real enthusiasm [sic]. It has been my endeavor to make it possible for the German people to see the facts calmly and objectively." The Propaganda Minister told his listeners that this gathering was to launch a series of meetings which "would be a demonstration of the German people's confidence in victory." Goebbels' remarks tell us both about the change in the opinion of the German people during that second war winter and about the way Nazi leaders' minds work. They could conceive of enthusiasm only as "created," and of confidence in victory only as "organized." Goebbels himself found a word in 1934 to describe this phenomenon; he called it "organized spontaneity."

The growth in popular opposition gave new impetus

to the underground movement. A report that came from Berlin in April told us a part of the story. This report reached us with the aid of the Berlin correspondent of a well-known Swiss newspaper. It did not tell of any great events or sensational happenings. It is remarkable just for that reason; it soberly registered a series of small atmospheric changes. These changes were preparing the ground out of which great events would be born and these changes gave the underground movement new room for action.

We have reproduced the report in full:

"Generally speaking, the situation in Germany has deteriorated since last year. Consumption goods are insufficient and, more important, people have grown more tense and nervous. But this does not mean that the regime is weakening.

"In recent months, a characteristic change took place in the attitude of many of the young soldiers who were full of enthusiasm after the Polish campaign. They are 'fed up with it.' Their cocksureness is gradually vanishing, shaken by the crushing blows of their own experiences: the ruthless methods of warfare, the death of many of their comrades, the resistance and contempt of the populace in the occupied territories and, above all, the fact that 'there is no end in sight.' At the beginning of the war, a young metal worker in our plant volunteered for war service [machine repair work], chiefly because of the higher pay and the 'change.' Now he has had enough of it and wants to go back to his old job.

This is, however, out of the question. He told us that the prospect of a prolonged war had depressed most of his comrades.

"In air raid shelters discussion is sometimes very lively, not so much about war as about the food situation. People complain that the amount of work exacted from them is in no proper proportion to the amount of food they are supposed to get along on. They resent particularly that even the rations as 'provided for' on the rationing cards are not to be had; and then there is the illegal trade. Only the 'upper crust' can profit from it, a fact which does not make the whole system any more popular. In factories the workers enjoy relatively more freedom of speech at the present. A particularly favorable opportunity for discussions is on the night watch when your job is to extinguish fires started by incendiary bombs. Every night one-fifth of the working force is on duty. The next day the men who were in the night watch come back to work only at two or three o'clock in the afternoon; however, they have to do the usual day's work lest there be a decline in production. On the night watch political discussions about the war are much more frequent than in the air raid shelters. Sometimes conditions in the factory, questions of working hours and tempo are discussed. One can sometimes go amazingly far. There are not so many of the 'trouble makers' [Nazis] in the factories any more who used to make such discussions impossible; a great part of the Nazi followers, particularly the young fellows, are with the troops. The older workers who now form the majority in the factories can be relied upon. And those who are trained and know their way about find it easy to lead and influence discussion in any direction they like. So far all this must be done in a very subtle manner, avoiding the slightest appearance of organized political activity. . . .

"The old friends still meet privately at regular intervals, play cards, discuss things and exchange information. Though these meetings are not really political, they offer the individual an opportunity to speak openly among friends. The foreign broadcasts have been listened to more than ever before since the outbreak of the war. Thus, in our own small circle of trusted friends, we discussed Churchill's last speech, the coming spring offensive and its chances and the set-backs suffered by the Italians about which everyone is truly delighted. Most of us, however, have been too often disappointed by foreign radio news and feel skeptical about it. We know that we have got to wait. The power of the regime is omnipresent down to the last detail of everyday life and there is no chance yet of its faltering or wavering. And, as long as there is no major military defeat, no one expects anything of the kind. Most of the experienced people are of the opinion that the final decision must be reached in the West. In our discussions sometimes an attempt is made to draw the general outline of future developments; but we never really get very far since no one seems to know any more what it is all about. . . . Our interest in our friends who had to emigrate, in what they are doing and thinking, is as great as ever. You are not forgotten and are more in our minds than you perhaps realize."

What this report said was confirmed for us by a member of the French underground movement who was a prisoner of war in Germany from July, 1940, to May, 1941.

This French Socialist had not been in the prison camp very long before he had the following experience. He asked one of the guards, a German soldier, if he could get him a German newspaper, for example, the *Voelkischer Beobachter*. It was strictly forbidden for prisoners to read newspapers. The soldier (who was a former member of the Social Democratic Party) answered him: "Are you crazy? Why do you want to read a German newspaper? There's nothing in them but lies. I never read German papers. I told my old lady, 'If I die, don't you dare to put a death notice in the paper. If you do, nobody'll believe I'm dead.' "

The guards of this camp of about 100,000 prisoners were all older men, soldiers unfit for service on the front. They were all against Hitler and against the war. The only Nazis there were a young official in the camp administration, who used his post to keep from being sent to the front, and a large number of Gestapo officials there to observe the prisoners and the guards.

Those French prisoners who were skilled workers and were sent to war industries were amazed at what they found. They said that many of the German workers complained to them because France had given in so quickly. "If you had held out longer, we would already be rid of Hitler," one of the Germans told a new colleague. When the Frenchmen turned the tables on them and said that the German opposition hadn't put up any real fight either, the Germans shrugged their shoulders and said: "If we'd only known then . . ."

All the French prisoners who went to work in war industries reported that the Germans were practically all older men, even in the winter of 1940-41. They were friendly to the foreigners and almost all of them were against Hitler. The only questions they were interested in were: how long this war would last and how long they would have the Nazis running things. The Frenchmen could not get them to commit themselves on what they hoped for after the "day of reckoning" with their hated masters.

However, passive resistance was extensive. The men worked as slowly and as poorly as they could. French metal workers, who were happy to get their hands on a machine again after being in camp and working on farms, found that their fellow workers did not like their spirit. "Have you lost your minds?" They explained that they had worked for years to achieve the "proper tempo of work"—slow, but not so slow as to be suspicious. They told the French workers that with their high rate of speed—German workers have always looked down upon the French as slow and lackadaisical—they were just pleasing the Nazi slave drivers. "We take it easy," they said and they taught their new colleagues how to damage tools slightly, how to take a long time cleaning and polishing their machines and how to mislay a tool just at the moment they needed it.

In the past year reports have come from Dutch, Belgian, French, Danish and Norwegian "volunteer" workers about the conscious slow-down in German factories. A representative of the Norwegian underground movement told of one such instance:

"Many Norwegian workers who just returned from Germany have reported that they were surprised by the slow tempo of work there. These workers were not the so-called volunteers who last winter were sent off to Germany in groups. They were highly skilled metal workers who had been in Germany for a long time. When they were transferred into new factories, they frequently had the experience that one of the workers, who was considered by his fellows as a kind of 'unofficial leader,' would approach them and say: 'You don't want to overstrain yourselves. We work slowly here.' These statements amazed the Norwegians as did the openness with which they were made."

By the summer of 1942, the "work slowly movement" had reached such proportions that the Nazis had to admit it officially. For example, the coal mining division of the Ministry of Economy instructed all branch offices to conduct efficiency investigations in those coal mines where production was below average. At the end of

August, 1942, the Berlin *Lokalanzeiger* reported that some miners produced three times as much coal as others. An indication that the Nazis have found the decline in production grave and are trying to combat it was an article in the *Reichsarbeitsblatt,* by Dr. Sturm, an official of the Ministry, concerning a new regulation dealing with "breach of labor contract," "refusal to work," "enticement of labor" and "slowing down of output in contravention of obligation." Dr. Sturm was giving warning that Nazi officials intended to act with more severity against the underground leaders of the silent warfare in the mines, mills and factories.

Since the summer of 1940, the situation on the inner front has changed from the ground up. Instead of an invasion of England and the end of the war came a full-sized war with Russia and declaration of war by the United States. Both developments have profoundly affected the average German citizen. They confirmed what he had always feared, namely, that all of the misery of the First World War would be repeated up to and including the inevitable end. No campaign of mass meetings demonstrating the "German people's confidence in victory" can change their conviction that history will repeat itself.

As the hopes of a quick end to the war vanished and as the conditions in Germany became slowly but surely worse, opposition in all classes of the people reached proportions not equaled in all the preceding years of Hitler's rule. The first sign was that they began to talk more openly and more loudly than they had before, to complain about the small but so important problems of everyday life: bad food, too little sleep, disorganized transportation. (At the beginning of the war the Nazi press had occasionally remarked that "love of Fatherland has some relation to the stomach.") From petty troubles such as these the opposition moved on to the big problems of politics and religion; Catholics, Protestants, Democrats, Socialists and Communists were being pressed into a single front against the Nazi regime.

Country people became increasingly restive at the farm regulations. They hated being pestered with exact specifications concerning sowing and harvesting and with the increasingly annoying control by the bureaucrats of the Reich Farm Estate. Nazi officials were always in the barnyard finding out exactly how much milk the cows were giving, how much the farmer had harvested, to the last potato. They prescribed what every farmer had to deliver and where, while the farmer coveted the higher prices on the black market or wanted to barter his crops for some manufactured articles which he could not get in any other way. The Nazi judges have sent more and more farmers to jail for illegal selling and for what they call "black slaughtering"—for example, if a farmer kills his pig without express permission—but the action of the courts seems no longer to serve the purpose of deterring potential offenders.

The problems of the peasants are aggravated by the absence of so many farmers and their sons on the front.

There is not enough foreign labor to keep up the work, and every village is mourning its sons who have fallen in Russia. There are villages where most of the male population will never come back, because an entire regiment recruited locally has been wiped out. No one knows how great the losses have been. No one believes official figures and fantastic rumors enjoy widespread credence.

Most people have their own system of estimating casualties. A soldier from central Germany, an old Social Democrat, was asked about German losses by a Norwegian acquaintance. He said that no one took the figures published by the High Command seriously. "You can always multiply Goebbels' figures by three when he is talking about our losses and you can divide them by three when he is talking about the losses of the enemy; then you may be somewhere near the truth."

The extent of losses is the most frequent subject of conversation and bitterness in Germany, and the next is the food scarcity. Older people are making ominous comparisons with the hunger years of 1917 and '18. More frequently than formerly the shops do not have the food to which people's ration cards entitle them. Housewives must stand in line for hours in order to get a few vegetables or a little fruit. In some districts of western Germany rationing of vegetables was introduced during the summer of 1942. The highly organized black markets play a sinister role. If you have enough money and good connections, you can still buy almost anything. Meanwhile, foodstuffs intended for general consumption simply vanish. For example, the *Oldenburgische Zeitung* reported that fifty to seventy thousand double hundred-weight of fruit that had been stacked up ready for distribution had disappeared and the police had not been able to find a trace of it. The paper dwelt on the economic consequences of such theft and stated that in 1939 the apple-butter industry had been able to get 120,000 tons of apples, but that in 1941 though the harvest had been as great it could get only 19,000 tons. The papers are filled with accounts of grave sentences given to persons found guilty of selling goods on the black market. They also publish answers to some of "many letters" received from the public, expressing disapproval of the severity of punishment. The *West Deutsche Beobachter* answered a reader who had written: "Why should a man have to spend so many years in jail because of a few bushels of plums?" by saying, "If our courts do not act ruthlessly, we shall have a repetition of 1918."

It is especially infuriating to the ordinary person that the Nazi big shots themselves buy in the black market. In this matter of the Fatherland and the stomach the German people have reacted very clearly. The *Schwarze Korps*, weekly organ of the S.S., felt called upon to defend Nazi officials in an article entitled *Speak for Yourself, Mueller*.

It accuses Mueller (the proverbial man in the street) of incessant whispering and the spreading of rumors to the effect that the Nazis do not keep ration regulations and that they enjoy special privileges. The "Muellers," the paper charges, are of the opinion that the courts of Germany have two standards of justice, that they are amenable to bribery and that the sentences they give to Nazi functionaries are too light. The S.S. organ expresses indignation that every time a Nazi functionary is on trial, "if the judge condemns him to death, the Muellers cheer unanimously, and if he is only sent to prison, they complain." When the papers carry an account of the trial of a Nazi and he only gets five years, the Muellers whisper about the "pull" that the accused used and are convinced that the judge was bought. The article ends with a protest: "The State cannot help it if, before his crime was discovered, the accused man was a pillar of the National Socialist Party." Perhaps the most significant sentence in the article is: "No one can expect the State to condemn more and more Nazi functionaries just to make the Muellers of Germany happy."

The petty irritations of daily life are aggravated by the more serious problems, by fear of R.A.F. raids and of the "Americans who are on their way," by the misery of the refugees from bombed cities, by the anxiety of families for the soldiers at the front, by fear and doubt about the future. There is every indication that the Germans can't take it!

Nazi leaders even had the nerve to refer to the resistance that the people of Britain have shown. Churchill could promise the people of the British Isles, "blood, sweat and tears," because he knew that they are fighting for their freedom. In an article in *Das Reich* in August,

1942, Dr. Goebbels tried to balance against the sufferings of the war "the end that is to be achieved." He wrote: "I admit that it is bitter that our sufferings have to be concentrated in such a relatively short space of time; sometimes we are so weighed down that the weak-hearted feel that it is really unbearable." Then the German Propaganda Minister tried to exorcize the sorrows of the present with the help of historical illustrations. "Who today still speaks of what the German people had to endure in the Thirty Years War, the Seven Years War or, for that matter, in the World War?" Dr. Goebbels' words tell us clearly enough what the German home front is like.

The press warns the people at home not to disappoint their heroic soldiers on the battlefields. "Our men in the field look at home through the eyes of the individual soldier," wrote the newspaper *Westmark*, at the end of July. "If the home front fails, for what is he risking his life? The morale and the efficiency of our fighting front are directly dependent on the morale at home."

Nor has the increase in discontent even spared the Nazis' own state machinery. Casualties in Russia, raids on inadequately defended cities, the hardships of scarcity, the shocking prospects for the fourth winter of war and especially a growing realization of the uselessness of all these sacrifices, have served to revive the differentiation which existed when the Nazis first inherited the extensive state administrative machinery. In purely technical offices it was neither necessary nor practical to remove many docile civil servants simply because they had served under a previous regime. But we know that difficulties have arisen. The best proof was provided by Hitler's speech before the Reichstag on April 26, 1942. Hitler demanded that it be "expressly understood that any man who did not do his duty should immediately be removed, no matter who he was or what well-earned rights he might possess." Why does the Fuehrer need any new confirmation for this? He needs it to intimidate public officials who have begun to try to find some insurance so that they will be prepared in case the regime they have so obediently served for a decade should collapse.

Hitler not only demanded the right to remove any public employee without further ado. He also demanded that the Reichstag make him "Supreme Judge of the German people," and he ordered the judges to "recognize as law what *I* order." A further step in the same direction was taken in August, when Hitler appointed the President of the People's Courts, Dr. Thierak, a man with thousands of terror sentences on his conscience, as Minister of Justice for the German Reich. In the decree naming Dr. Thierak to his new office Hitler stated: "I charge and empower the Reich Minister of Justice to create a National Socialist system of justice in accordance with my program and my instructions. In doing so he may depart from existing law." That last sentence tells us the troubles that Hitler has encountered among the officials of the German courts. Undoubtedly, certain

older officials have insisted on sticking to former inter-
pretations of the law. But, under the steadily growing
pressure of the war, neither the old theories of law, nor
even the original formula for Nazi law—"that is right
which serves the German people"—any longer suffices to
guarantee the maintenance of the Nazis' state power.
The last veil has been torn away. In Hitler's Germany,
justice is the word of Hitler.

On October 1, 1942, the B.B.C. gave a summary of
the executions for political crimes in Germany that were
reported by the Nazis during the month of September.
This list, which is certainly incomplete, records the exe-
cution of more than forty men and women.

Frankfurt and Karlsruhe—fifteen people, among them
one woman, were executed. They were accused of high
treason, attempts to organize "communist cells" and circulation of foreign radio news.

Mannheim—fourteen people, including one woman.
Charge: organization of a new Communist party nucleus
to undermine the German home front and the army,
the dissemination of enemy radio news.

Oldenburg—one man executed. Charge: espionage for
a foreign power.

Breslau—two armament workers executed. Charge:
acts of sabotage.

Berlin—two persons executed, one of them a twenty-
one-year-old girl. Charge: espionage for a foreign
power.

Munich—one man executed. Charge: high treason and
attempted aid to the enemy.

Graz—a number of persons executed. Charge: formation of a communist organization.

Vienna—three persons executed, one of them a woman. Charge: high treason, undermining the German armed forces, espionage for the enemy.

The next day, October 2nd, Reuters announced in a dispatch from the German frontier:

"It has been learned that forty-six Germans were put to death following Hitler's declaration, in his speech of September 30th, that saboteurs within the Reich would be dealt with ruthlessly. Charges against the executed ranged from high treason and espionage to the dissemination of news from foreign broadcasts."

Likewise in the course of September, the Berlin correspondents of Swedish newspapers reported the following incidents:

September 13, 1942: "A middle-aged couple from Kassel, previously sentenced for treasonable acts, were executed when it was found that they had resumed activities after their release from prison. They were accused of listening to foreign broadcasts and spreading enemy news."

September 4, 1942: "Seven Germans were arrested for listening to English broadcasts. Two of them, an artist and a clergyman, were sentenced to death. The others received long prison sentences to deter all those who . . ."

On September 9th, the Danzig Nazi paper, the *Vorposten*, published the following warning:

"Repeatedly the courts must deal with persons guilty of listening to foreign broadcasts. Punishments are severe. There is no point in trying to evade the law. The only result is misfortune for the culprit and his family. There are incurables; one can have no compassion for them; they will feel the full weight of the law. But some people violate the law because of carelessness or neglect; we are addressing ourselves to them today. One continually hears remarks, such as that the accused did not mean anything by listening to foreign broadcasts. This is a poor excuse. Some people say that they have only listened to the music programs; others that they have tuned in on foreign stations accidentally. We know of many instances where a woman has listened to forbidden broadcasts and then told her husband what she heard or a man has listened and told his wife. Equally bad are the cases where one person is asked to listen to the news in order to tell it to others. It must be understood: The fact that an individual does not listen himself is irrelevant. 'Listening' means learning the content of broadcasts. It is immaterial whether an individual himself sits at the radio or whether some one else does the work for him. It is useless to try to evade the law. Listener, be honest with yourself."

In reporting the Frankfort and Mannheim death sentences the B.B.C. gave the names of the persons executed.

We know some of these most recent victims of Nazi terror. By questioning people from the same cities, now in the United States, we have been able to learn more of their background and of their activity. They are people who were active in the labor movement, in the Socialist youth movement and the Social Democratic Party, a decade before Hitler seized power. The Nazi assertion that they are "Communists" is only another propaganda lie.

We know that some of them were working underground as early as 1933. We know that until 1936, at least, they were in contact with groups abroad. Exact information about their activity in the last few years is not available; however, we can tell from the names that these men and women maintained some kind of connections throughout the years. Further, we know that most of them were workers in industrial plants. There is no doubt that the "treasonable" acts that they carried on, in distributing information and organizing anti-Nazi units, were directed, at least in part, to their fellow workers, that they were trying to weaken the Nazi war machine at its base, in the armament factories.

During these last years, the first signs that the Nazi regime was weakening, the growth of widespread opposition in Germany, the feeling that "something must be done" had driven them, and certainly thousands of others as well, to increased activity. These men and women, who came from the old democratic movement, are today the vanguard of the forces which are re-forming on the battle front inside Germany.

Thus has the last act of the bloody drama of National

Socialist rule begun. The National Socialist Party rose to power, carried on the wave of a revolutionary movement, in the great crisis years of 1931 and '32. With an irresistible, offensive will it overcame seemingly immovable obstacles, and for a time, if it did not win over the overwhelming majority of the German people, it did neutralize them. On this foundation, it built up a military power which could bend all of Europe to its will. But, in spite of this success, during the last years the basis of the rule of this most modern of all regimes of force has become narrower and narrower. It is true that in the summer of 1942 the real power of the Third Reich is still unshaken. However, the second most vital instrument of this, as of every totalitarian state—its propaganda—already shows clear signs of a basic change.

For the first time since the Hitler regime became the decisive power in Europe the Nazis have been forced on the defensive in their propaganda. It is a long way from the militant words we used to hear about the "nations who oppress innocent Germans," "the stolen colonies that must be returned," the "Blitzkrieg" and the "Kraft durch Freude war," the "victories in the East and in the West," "the enemies who will never rise again," to an article which Dr. Goebbels published in *Das Reich* on November 9, 1941. He said, "All the sorrows and burdens that we must bear during this war would pale before the inferno that awaits us should we lose it. . . . The chance which the German nation has today is its greatest chance, but at the same time it is its *last* chance."

Even on the defensive, Goebbels is a master of propaganda. Probably no propaganda line of his has ever enjoyed more success than this one threatening the German people with catastrophe if they are defeated. The Germans are completely aware of the crimes that the Nazi regime has committed. They are desperately afraid of the consequences of the hatred that has gathered in Europe, afraid that the barbarity of their war leaders will be avenged on the German people.

Goebbels knows exactly how to make use of these fears for his own purposes. In his propaganda line he says simply: "If we are caught together, we shall hang together." An American, Theodore Kaufman, published a book entitled *Germany Must Perish*, in which he demanded the sterilization of forty million Germans. In Germany Goebbels saw to it that it became a "best-seller." Hundreds of thousands of copies have been distributed. It has been Goebbels' concern to see to it that scarcely anyone in Germany should know what really is in the Atlantic Charter. Most people think that it is a plan to cut up Germany into small states. But he has called the services of his entire apparatus into play to "popularize" the "Black Record" theories of Lord Vansittart.

If the United Nations want to shorten the war, then they must break the defensive positions of the Hitler regime. The first decisive break-through can come on this front; the German home front can be opened up. In their own propaganda, the Nazis concentrate on warning of the frightful consequences if the home front fails. There is nothing the Nazis fear so much as the "stab in the back" of German anti-Nazis. The United Nations must give those enemies of Hitler, who are at the back of his armies, the dagger with which they can stab. Today, that dagger means—clear and unmistakable war aims.

In his speech on August 31st of this year, in launching the Winter Help Campaign for the fourth winter of war, Hitler told the Germans that the enemies of his system intended to "reduce the German people to a slavery worse even than that of the Versailles dictates." He said that what they plan is "the brutal destruction of National Socialist European States which are opposed to their capitalism" and "not a better social structure." Why should Hitler talk this way unless more people in Germany are beginning to believe in a "better social structure" than he can offer them; unless they are becoming less impressed by the Nazis' monotonous references to "Wilson's treason" and the "trickery of the fourteen points."

The situation in the Third Reich is just now beginning to be ripe for a conscious program of psychological warfare and war aims of unmistakable clarity. It is vital that the United Nations take the offensive in this sphere. However, at the same time, the mistakes of the first months of war must not be repeated, one must not be blinded by false hopes. Psychological warfare is not magic. The walls of Jericho collapsed from the blare of trumpets. During the last ten years, whole nations have collapsed from the blare of the trumpets of Nazi propaganda. But we can expect walls to collapse only when their defenders do not believe firmly enough and do not put enough energy into their defense. The Nazis know that they are fighting for their lives. The Nazi fortress will not fall from propaganda arguments; it must be stormed.

After the beginning of the war, when the first English leaflets fell on Germany, the anti-Nazis were delighted. But by the end of October, 1939, an underground worker in western Germany wrote: "Leaflets are no good without bombs." Psychological warfare is like every method of modern warfare; it is only *one* of the weapons. The question is not whether we should have this weapon or that weapon, freight boats or transport planes, bombers or fighting planes, psychological warfare or military warfare. Total warfare demands the use of *all* weapons. They must be coördinated and the proper balance between the various weapons must be maintained. The Nazis have taught us a lot in this regard.

The Nazis were able to give the preparations for their military offensive a thorough psychological foundation. The United Nations will be able considerably to shorten the war, if they prepare for their coming military offensive by planned disruption of the home front of Hitler Germany. The precept of the hour is: bombs *and* leaflets, military offensive *and* psychological offensive, unrelenting warfare *and* clear war aims.

10

The Coming Revolution in Germany

Autocracy on the one hand and the impulse to freedom on the other have been the two great forces of human society which have struggled against each other throughout history. Often during the centuries tyrants have seized power and set up autocratic rule. In the end, this autocratic rule has always been broken. Great nations have been bound in fetters and they have always thrown them off. Empires that spanned the world have been founded on armed might. Through armed might and inner disruption they have gone down again. The advance of human freedom has been halted; but always it has marched on once more, stronger than before. For a human being can be a man only when he is free; because of his profound awareness of this, he has always raised himself up from the deepest oppression with the cry: Down with tyranny.

The world has witnessed the collapse and the overthrow of many systems of tyranny and dictatorship. True, it has not yet witnessed the collapse of a modern totalitarian regime. If we want to find an answer to the question—how can Nazi rule be overthrown and the Third Reich wiped off the map?—it will help us to consult the experience of history. But we must always be circumspect in relying on historical precedent.

The events of the collapse of the three great autocracies of Europe at the end of the First World War are still fresh in the minds of the older generation. Century-old dynasties and regimes which seemed proof against change broke down in a twinkling; venerable crowns rolled in the cyclone of revolutions, out of which emerged movements, leaders and personalities for the most part unknown to the world. Who, outside of the narrowest circles of European Socialists, had heard of the Bolsheviks before 1917? Before the First World War, who would have thought of Soldiers and Workers Councils? Who could have identified Lenin before Czarism was swept away on the waves of the Russian Revolution? Who would have dreamed that the Socialist poet, Kurt Eisner, would become the Premier of Bavaria, only to be murdered later by German nationalists? Who would have seen in the young assistant of Masaryk, Eduard Benes, the European statesman and future president of a Czechoslovak Republic?

From Camille Desmoulins, unknown Paris attorney, who directed the storming of the Bastille on the 14th of July, 1789, to Richard Mueller, the trade unionist who organized the strike of Berlin metal workers in January, 1918, and played an important role in the overthrow of the Hohenzollern regime, a chain of unknown people have been the pioneers in the struggle for freedom. The story of Leon Trotsky, habitué of Vienna's Café Central, is familiar. When the Police President of Vienna heard the news of the October Revolution, he refused to believe that the leader and strategist of the Bolsheviks and the chess-playing intellectual of the local café were one and the same.

These revolutionary movements, groups and leaders, insignificant until the moment when they filled the headlines of the world's newspapers, have made history. Their deeds have revamped the countenance of the earth. It is irrelevant, whether they have endured or whether they have been beaten; what they once achieved has become a part of the world's history for all time, it cannot be erased, it cannot be changed, its effects are inescapable.

How do unknown groups, movements and parties grow to a power which can overthrow old and venerable states? How do leaders known only in the smallest circles win the support and the confidence without which they would not be able to overthrow firmly established governments? How does a new and a revolutionary authority usurp the place of the old authority?

History gives us the answer to these questions. We know that when the majority of the people is unwilling to continue to live under the existing rule, we have the first prerequisite for a revolutionary change. If we ask, what is the situation in this respect in Nazi Germany today, our answer must be that in the year 1942, in Nazi

Germany, this first prerequisite for revolution is to a great extent present. In the preceding chapter we have given many examples in support of this diagnosis: from lack of enthusiasm for the war, even at the outset, to apathy and indifference toward great Nazi triumphs; from generally growing opposition since the war has really come home to Germany, to the numerous, largely passive, manifestations of resistance. The best proof comes from the Nazis themselves, who have found it necessary to repeat over and over again: Either we win or the entire German people will go down.

But, if this is the case, why isn't Hitler overthrown? Why is there no revolution in Nazi Germany? This is the sense, explicit or implicit, behind most of the questions asked in the anti-Nazi world today about the behavior of the German people. The answer to these questions is that, in the modern world, revolutions almost always come as a result of the defeat of an autocratic regime in war. That was true of the chain of revolutions which swept away absolutist regimes in 1917-18. It was the same in 1871, when Napoleon III's Bonapartist regime collapsed. The fact that the majority of a people no longer wants to live under existing conditions is a decisive, but only the first, prerequisite for revolution. The second, and equally indispensable, prerequisite is—in the words of Lenin—that the ruling class can no longer maintain its rule under the given conditions. One may disagree with Lenin in almost every point, but one must grant that he had some understanding of revolutions.

There is room for differences of opinion as to whether, in 1942, a sufficient majority of the German people already reject the Nazi rule. No one can doubt that the overwhelming majority of the people of the occupied countries rejects the Nazis and is waiting for the day of reckoning with the oppressors. But the Nazis have not yet in any way shown themselves seriously incapable of maintaining their rule of terror under today's conditions. Their power is still not shaken, in the occupied countries or in Germany. Their armies are still victorious. There is one vital difference between the regime of the Nazis and previous autocratic regimes. The core of their power machine, Hitler's S.S., Elite Guard, cannot be disrupted as could that of the Czars, the Hohenzollerns and the Hapsburgs. It is immune to revolutionary infection. It has to be beaten from outside. As long as this force, the heart of Hitler's organization, is not, at least, completely isolated from the masses of the people, not the slimmest chance exists of seriously threatening the regime, to say nothing of destroying it.

This fact must be faced honestly: we shall have to travel a long distance before we find conditions under which the Nazis will no longer be able to maintain their rule. How quickly we can cover this distance depends largely on the war. Great victories for the Nazi armies will mean delay, defeats will hasten the end. The battle against the existing rulers, against the leading powers and the old authority, does not begin only when the guns begin to speak. Once that point has been reached, we are already in the final stage of the battle. Before that final stage a series of engagements must be fought and won. Although the way to the revolutionary overthrow of the Nazi regime is still far, the first steps on this way are already behind us, steps of crucial importance.

We have implied that, in a revolutionary situation, the decisive factor is the emergence of a new authority, which first undermines the old, then overthrows it and finally replaces it. Such a new authority is growing up before our eyes in Nazi Germany. To be sure, it is still not a calculable factor. It is not even a positive factor today. It is much more a tendency, a vague and unorganized stream. It is more an attitude of mind than a movement. But it is the attitude of masses of the German people, of the overwhelming majority of the German people and that is what gives it importance. It is only one step from this attitude of the masses to a movement of the masses. And from the unorganized movement to an organized movement is just one more step. An organized mass movement in Germany would be a revolution, but the two intermediary steps are big steps and we are still far from that.

If we are still far from a serious movement among the German people, there have, however, already been a number of extremely significant illustrations of a new anti-Nazi authority. We have passed the period when

330

the Nazi leaders could completely silence such manifestations of another authority. They have begun to reason with it. They have felt forced to defend their regime and their deeds against the reproaches of this new authority. It is making its first appearance in the guise of rumor and rumor has become a dangerous force against the Nazi rule, a mighty weapon of the anti-Nazi opposition.

For example, note how Nazi Gauleiter Buerckel defends the Nazi state against this enemy. In the middle of July, 1942, in a speech at Kaiserslautern, he said:

"Most extraordinary rumors are being spread: For example, the rumor that the savings-bank accounts of fallen soldiers will be confiscated by the state. It is superfluous to say that this is absolutely and completely untrue. Especially this rumor is a crime and spreading it is criminal. In the future rumor mongers will be punished with extreme severity."

Shortly before Buerckel's speech, the official Nazi publication for Hessen and Nassau issued the following warning: "People who spread rumors undermine confidence and the national power. This is not a question of protecting National Socialist leaders, but the whole nation. Rumor mongers will be punished without mercy. Communist agitators who had expected three years' imprisonment were surprised when they were sentenced to death. They were undermining national security and serving the interests of our enemies. Rumor mongers are considered to be no less than servants of our enemies and it is the determination of the National Socialist Party to eradicate them from the community."

Why have the Nazi leaders suddenly gone all out against rumor mongers? There have been rumors and there have been people who spread rumors ever since the Nazis came to power. Rumors are an inevitable by-product of censorship; the stricter the censorship, the more numerous the rumors. The less confidence people have in the information they are given, the more likely they are to believe rumors. Until the summer of 1942, the Nazis did not take rumors particularly seriously. Of course, Goebbels has often thundered against grumblers and rumor mongers and they have been sent to prison when caught by the Gestapo. On the other hand, Goebbels has put rumors to work in the service of his propaganda with great success. Every time the press of the world has reported crises in the Third Reich, manifestations of imminent economic collapse, generals' revolts and such matters, Goebbels' well-organized whisper propaganda has won a new victory. However, in the third year of the war, this very weapon is beginning to turn against Goebbels and against the Nazi regime. Faith in the statements of the Nazi leaders has been so shaken that the average German is more willing to believe any rumor he hears than to trust official pronouncements. That is why leading Nazis are now launching such a concerted drive against rumor mongers. They fear their own weapon of whisper propaganda.

An official German broadcast late in July, 1942, af-

forded convincing evidence of Nazi fear of rumor. As
no one believes so much as a word that comes from
Goebbels' apparatus, a speaker was commandeered from
the army to refute rumors about mercy killings of in-
curably wounded soldiers. The *New York Times* reported on this special broadcast from the Psychological
Service of the German army as follows:

"The spokesman first turned against rumors in general, 'including German-manufactured rumors,' which
he said had received too ready credence among the
German people.

"As an example he specifically referred to reports
that wounded German soldiers from Norway refused
to be repatriated aboard the hospital ship *Adolf Hitler*.
Two hospital ships, the *Berlin* and the *Adolf Hitler*, are
plying between Norway and Germany, but only the
soldiers repatriated aboard the *Berlin* reach Germany
alive, according to these rumors, as recounted by the
spokesman.

" 'The rumors are completely absurd,' said the speaker,
but 'I could not deny that a certain percentage of the
more seriously wounded die and are buried at sea, naturally, with all military honors and enveloped in a Swastika flag.' The real explanation, he said, is that, while
the hospital ship, *Berlin*, is reserved for slightly wounded
cases, the *Adolf Hitler* takes on all serious cases."

The fact that an officer spoke in this case instead of
one of Goebbels' underlings does not make his statements more credible. One can scarcely believe that, with

only two ships available, the wounded are strictly separated into light and serious cases. That, however, is irrelevant to our point. Much more important than the fact that there is a rumor that the *Adolf Hitler* is a "Death-Ship," is the fact that great numbers of people believe it. Nor is that the only interesting point. The military psychologists spoke quite openly about "German-manufactured rumors." Previously, Goebbels had always placed responsibility for rumors on "criminal propaganda from abroad." The officer told the truth, namely, that the rumors against which he was protesting were manufactured and circulated within Germany by an organized opposition. The Nazis have thus officially confirmed a fact which heretofore we could only assume to be true.

It is the recognition of this that upsets the Nazi leaders. They know better than anyone else in the world the power of organized whisper propaganda, having used this weapon against the whole world for years. Now it is being used against the Nazi regime by an anonymous foe, a foe whom they cannot locate and cannot silence. They can execute every rumor monger they find; but new ones will always take their places, because spreading rumors is only an external symptom of the inner attitude of a vast section of the German people.

Naturally, the Nazi leaders do not admit that rumor mongering and whisper propaganda are already a mass manifestation. Buerckel speaks only of "a few people who disturb unity." In his Kaiserslautern speech he said:

"It would be wrong if one overlooked this small minority, considering their activity unimportant. Every day this war is prolonged produces more bleaters and grumblers." If this is already an astonishing admission, the following sentences show even more clearly how seriously the Nazi leaders take this "small minority." Buerckel said: "Do not tell me that a colossal fighting front cannot be disturbed by such a thing. In 1918 we saw its effect." Ever since the war started, the Nazi leaders have tirelessly repeated the same formula: there can be no repetition of 1918. By the middle of 1942, we find them beginning to admit that a repetition of 1918 is not impossible.

Is it not ironical that, in the summer of 1942, while the German armies are marching victoriously across the Don to the Caucasus, anti-Nazi whisper propaganda is finding credence among the German people, that they are ready to believe rumors about the "Death-Ship," *Adolf Hitler?* Could we ask for any better proof that the situation has changed in Hitler's Reich?

At the same time we should not overestimate these symptoms of the beginnings of disruption. But a beginning has been made, an entering wedge is already there, an engagement has been won. These signs show that great masses of the German people no longer want to live under Nazi rule. The Nazis are indeed still too powerful, too confident and too victorious for such shocks seriously to shake their actual power. But it is not unduly optimistic to read one thing out of these symptoms. The way from the height of unchallenged might of Nazi power to the depths of collapse is shorter than most people believe, and the first steps along this way are already behind us.

What are the next steps leading to a revolutionary uprising against the Nazi regime? What forces will be in the vanguard of the fight? To what groups can we look for the leaders of the movement that will overthrow the barbaric system? What will be the process of disintegration, of collapse and finally of complete demolition of this totalitarian power?

It is as necessary as it is perplexing to seek answers to these questions. It is necessary because an accurate evaluation of the forces gathering against Hitler within the borders of Germany can help to shorten the war. It is perplexing because every attempt at an answer is inevitably hypothetical, simply because we are reckoning with many unknown factors, because mass movements are always unpredictable. It is for these reasons that in our own prognosis we want to confine ourselves strictly to the lessons of our own experiences in a decade of Nazi rule.

In beginning to discuss the chances of a revolution against the Nazis, we immediately run into one widely held conception, a conception which distorts the vision even of good observers. It is the belief that "decent" and "more moderate" elements in the Nazi regime will one day gain the upper hand and liberate the world from the modern demon, Hitler. Since the Nazi regime first came into existence, a large part of the public in Germany and in the rest of the world has waited and hoped that eventually the scourge would simply vanish. Despite disappointments, despite the fact that time after time hopes of this kind have been blasted, despite all the catastrophes we have lived through, this myth has persisted. There are still many, far too many, people who expect the Nazi regime to be undermined by forces within itself, forces represented in the regime and with interests closely tied up with it.

People still await from the "decent" industrialists, the conservative bureaucrats and the "moderate" generals deeds which, during ten long years, they were unable to decide on, deeds which they did not even want themselves. A miracle is supposed to bring the overthrow of Hitler, a sudden gift to the world. But the time of miracles has passed and it is time to realize that there is no easy way out of the Hitler era; there is only the hard way.

Experiences throughout a decade prove what we maintain to be a fact: the Nazi regime will not be overthrown by the "conservative opposition," by a generals' revolt or a palace revolution, no matter how hard we wish it. The Nazi regime will only go down in the face of a revolution of the masses of the German people. That does not mean that oppositional industrialists, conservative officials and mutinous generals cannot be instrumental at the moment when the power of the Nazis is broken. But their record since 1933 proves that there

337

is absolutely no prospect of their rising up to action before the popular revolutionary movement against Hitler has gathered so much force that it cannot be stopped. It is highly probable that certain groups in the Nazi regime will try to save themselves by going over to the revolution. But they won't attempt it until Adolf Hitler's ship has begun to sink. Their record has demonstrated that they have had no inclination to mutiny under their lunatic captain and steer the ship into a safe harbor. Like rats, they will only desert when it sinks.

This is a harsh statement, but a summary of the history of ten years of the opposition *within* the Nazi regime will show unmistakably that we are right.

1933—Hitler's "National Government" was installed. The conservatives had an overwhelming majority in this government. They confidently believed that they would be able to "tame" Hitler with their moderating influence. Privately they anticipated that, having the responsibility of governing and fulfilling his promises, Hitler would "be discredited." Furthermore, they believed that, with the support of President von Hindenburg and the army, they would be strong enough always to hold Hitler within definite limits and if necessary get rid of him. In the General Staff there was a pessimistic opinion and an optimistic opinion. The optimists believed that Hitler's rule would last only six months, the pessimists gave him two years.

1934—The conservatives had already been rendered completely impotent. Their leader, Hugenberg, had "retired." The other conservative ministers continued to serve the Nazi state as obedient officials. However, the army was still rather complacent. It considered itself a "dictatorship within the dictatorship." The army demanded of Hitler that the Storm Troops be robbed of their power. Hitler acceded to this demand; he cut off the head of the so-called "second revolution" in the bloody night of June 30, 1934, when Roehm and his leading subordinates were "liquidated." On this occasion, Hitler promised the generals that the army would remain the "only armed body in the nation." The incident marked the last great victory in Hitler Germany for the leaders of the army.

1935-36—By this time Hitler was no longer only Reich Chancellor. He had become the successor of President von Hindenburg and the "leader" of the German people. This was the price that the army had paid for June 30, 1934. From that point on every step was a compromise in Hitler's favor. The leaders of the army had demonstrated that they had not the slightest understanding of the basis in mass psychology on which a modern power state rests. Hitler towered over his generals. He had General von Schleicher and General von Bredow murdered along with Roehm. In this act he had shown the German people who was the real master in the house. To get *Wehrfreiheit* (the repudiation of the disarmament clauses of the Versailles Treaty) the generals had given up their professional army and accepted Hitler's mass army. Young soldiers, trained by the Nazi

339

organizations, streamed into the army. Soldiers and officers swore their allegiance to Hitler. Hitler got the upper hand in the army too. The occupation of the Rhineland in the spring of 1936 incontrovertibly demonstrated this fact. The generals maintained that the risk was too great. Hitler disagreed and Hitler proved to be right that time and every time during the years to follow, through the victories in the west. In every crisis, from that day on, Hitler's point was upheld. The generals, like the conservative cabinet ministers, were reduced to the role of technical advisers of Hitler.

. *1937-38*—The real test came when Hitler determined to initiate his plan of expansion by bringing Austria back into the Reich. The General Staff opposed his decision, but the position of this military body had already been so weakened that there could be no doubt whose will would prevail. Hitler settled this crisis by naming himself Commander-in-Chief of the army, by dismissing General von Fritsch and other generals and by putting Von Brauchitsch and Keitel at the head of the armed forces. Five weeks later, the army was able to march in review before the Fuehrer in Vienna. Then, following his triumph at Munich in September, 1938, Hitler could permit himself to take the religious element out of the soldiers' oath of allegiance, to hand pre-military training over to the same Storm Troops whose power had been destroyed in the summer of 1934, and to forbid any recognition within the army of Kaiser Wilhelm's eightieth birthday. Because the army was unable to maintain the prohibition against army officers belonging to the Nazi Party, General von Beck resigned in October, 1938. From that time on, the only way in which a general could openly express opposition was to retire.

After three years of war, the position of the army leaders has been weakened further. We have been hearing reports about an imminent revolt of the generals, combined with industrialists and other conservative elements, at recurrent intervals, at least once before every attack on a new victim. As a rule, Goering's name has been associated with such alleged plots. However, the facts show us that every time Hitler has found opposition of some kind to his plans, there has not been revolt, but a few generals have been shifted about or, as has been more frequent during the last years, a few generals died at the convenient moment. Hitler has always been able to carry his own point. Generals change, but Hitler remains and changes the generals to suit his own needs. The most recent example of this vicious circle was the resignation of Von Brauchitsch following the failure of the offensive before Moscow at the end of 1941. Hitler has since called him back into service.

No, the generals of the German army are not capable of overthrowing the Nazi leadership. And why should they? They have the Nazi regime to thank for the fulfilment of their dearest dreams. Hitler rearmed Germany. He rebuilt Germany's military might and raised the social position of the officer. Furthermore, all of the

341

generals in leading positions today owe to Hitler the
rank they now enjoy. Brauchitsch, Keitel and Bock
would never have risen so quickly in the old army leadership of Schleicher, Hammerstein and Fritsch. Certainly not without war. Why should the field marshals
revolt now? What have they to gain? They could only
lose. In the best circumstances, the most they could
expect would be to save their own skins. After the defeat of the Nazi regime, a peaceful world order will
have to see to it that the forces that made Hitler great
will not again have a chance to send the world into a
catastrophic war. After Hitler, there will no longer
be a place in the world for German generals, and in the
name of peace we cannot dare to give them a place.
They know that. Can anyone take it amiss that they
should not find such prospects attractive?

Moreover, most of the leading officers of the German
army are not only co-responsible for the crimes of the
Nazi regime, but also for very specific atrocities. Does
anyone believe that the world will forget that? There
are names among the leading generals of the army that
have the same ring as those of the hangman Heydrich,
of Terboven, and of Frank—for example, General von
Falkenhausen, General Christiansen, General von Stuelp-
nagel. These generals know what they can expect. They
are going to defend their lives just as the Himmlers, the
Dalueges and the Death's Head S.S. will defend theirs.

Moreover, if some of the less involved higher officers
of the army should think of revolt, Hitler has already

provided that such an attempt should have little chance of success so long as the Nazi power is not completely broken. First, a large section of the younger officers and many of the soldiers are so strongly influenced by Nazism and particularly by Hitler that their loyalty to the Fuehrer is greater than their obedience to the generals. Secondly, Hitler saw to it that the army did not remain the "only armed body in the nation." Alongside the army is the *Waffen S.S.* which belongs unqualifiedly to Hitler. Hitler broke his promise of June 30, 1934, as he has broken many promises. The leaders of Germany's army are prisoners of their own politics.

Today Hitler uses every occasion to speak of the army *and* of the S.S. In December, 1941, when Field Marshal von Brauchitsch retired, ostensibly because of his failing health, in his announcement Hitler said: "Whatever I can do for you, my soldiers of the army and Elite Guard, shall be done." In his "great speech" on April 26, 1942, Hitler was particularly emphatic in describing the "model courage and the firmness of my brave S.S. Divisions and my S.S. Police Units." Hitler can rely on his S.S. He protects them and they protect him.

Hitler was farsighted enough to clip the wings of the army not only in the Third Reich, but also carefully to delineate and delimit their influence in the occupied countries. It shows how little Hitler leaves to chance.

When the British Commandos made their raid on the Lofoten Islands on March 4, 1941, they seized secret

documents describing the relationship between the army and the S.S. in the occupied territories. We quote from the *Program for the Coöperation of the German Army with the German Security Police (S.S.) in Norway:*
"Independent action on the part of the Wehrmacht is only to be envisaged:

(1) at the request of the German Security Police; or
(2) if units of the German Security Police cannot be immediately summoned to the scene of action,"

and in such cases reports are to:

"be communicated without delay to the leader of the appropriate local executive command of the Security Police."

The most important document concerning the role of the *Waffen S.S.* fell into the hands of British troops in Libya. It is a memorandum on the *Thoughts of the Fuehrer on the Waffen S.S.*, and was recommended for the widest possible distribution by the chief of the High Command of the German army. The contents of the document are most revealing. It reads as follows:
"Confidential. In Re: *Waffen S.S.*

"On July 6, 1940, the Fuehrer, on the occasion of the formation of the S.S. Division *Leibstandarte Adolf Hitler*, enunciated the following summary principles concerning the need for the Waffen S.S. The Greater German Reich, in its final form, will include within its

344

borders not only peoples who are necessarily friendly to the Reich. Therefore it is essential that a State Police Troop be maintained which will be able, in any situation, to represent the authority of the Reich and to carry out that authority. Only a State Police can fulfil this task, a police made up of men of the best German blood, who identify themselves without reservation with the *Weltanschauung* of the Greater German Reich. Only a contingent composed of such men will resist in critical times disruptive influences. Such a contingent will feel a pride in its integrity and will therefore never fraternize with the proletariat and with that underworld which undermines the fundamental idea. In the Greater German Reich of the future, a police contingent will possess the necessary authority with the other *Volksgenossen* only if it is of a military character. As a result of the military events they have witnessed and of their education by the Nazi Party, a 'stocking-knitting' police, like that of 1848, or a police of civil servants like that of 1918, can no longer wield authority. That is why it is necessary that this State Police go to the front in its own units to prove itself and sacrifice its blood just like every unit in the ranks of the army. After they have been tested in the field and returned home, the units of the Waffen S.S. will possess the authority to carry out their duties as a State Police. This use of the Waffen S.S. within the country is also in the interests of the army. It can never again be tolerated that, in a critical situation within the country, the army, based on popular

military service, turn its weapons against its own Volksgenossen. A step of this kind is the beginning of the end.
A state which has to turn to such means is no longer able
to use its army against the enemy abroad and thus must
give up. Our history affords enough tragic examples of
this. For all future time the army will be reserved exclusively for use against the enemies of the Reich abroad.
In order to guarantee the high quality of membership
in the units of the Waffen S.S., its units must always be
restricted. The Fuehrer envisages this restriction in speci-
fying that in general the Waffen S.S. shall not exceed
in numbers five to ten percent of the peace-time strength
of the army."

The basic conceptions governing Nazi domination
were always hidden behind a fog of propaganda. These
"Thoughts of the Fuehrer" concerning the Waffen S.S.
help us to disperse the fog. This invaluable document
contains three points of special significance:

(1) Hitler admits that he does not consider the army
an institution which identifies itself with the Nazi
Weltanschauung "without reservations." Consequently
it is not, in his opinion, immune to disruptive influences.

(2) Hitler fears the German "proletariat," and an underground movement that might grow out of it, as
he fears no other enemy. The German soldiers may
not "fraternize" with what he calls the "underworld."

(3) Hitler forced the army leaders to a characteristic
compromise. The Waffen S.S. "shall not exceed in numbers five to ten percent of the peace-time strength of

346

the army." The very vagueness of these formulations shows that Hitler has had as little idea of keeping these promises as he had of keeping the one that the army would remain the "only armed body in the nation." The Waffen S.S. already includes far more than ten percent of any conceivable peace-time German army. The generals, as usual, took the path of least resistance and have continued to serve Hitler.

By these statements about the role of the Waffen S.S. Hitler has simplified our task. He has shown up the myth of revolting generals in the proper light. Further, on his authority, we have confirmation that he considers the German working class his real enemy. With this evidence, we can dispense with complicated analyses and other arguments. The workers of Germany, with their Socialist traditions, their philosophy of freedom, their organizational experience and their irreconcilable opposition to Nazism, are the principal opponents of the Nazi movement. To be sure, they are not the only oppositional forces. There are other groups, religious, intellectual, middle class and agrarian, of which the strongest is the powerful Catholic opposition. This opposition represents primarily the peasants and the urban middle class of western and southern Germany. However, the workers who were formerly organized in the Socialist parties and in the trade unions will, because of their numerical superiority, their key positions in the vital industries and their old experience in the struggle, furnish the backbone of the popular anti-Nazi movement, which

347

will overthrow the Nazi regime. Throughout the years before and following Hitler's taking of power, they have demonstrated that they were anti-Nazi "without reservation," and that they still are.

Once the mass movement of the German people has gained enough strength, great forces will swarm into its ranks from among the millions of "volunteer" workers from France, Holland, Norway and other oppressed countries. And, if Hitler's armies suffer serious and obvious defeats, if confidence, even in leading Nazi circles, is shaken by these defeats, then a day will come when this mass movement will take on a revolutionary form and that which Hitler fears will happen: the soldiers of the German army will begin to fraternize with the rebellious people. Then a new anti-Nazi authority will win through and take over the leadership in the fight for freedom. When that day comes, the final conflict against Hitler domination will have come and not before.

In March, 1917, in Petrograd, Cossacks were called out as the last support of the Czar. As they rode into the streets the people who were demonstrating cried out: "Don't shoot, Brother Cossacks." There were several minutes of tension during which no one knew what the Cossacks would do. But the unbelievable happened. One Cossack leaned over and picked a young girl, a student, out of the front row of demonstrators, raised her to his saddle and kissed her. The ice was broken. Instead of shooting as they always had before, the Cossacks fraternized with the people.

348

This incident of the Cossacks was the personification of that moment when both prerequisites for a revolution coincided: namely, the people were no longer willing to live under the existing authoritarian rule and the regime was no longer capable of maintaining the conditions necessary for its rule.

In Russia this moment was born of riots in the marketplaces, hunger revolts and strikes. And as in Russia so in Germany the overthrow of the rule of the Hohenzollerns and, in Austria, the overthrow of the Habsburgs, were initiated by desperate women standing in queues, by hungry workers who struck. And the soldiers and sailors came to their aid at the moment when the ruling authority disintegrated. The sailors in Kiel who mutinied on November 4, 1918, the soldiers in the Berlin barracks, who fraternized with the masses of the workers on November 8th and 9th, the Austrian and Czech soldiers who began deserting the Italian front in October, 1918, and making their way home, their guns in their hands, sealed the fate of the Central Powers and brought the war to an end.

It will not be different in the present war—demonstrating women, workers engaged in passive resistance, deserting soldiers, are no longer rare in Germany in the third year of Hitler's war. The Nazis have begun to appeal to the people at home not to give the soldiers, who are sacrificing everything on the battlefields, the example of "a collapsing home front." They prescribe exactly what relatives are to write in their letters. They

349

try to exorcize the spirit of 1918. In the summer of 1942, the attitude of the German people is coming more and more to resemble that of 1918.

There are, however, two vitally important differences from the situation in 1918. Today we know enough about the Hitler guard to compare these murderers, with their death's-head symbol, with the Cossacks of 1917 and the German soldiers of 1918. Can anyone imagine the S.S.—the "black death"—fraternizing with hungry demonstrators? We cannot.

The second decisive difference from the situation in 1917-18 is that in Nazi Germany the opposition has no legal status. The opposition had representatives in the parliaments of Russia, Germany and Austria, leaders who were known to the entire population. There were Bolshevik deputies in the Russian Duma in 1914. Germany's Social Democratic Party polled more than 8,000,000 votes in the Reichstag elections of 1912. The Social Democrats were a mass opposition and their leaders were known throughout the land. Not only were they in the Reichstag; they were in the provincial legislatures, in the city councils and in the municipal governments. The trade unions had played an important part in the organization of the war industries. The same situation existed in Austria-Hungary. And in the parliament in Vienna, in addition to the Social Democrats, the national opposition of the Czechs was a powerful force. Close associates of Masaryk were in parliament during the war. But, since 1933, in Adolf Hitler's Germany,

THE COMING REVOLUTION IN GERMANY

the opposition has had no legal status at all, neither in the Reichstag, nor in provincial and municipal administrations. The Nazi rule is a total rule.

How, under such conditions, can a new authority develop and accredit itself with the people? How can men win the confidence of the people, when, for a decade, they have been cut off from any possibility of proving themselves in the public eye?

In answering this question we must be clear about one thing: that the reconstruction of a democratic authority in Germany cannot come from above, cannot be a centralized authority. An authority, based on the confidence of the people and on responsibility to the people, will have to come from below, from the people themselves. It will have to begin in all of those places where people come together in a modern society, in great working-class dwelling blocks of the cities, in the small villages, in the factories. Wherever social functions are carried on in a sphere limited enough for the individual to encompass, people can be chosen for these functions who are known and who enjoy the confidence of their fellows. In other words, the rebirth of German democracy will begin in the smallest cells of the social organism. Moreover, it is only in this way that the poison of Nazism can be completely eliminated.

It is difficult to do more today than to outline these very general prerequisites for the re-establishment of a government of the people, by the people and for the people in Germany. Much will depend on the form

351

which the final crisis in the Nazi regime takes; much will depend on the strength of the revolutionary movement and much will depend on what the victorious military powers of the United Nations do. One can, however, call attention to certain possible developments, certain trends which can influence the revolutionary process.

When Nazi authority does not extend any further than the S.S. machine-gun and cannon reach, the necessities of daily life, food, transportation, the maintenance of order and the protection of the safety of the ordinary citizen will force the spontaneous development of local authorities. When the Nazi authority collapses, its entire system of laws and law enforcement will also collapse. On that day, what farmer will deliver food, what grocer will want to sell it? Who will recognize food-ration cards and travel permits and all the other crutches of the Nazi economy of scarcity? Danger of complete anarchy will exist, total disorganization and starvation, unless the orders of a new authority can immediately replace the old. The workers in each factory, the dwellers in each housing block, the inhabitants of each village will have to find a means of preventing entire collapse. In the places of Nazi officials, who have fled or been killed, they will have to put men of their choosing to care for the water supply, for the distribution and rationing of food, for transportation and for all the small but indispensable functions of modern community life.

352

In the districts where the Nazi authority has been removed by the invasion of troops of the United Nations, the same problem will not exist, as the military authorities will take over. But it is not military action alone that can cause the downfall of an authoritarian power. In 1917, the German troops did not penetrate into the heart of Russia. The Czarist regime had collapsed long before. And, in 1918, when Germany collapsed, the Allied troops did not occupy Germany. Ludendorff gave up the hopeless battle while the German troops were still deep in French territory. The Nazi regime will probably be able to defend some part of Germany longer than could another kind of autocratic regime, but its authority will break down more quickly in other districts. It will collapse when the soldiers of the German army fraternize with the revolting people and turn against the S.S. It may collapse while German troops are still far outside of German borders. It is unlikely that Hitler's rule will have to be broken in the belt of occupied countries around Germany, land for land and district for district. An important defeat on a decisive front will probably suffice to disrupt the military power of the Nazi regime and thus to bring the ultimate disintegration of its authority. In Norway, Holland, Belgium, Yugoslavia and all the other occupied countries, the authority of the conquerors will be replaced by the legal governments of these countries. Benes' provisional government will take care of Czechoslovakia, a temporary solution in France will be furnished by the Free French. But the democratic emigrants from Germany do not even have a united, representative body abroad. And it would be a long way from such a representative body to its recognition by the United Nations even if there were a possibility of establishing one.

At the moment the Nazi rule collapses, who will enjoy the confidence of the people even in very limited districts? There is no doubt that first of all it will be men and women who, in their attitude and their behavior toward the Nazis, have shown that they are worthy of trust and who develop the initiative in the crucial days to solve the difficult problems of the immediate transitional period. Among them will be former functionaries of the democratic parties with experience in administrative matters, trade union officials who know how to handle industrial problems as well as those of the labor organizations, clergymen with a record of opposing the Nazis, men and women who have proved their anti-Nazism through terms in prisons and concentration camps, soldiers and officers who stand on the side of the people in the crisis. In many cases the new authority will arise out of bloody battles with S.S. troops. Factories, homes and whole cities will have to be defended against them. The most courageous, energetic and capable anti-Nazis will appear in the first ranks during those days. Those who prove themselves in that difficult time and survive will have earned the trust of their neighbors and their fellow workers.

354

THE COMING REVOLUTION IN GERMANY

But we should not go too far in our predictions of what will happen. We have tried to analyze the conditions under which the Nazi regime will finally break down. The form the final crisis will take, the strength the popular revolutionary movement will manifest, are matters for speculation only. That is why we have limited ourselves to drawing general conclusions from the known facts in the German situation and from the experiences of history.

If we are to win, not only the war, but also the peace, then a democratic Germany must emerge in the place of the aggressive Germany. If the people of the world are, once and for all, to end the period of barbarism, then those conditions must be removed which have made Germany play the aggressive role in a world conflagration twice within a quarter of a century. If freedom is really to be secured, it must be freedom for all the peoples of the earth.

The German underground movement is cut off from any possibility of expressing its opinion regarding the Atlantic Charter and other post-war proposals like those of Vice-President Wallace, Secretary Hull or Under-Secretary Welles. However, in a pamphlet, *The Coming World War*, published shortly before the outbreak of formal hostilities, the underground movement did indicate the conditions which it felt would have to be fulfilled if we were to be sure that there would be democracy in Germany.

In order to achieve this democratization of Germany

355

three steps must be taken and completed within the country: "The destruction of the positions of power and the economic bases of the Fascist regime; the replacement of its machinery of terror by democratic self-government of the working people; the replacement of war economy by planned economy based on the needs of the people." Always before in German history, the forces of democratic revolution have been stopped short before achieving their goal. This time the process must be carried to its completion.

"The first international task of the German revolution," the German Socialists explain, "is the liquidation of German imperialism. Because of the tension caused by Germany's high industrial potential on the one hand and its delayed political development on the other, German capitalism became one of the factors most responsible for war during the last fifty years. The Socialist revolution, on the other hand, will make Germany a chief factor in the creation of peace and coöperation in Europe because it will remove the cause of the old drive for expansion. The raising of the consuming power of the masses by the expropriation of monopoly capital and large landholders, will make possible the diversion of German productive power from armaments, autarchy and heavy industry to production for the domestic market. Socialist organization of foreign trade will put the exchange of surplus industrial products for raw materials and food on the basis of coöperation and equality rather than on the basis of blackmail and exploitation.

"Therefore, revolutionary Germany will need no Lebensraum outside its own frontiers. It demands no share in colonial oppression. Above all, it will liquidate, once and for all time, the subjugation of the nations of central and eastern Europe by German Fascism, by giving full right of self-determination to those nations.

"The aim of the foreign policy of German Socialists is a European Federation; for, a truly democratic solution which, at the same time, will provide for self-determination by all nations must be a federal solution; it can only have as its goal the free economic coöperation of nations, which enjoy extensive autonomy, but are not split up by customs' and military barriers."

These are the basic conceptions with which the German Socialist underground movement is facing the problems of post-war settlement. This spirit is in the tradition of the German labor movement which became a great movement in its struggle to free the people from the yoke of autocracy. It is out of this spirit that the irrepressible resistance against the Nazi regime has grown, a resistance that has cost inestimable sacrifice and will cost more. And it is this spirit that gives us a guarantee that a peaceful, democratic and free Germany will come into being in a world of free peoples.

THE END